ISBN 978-1-332-04690-4
PIBN 10275473

GENEALOGICAL ACCOUNT

OF THE

DESCENDANTS IN THE MALE LINE

OF

WILLIAM PECK,

ONE OF THE FOUNDERS IN 1638 OF THE COLONY

OF

NEW HAVEN, CONN.

BY DARIUS PECK.

HUDSON:
BRYAN & GOELTZ, STEAM BOOK PRINTERS.
1877.

PREFACE.

———◆———

The general indifference of the public in regard to works of this kind, would seem to be a sufficient apology for the want of a prefatory introduction; but some explanation is due to those whose ancestors or descendants are named, and to others who are interested in similar researches.

Having been forcibly reminded, a few years since, of his lack of information in relation to his ancestral kindred, the author immediately instituted inquiries on the subject, and has since pursued them as opportunity and limited intervals of leisure from business avocations have permitted. The following work contains the result of those inquiries. Its publication has been assented to in deference to the wishes and for the gratification of many of the descendants, now living, and with a view to preserve, as far as attainable, in a brief, systematic and permanent form, the history and genealogy of the family. In some cases it is but little more than the collation and arrangement of the researches of distinguished genealogists and antiquarians, with the aid of such additional light as has been afforded by recent investigations. These investigations, have, from several causes, been prosecuted with great labor, difficulty and embarrassment. Much time, care and attention have been required to expose and correct the errors, and supply the omissions, in the early annals of the colonies relative to some members of the family and the events with which they were connected.

The common ancestor, WILLIAM PECK, was among the first of the early settlers of New England. Shortly before, and soon after his migration. the arrival of several others of his surname, but evidently not of his kindred, the most of them the progenitors of a numerous posterity, contributed to the wide extension of his name in this country; and one of the most perplexing difficulties has been to identify his descendants, and distinguish them from those of others of the same patronymic.

His sons, and a large majority of their posterity, soon left their paternal homes to dwell on the borders of the then unbroken wilderness; and in the inchoate settlements and in the new and changing civil organizations where they resided, had not the opportunity and were without the usual facilities, if desired, to make and preserve a record of their descendants. The family genealogy as far as known, was, therefore, chiefly perpetuated by tradition, generally unreliable as evidence, and only admissible after the severest scrutiny and confirmation from authentic sources.

The facts and materials embodied in the following pages have been gathered from cotemporary history, from family, town, church, probate, colonial and state records, and from a very extensive correspondence on the subject.

Though completeness of detail and entire accuracy in works of this description are impracticable, yet the author trusts that whatever could be done by long and patient research, and unwearied industry has been accomplished. His conclusions have only been stated when thought reasonable, and when absolute certainty was not attainable; and his expectations in regard to the work will be fully satisfied if it shall be deemed a worthy monument to the memory of his ancestors, and a valuable contribution to the historical and genealogical collections of the present day.

Acknowledgment is cheerfully made of the aid and co-operation of others in this undertaking. Especially should be named the distinguished historians and antiquarians, Samuel H. Congar and William A. Whitehead, of Newark, N. J., Sylvester Judd, of Northampton, and James Savage, of Boston, Mass., F. W.

Chapman, of Prospect, P. M. Trowbridge, of Woodbury, Henry Bronson, William S. Porter and Henry White, of New Haven, Connecticut; and, also, without invidious distinction, Royal R. Hinman, Ira B. Peck, Tracy Peck, Charles W. Wardwell, Henry K. Peck, Nathan Peck, Alfred Peck, Augustus L. Peck, Benjamin Peck, George Warner Peck, Jasper C. Peck and Samuel Griffin Peck, whose efficient assistance, sympathy and encouragement will always be gratefully remembered and appreciated.

HUDSON, N. Y., January 1, 1877.

EXPLANATORY NOTE.

The numbers in brackets, running through the whole work, show the number of each ascertained individual in the male line descended from the common ancestor, WILLIAM PECK and the number at the end of the name of any, indicates the number of his oldest child. By the aid of these numbers, together with the caption at the head of each family of children the connection of every one is at once seen, and the ancestors or descendants may be traced, backward or forward, with the greatest facility. The generation commences in the body, and is continued at the top, of the page. The names of those having children are necessarily repeated in the caption of their children, but without change of their numbers.

ABBREVIATIONS.

b. born ; m. married ; unm. unmarried ; dau. daughter, and d. died.

GENEALOGY

FIRST GENERATION.

[1] WILLIAM PECK[1] (2) was one of the founders of the New Haven Colony in the spring of 1638. With his wife, Elizabeth, and his son, Jeremiah, he emigrated from England to this country probably in the company of Gov. Eaton, Rev. John Davenport, and others, in the ship Hector, arriving at Boston, from London, June 26, 1637.[2] This company was principally from the city of London, where Mr. Davenport had been a celebrated minister, and consisted of many wealthy merchants, and others of great respectability from London, and of farmers from Yorkshire, Hertfordshire and Kent, and some from Surrey and Sussex.[3] They had suffered much from the intolerance and persecution of Archbishop Laud during the reign of Charles I., and the object of their emigration was the unmolested enjoyment of civil and religious liberty.

A persistent effort to trace the line of his progenitors involving much time and a large expense, has proved unsuccessful. He was born in the city of London, or in its vicinity, in 1601, and was there married about the year 1622. His son, Jeremiah, was his only child at the time of his emigration.

1. His surname was often written by him, and by his oldest son; Rev. Jeremiah Peck, with a final "e," but it was dropped in the latter part of their lives.

2. Trumbull (Hist. Conn. Vol. I., 95) states the date of the arrival to have been *July* 26, 1637, and some have copied his mistake.

3. No list of the names or English homes of this company can anywhere now be found.

He was one of the original proprietors of New Haven, his autograph signature being affixed to the fundamental Agreement or Constitution dated June 4, 1639, for the government of the infant colony.[1]   He was admitted a freeman of the colony October 20, 1640 ; was a merchant by occupation, and a trustee, treasurer, and the general business agent of the Colony Collegiate School, established on the basis of the Hopkins fund.   He is usually named in the records with the title of "Mr.," then a prefix of respect and distinction ; and from 1659 until his decease was a deacon of the church in New Haven.   His wife, Elizabeth, died December 5, 1683, and he subsequently married Sarah, the widow of William Holt, and died October 4, 1694, at the advanced age of 93 years. His children were all by his first wife, and were 1. *Jeremiah*, 2. *John*, 3. *Joseph* and 4. *Elizabeth*, all of whom, together with his second wife, survived him, and are named in his last Will and Testament.[2]   His home lot of about an acre, and his dwelling house and shop or store in New Haven, were, at the time of his decease, on the southeasterly side of, and fronting on, Church street ; the lot extending from Centre street northerly in front on Church street towards Chapel street about one hundred feet, and extended easterly from Church street a few feet beyond Orange street.   The front on Church street is now covered by the Connecticut Savings Bank building on the corner of Church and Center streets, the "Clark" building, so called, and the building known as the Odeon.   His grave is in that part of the. old burial ground now under the Center Church in New Haven.   His gravestone, however, is in the new cemetery in the northern part of the town, having, with the monuments and tombstones of others whose graves are covered by the said church, been removed thither in 1821.

---

1. This is said to have been one of "the first examples in history of a written constitution organizing a government and defining its powers."

2. His Will, dated March 9, 1688-9 (1689 as we now date), was left for probate October 11, 1694, and is recorded in the Probate Records of New Haven, Book II, page 176.

SECOND GENERATION.

CHILDREN OF WILLIAM PECK (1) AND ELIZABETH, HIS WIFE.

[2.] 1. JEREMIAH (6) was born in the city of London, England, or its vicinity, in 1623, from whence, in 1637, he came with his father to this country.   Little is known of his early history, except that he had a good education, acquired in part before he left England.   He is said by Cotton Mather to have been bred at Harvard College, but, though probably a student, his name does not appear in the catalogue of the graduates of that institution.   He married Johannah Kitchell, a daughter of Robert Kitchell,[1] of Guilford, Conn., Nov. 12, 1656.   He was then, and for some time previously had been, preaching or teaching school at Guilford, and he continued to be thus engaged until 1660, when he was invited to take charge of the Collegiate school at New Haven, Conn.   This was a colony school, and had been instituted by the General Court, in 1659. It was open to students from other colonies, and in it were to be taught Latin, Greek and Hebrew, and young men fitted for college.   He accepted the invitation, and removing from Guilford to New Haven, entered upon his duties as its instructor and continued to discharge the same until the summer of 1661, when the school was temporarily suspended for want of adequate support.   It was revived, however, after a few years, and has continued and flourished until the present day under the name of the Hopkins Grammar School.   In the autumn of 1661 he was invited to preach at Saybrook, Conn., where there is much reason to suppose that he was ordained, and where he settled as a minister, succeeding Rev. James Fitch ; the agree-

---

1. Robert Kitchell came to New Haven in the company of Eaton, Davenport and others, in 1638, and in 1639 settled in Guilford, Conn., being a prominent man and one of the first planters of that town.   He was one of those who migrated from the New Haven Colony to Newark, N. J., in 1666, where he died about 1672.   His only son, Samuel, migrated thither about the same time, died there April 26, 1790 and was a man of high standing and respectability.   The wife of Robert Kitchell died in Greenwich, Conn., in 1682, while residing there with her dau., the wife of Rev. Jeremiah Peck.

ment of settlement being dated September 25, 1661. After a few years there was some dissatisfaction with his ministry, and a misunderstanding as to the provisions of his agreement of settlement, which being amicably arranged he left Saybrook removing to Guilford early in 1666. He was then, and for some time had been, together with numerous other ministers and churches in the New Haven and Connecticut Colonies, decidedly opposed to what was called the "Half-way Covenant," adopted by the General Synod of 1662, and with many of the leading ministers and the people of the New Haven Colony was especially and irreconcilably hostile to the Union of the New Haven and Connecticut Colonies under the charter of Charles II., which, however, after a protracted struggle, was finally effected in 1665, and he resolved to emigrate from the colony. Removing from Guilford in 1666, he became one of the first settlers of Newark, N. J. His home lot and residence in Newark were on the northeasterly corner of Market and Mulberry streets. He does not appear to have officiated as a minister at Newark. He preached to the neighboring people of Elizabethtown soon after his removal to Newark, and finally settled there as their first minister in 1669 or 1670. In 1670, and again in 1675, he was invited by the people of Woodbridge, N. J., and in 1676 by the people of Greenwich, Conn., to settle with them in the ministry, but he declined these several invitations. In Sept., 1678, he was again invited to settle as a minister at Greenwich, and in Oct., 1678, he had a similar call from Newtown, Long Island, N. Y. He accepted the last call from Greenwich, and removing thither late in the autumn of 1678 from Elizabethtown, N. J., he became the first settled minister in Greenwich, Conn., where his pastorate was a very quiet and useful one, and only disturbed by his refusal in 1688 to baptize the children of non-communicants, allowed by the "Half-way Covenant," the introduction of which still agitated the churches in Connecticut. Though sustained by a majority of the members of his church, the dissatisfaction of the minority probably led to his resignation in 1689. He then

commenced preaching in Waterbury, Conn., and having received and accepted the unanimous invitation of the residents
of that town to settle with them in the ministry, he removed
thither early in 1690, and became the first settled minister of
the church in Waterbury in 1691.   He was then nearly seventy
years of age.   In a few years his health gradually failed, but
he continued the pastor of the church and discharged the most
of his official duties until his decease at Waterbury, June 7,
1699.   He seems to have possessed considerable energy and
ability, and to have been a man of much usefulness, both as a
teacher and minister in the frontier settlements, among the
early colonists of this country.   His wife survived him, and
died in Waterbury in 1711.   His Will, dated Jan. 14, 1696-7,
and that of his wife, dated Oct. 7, 1696, (in the form of Deeds
of Gift) are recorded, the former at page 6 and the latter at
page 103 of Volume I. of the Waterbury Land Records.

[3.]   2. JOHN, (12) b. in New Haven, Ct., probably in 1638;
m. Nov. 3, 1664, Mary Moss, dau. of John Moss, of New Haven,
where he settled; was admitted a freeman of the colony in
1669, and resided in New Haven until 1672.   He then removed
to Wallingford, Conn., and resided there until his decease.
The title of "Mr." and "Lieut." are prefixed to his name in the
Wallingford records.   He d. at Wallingford in 1724.   His wife
d. there Nov. 16, 1725, aged 78.

[4.]   3. JOSEPH, (32) b. in New Haven, Conn., in Jan. 1641;
was baptized there Jan. 17, 1641; m. Sarah ——— and about
1662 settled in East Saybrook, Conn., afterwards, in 1667, in-
corporated into the town of Lyme, and d. in Lyme Nov. 25,
1718, where his wife also d. Sept. 14, 1726, aged 90.   Their
gravestones are still standing in the old Lyme cemetery.   He
was a prominent man in Lyme, being many years a townsman,
Surveyor, Recorder, Justice of the Peace and Deacon of the
Church.

[5.]   4. ELIZABETH, b. in New Haven, Conn., in April, 1643;
was baptized there May 7, 1643, and in 1661 m. Samuel Andrews, son of William Andrews, of New Haven, where they

resided until 1672; then removed to Wallingford, Conn., and there both died. He died October 6, 1704, aged 69, but the date of her death is not found. Their children were, 1. *Samuel*, b. Feb. 1, 1662, who d. March 1, 1662; 2. *Samuel*, again, b. Aug. 30, 1663; 3. *William*, b. Feb. 9, 1665; 4. *John*, b. July 4, 1667, d. young; 5. *Nathaniel*, b. Aug. 2, 1670; all born in New Haven; and the following, all born in Wallingford: 6. and 7. *Twins*, b. May 30, 1673, and both d. the same day; 8. *Elizabeth*, b. July 17, 1674; 9. *Mary*, b. March 27, 1677; 10. *Joseph*, b. in March, 1679; 11. *Margery*, b. Jan. 15, 1681; and 12. *Dinah*, b. July 25, 1684. She has a very numerous and widely scattered posterity.

THIRD GENERATION.

CHILDREN OF JEREMIAH PECK (2) AND JOHANNAH, HIS WIFE.

[6.] 1. SAMUEL, (30) b. in Guilford, Conn., Jan. 18, 1659; came to Greenwich, Conn., with his father in 1678; was well educated; m. Nov. 27, 1686, Ruth Ferris, said to have been a dau. of Peter, a son of Jeffrey Ferris, of Stamford, Conn.; became the progenitor of the numerous Greenwich families of his surname; was a man of large wealth and influence; for about fifty years was a Justice of the Peace, and held other important positions in Greenwich, where he died April 28, 1746. His wife d. there Sept. 17, 1745, aged 83. Their gravestones are still standing in the old Greenwich cemetery.

[7.] 2. RUTH, b at New Haven, Conn., April 3, 1661; m. June 1, 1681, Jonathan Atwater, son of David Atwater, of New Haven, where they settled and resided until their decease. Their children, all b. in New Haven, were 1. *Joshua*, b. Feb. 21, 1682, and d. March 16, 1682; 2. *David*, b. Aug. 5, 1683 · 3. *Jeremiah*, b. Jan. 31, 1685; 4. *Mary*, b. Dec. 31, 1686; 5.

Ruth, b. Dec. 31, 1688 ; 6. *Jonathan*, b. Nov. 1, 1690 ; 7. *Lydia*, b. April 18, 1693, and d. Aug. 2, 1694 ; 8. *Joseph*, b. Dec. 9, 1694; 9. *Stephen*, b. Dec. 4, 1696, and d. Oct. 23, 1704 ; 10. *Damaris*, b. Oct. 9, 1698 ; 11. *Lydia*, again, b. July 31, 1701, and d. March 30, 1708. In the Will of her father, William Peck (1), her husband was a devisee of an acre or more of land in New Haven, where he was a man of distinction, and d. June 3, 1726, aged 70. The date of her death is unknown.

[8.] 3. CALEB, b. at Saybrook, Conn., in 1663 ; came with his father to Greenwich in 1678 ; was probably unm.; resided in Greenwich until about 1810, when he removed to Newtown, Long Island, N. Y., and afterwards to Concord, Mass., and there d. March 10, 1725. It does not appear that he left any descendants.

[9.] 4. ANNE, b. at Saybrook, Conn., in 1665 ; m. in May, 1790, Thomas Stanley, son of Capt. John Stanley, of Farmington, Conn., where they settled and resided, and where he d. April 14, 1713, aged 64 years, and she d. May 23, 1718. They had two children, 1. *Thomas*, b. Oct. 31, 1696, who d. Oct. 13, 1756 ; and 2. *Ann*, b. May 14, 1699, who was living in Farmington in 1728.

[10.] 5. JEREMIAH, (39) b. at Guilford, Conn., or Newark, N. J., in 1667 ; came to Waterbury, Conn., with his father in 1690 ; m. June 14, 1704, Rachel Richards, dau. of Obadiah Richards, of Waterbury, and settled and resided there until his death in 1752. He was highly respectable, a man of large wealth, a collector of the town rates in 1703 ; constable in 1713, 1717 and 1723 ; a Deputy to the General Court of Conn. in May, 1720 and 1721, and appointed one of the first Deacons of the Northbury Church in Waterbury in 1739, and officiated as such until 1746.

[11.] 6. JOSHUA, b. at Elizabethtown, N. J., in 1673 ; came to Waterbury with his father in 1690 ; was unm. and d. there Feb. 14, 1736.

CHILDREN OF JOHN PECK (3) AND MARY, HIS WIFE.

[12.]　1. MARY, b. in New Haven, Conn., March 4, 1666 ; m. John Doolittle, of Wallingford, Conn., Feb. 16, 1683 ; resided in Wallingford and d. there Sept. 1, 1710.

[13.]　2. ELIZABETH, b. in New Haven, Conn., in Jan., 1668, and d. there Jan. 16, 1668.

[14.]　3. JOHN, b. in New Haven, Conn., March 16, 1670, and d. there March 22, 1670.

[15.]　4. JOHN, again, (48) b. in New Haven, Conn., in Aug. 1671 ; came with his father to Wallingford, Conn., in 1672 ; there m. 1. Susanna Street, dau. of Rev. Samuel Street, the first minister of Wallingford, May 23, 1694, who d. April 21, 1704, aged 29 ; m. 2. Mary Bradley, July 21, 1706, who d. June 12, 1737, and m. 3. Martha Stent, May 24, 1738, who survived him and d. in Wallingford, May 25, 1771, aged 87.　He was a deacon of the first Congregational church in Wallingford, and resided there until his death which occurred June 28, 1768, at the advanced age of nearly 97 years.　Outliving all his children, he disposed of his property by Will to his grandchildren, the last codicil to which was made shortly before his decease[1]. Some of his descendants still reside in Wallingford upon the premises which were the homestead of his father more than two centuries ago.

[16.]　5. ELIZABETH, again, b. in Wallingford, Dec. 29, 1673 ; m. John Merriman, son of Capt. Nathaniel Merriman, Nov. 20, 1690, and d. in Wallingford about 1723.

[17.]　6. LYDIA, b. in Wallingford, May 1, 1677, and probably d. young.

[18.]　7. RUTH, b. in Wallingford, July 20, 1679 ; m. Samuel Lathrop, Feb. 3, 1704, and d. Jan. 8, 1738.

[19.]　8. ABIGAIL, b. in Wallingford, March 16, 1682 ; m. David Austin, of New Haven, in 1698, and probably d. there.

---

1. His Will and the codicils thereto are recorded in Book X, of the New Haven Probate Records.　In it Jan. 26, 1762, he erroneously calls himself aged 92, taking for his own the date of the birth of his brother John (14) probably not being aware that there were two Johns in the family.

[20.] 9. ANN, b. in Wallingford, Nov. 3, 1684, and d. in infancy.

[21.] 10. ANN, again, b. in Wallingford, in March, 1686 ; m. 1. Nathaniel Yale, Feb. 11, 1704, and m. 2. Joseph Cole, April 11, 1715, and d. in Wallingford, Feb. 26, 1716.

CHILDREN OF JOSEPH PECK (4) AND SARAH, HIS WIFE, ALL BORN IN LYME, CONN.

[22.] 1. SARAH, b. Aug. 4, 1663 ; m. May 2, 1684, Matthew Gilbert.

[23.] 2. JOSEPH, b. March 12, 1667, and d. in Lyme, Oct. 10, 1677.

[24.] 3. ELIZABETH, b. Sept. 9, 1669 ; m. Dec. 6, 1686, Samuel Pratt, being his second wife, and d. in Lyme, Aug. 29, 1688.

[25.] 4. DEBORAH, b. July 31, 1672 and April 3, 1694, m. Daniel Sperry.

[26.] 5. HANNAH, b. Sept. 14, 1674 and June 25, 1696, m. Thomas Anderson, who d. in Lyme, May 7, 1746.

[27.] 6. RUTH, b. Aug. 19, 1676, and m. Jasper Griffin, April 29, 1696.

[28.] 7. SAMUEL, (51) b. July 29, 1678 ; m. 1. Elizabeth Lee, Dec. 28, 1699, who d. Aug. 29, 1731, and m. 2. Widow Martha Barber, of Killingworth, Conn. Jan. 25, 1732. He resided in Lyme, and d. there Jan. 28, 1735. His second wife again m. Peter Pearson, Jan. 8, 1736.

[29.] 8. JOSEPH, again, (61) b. March 20, 1680 ; m. Susanna ——— Oct. 3, 1704, and resided and d. in Lyme.

FOURTH GENERATION.

CHILDREN OF SAMUEL PECK (6) AND RUTH, HIS WIFE, ALL BORN
IN GREENWICH, CONN.

[30.] 1. SAMUEL, (68) b. in March, 1688;[1] m. Elizabeth
——— in 1715; was a carpenter by trade, and also a farmer
owning a farm in that part of the town of Greenwich called
Old Greenwich, where he resided and d. in Dec. 1733. His
widow, in 1735, again m. John Clogston, and soon afterwards
removed from Greenwich to Reading, Conn., where she died[2].

[31.] 2. JEREMIAH, (72) b. Dec. 29, 1690; m. Mary Johnson; was a farmer in Greenwich, and d. there about 1765. His
wife survived him.

[32.] 3. JOSEPH, b. May 1, 1692; was unm. and d. in
Greenwich about 1761.

[33.] 4. DAVID, (85) b. Dec. 15, 1694; m. Elizabeth ———;
was a farmer and resided in Greenwich until about 1743, and
then removed to the adjoining town of North Castle, Westchester county, N. Y., where he died about 1756, his wife surviving him.

[34.] 5. NATHANIEL, (87) b. Aug. 15, 1697; m. Dec. 4,
1722, Mary Pardee, of New Haven, Conn., who d. in Greenwich, Jan. 6, 1758. He was a prominent man, and for several
years a Justice of the Peace of the town of Greenwich, where
he d. in 1765.

[35.] 6. ELIPHALET, (99) b. in 1699; m. Sept. 16, 1732,
Deborah Lockwood, dau. of Robert Lockwood of Greenwich;
was a farmer in Old Greenwich and resided there until his
death, about 1770.

---

1. The day of the month is obliterated in the Greenwich town record.

2. She had by her second husband two daughters, born in Reading, viz: *Mary*,
b. in 1737, m. Amos Sanford, lived in Sharon, Conn. and d. there March 13, 1816;
and *Abigail*, b. March 22, 1738, m. Capt. Enoch Parsons, who settled in Sharon, Conn.
where she d. June 6, 1807. Betsey, a daughter of Capt. Enoch Parsons and Abigail
his wife, was the wife of Calvin Peck (236.)

[36.] 7. THEOPHILUS, (107) b. in March, 1702 ; m. Feb. 5, 1728, Elizabeth Mead, dau. of Benjamin Mead, of Greenwich, who was b. in Nov. 1703, and d. Nov. 17, 1783, aged 80. He was the owner of an extensive tract of land in the northern part of the town of Greenwich, called Pecksland and Round Hill, where he resided until his death, Nov. 7, 1783.

[37.] 8. PETER, (119) b. about 1704 ; m. Sarah ————— ; resided in Greenwich, Conn., and d. there about 1759. His wife survived him, and soon after his death removed with his children to New Milford, Conn. where she probably died.

[38.] 9. ROBERT, (125) b. about 1706 ; m. Deborah Reynolds of Stamford, Conn. and resided in Greenwich until his decease in 1749. His wife d. in Bedford, N. Y., Nov. 4, 1787, aged 84.

CHILDREN OF JEREMIAH PECK (10) AND RACHEL, HIS WIFE, ALL BORN IN WATERBURY, CONN.

[39.] 1. JOHANNAH, b. April 12, 1705 ; m. Joseph Galpin, and resided and d. in Woodbury, Conn.

[40.] 2. JEREMIAH, (131) b. Nov. 9, 1706; m. Mercy Northrup, dau. of Samuel Northrup of Milford, Conn., Jan. 14, 1740 ; was a farmer, and settled in Northbury Society in Waterbury, now the town of Plymouth, Conn., where he d. in 1750. His widow, March 3, 1754, again m. Joseph Luddington.

[41.] 3. RACHEL, b. May 10, 1709, and m. ————— Riggs. The place and date of her residence and death cannot be ascertained.

[42.] 4. ANNE, b. March 10, 1713 ; m. John Guernsey, son of Joseph Guernsey of Milford, Conn., Nov. 28, 1733, and resided and d. in Amenia, N. Y. She had four children b. in Waterbury, Conn.

[43.] 5. MARY, b. Oct. 1, 1715, and d. unm. in Waterbury, Conn., about 1753.

[44.] 6. PHEBE, b. Jan. 26, 1717, and m. ————— Weed. The place and date of her residence and death cannot be ascertained.

[45.]   7. RUTH, b. Feb. 8, 1719 ; m. Feb. 6, 1740, Rev. Mark Leavenworth, who, in 1740, was ordained pastor, being the third minister, of the church in Waterbury.   He d. there Aug. 20, 1797, in the 58th year of his ministry.   He was a chaplain in the Army during the old French War.   She d. in Waterbury, Aug. 8, 1750, leaving an only child, *Jesse*, who was a graduate of Yale College in 1759, d. in 1823, and was the father of General Leavenworth, of the U. S. Army.

[46.]   8. ESTHER, b. June 27, 1721, and d. probably unm. in Waterbury, Conn., before 1752.

[47.]   9. MARTHA, b. May 4, 1725, and m. Caleb Weed, July 7, 1742.   The place and date of her residence and death are unknown.

CHILDREN OF JOHN PECK (15) AND SUSANNA, HIS WIFE, ALL BORN IN WALLINGFORD, CONN.

[48.]   1. MARY, b. Feb. 3, 1695 ; m. Joshua Atwater, Jan. 17, 1723, and d. in Wallingford prior to 1740.   Her husband d. there Nov. 29, 1747.   She had a dau. *Mary*, who m. Thomas Johnson, of Middletown, Conn.

[49.]   2. SUSANNA, b. April 26, 1697 ; m. in 1717 Stephen Hopkins, of Waterbury, Conn., where she d. Dec. 2, 1725, and he d. Jan. 4, 1769.   She had two daughters and three sons.

[50.]   3. SAMUEL, (136) b. Oct. 19, 1704 ; m. Jan. 18, 1727, Mary Parmelee; resided in Wallingford where he was a prominent man, and d. there May 20, 1755.   His wife d. there Oct. 14, 1781, aged 75.

CHILDREN OF SAMUEL PECK, (28) ALL BORN IN LYME, CONN.

[51.]   1. ELIZABETH, b. April 26, 1702, and d. in Lyme, Jan. 15, 1705.

[52.]   2. ELIZABETH, again, b. May 14, 1705 ; m. Richard Ely, Jr., Jan. 23, 1724, and d. in Lyme, Oct. 8, 1730.

[53.]   3. SAMUEL, (149) b. July 12, 1707 and m. Alice Way, Nov. 7, 1728.

[54.]   4. WILLIAM, (155) b. Aug. 31, 1709 and m. Jemima Marvin Jan. 25, 1732.

[55.]   5. BENJAMIN, (158) b. March 6, 1711 and m. Sarah Champen, Feb. 8, 1734.

[56.]   6. ELIJAH, (168) b. Oct. 20, 1713 ; m. 1. Hepsibah Pearson, April 28, 1737, who d. Oct. 9, 1770 ; m. 2. Widow Jane Miner, Jan. 8, 1771, and d. in Lyme Aug. 6, 1771.

[57.]   7. JEDEDIAH, (181) b. June 1, 1717 and m. Tabitha Pierson in 1738, who d. in 1753.   He d. at sea in 1744.

[58.]   8. DANIEL, (183) b. March 4, 1721 ; m. Abigail Lord, Nov. 8, 1744 and d. in Lyme, March 1, 1751.

[59.]   9. SILAS, (186) b. Oct. 2, 1724, and m. Elizabeth Caulkins Nov. 4, 1746 ; first settled in Lyme ; served as a soldier in the French War, and after the treaty of peace in 1763, settled in Nova Scotia.   He afterwards removed back to Lyme, and was in the service in the Revolutionary War, and d. in Lyme in June 1808.

[60.]   10. MARTHA, b. June 4, 1733.   She was the only child of his second marriage.

CHILDREN OF JOSEPH PECK (29) AND SUSANNA, HIS WIFE, ALL BORN IN LYME, CONN.

[61]   1. JOSEPH, b. Aug. 13, 1705, and probably d. young in Lyme, Conn.

[62.]   2. JASPER, (192) b. Feb. 3, 1708 ; m. Sarah Clark Nov. 24, 1731, and d. in Lyme, Oct. 21, 1788.

[63.]   3. SARAH, b. March 17, 1710, and d. at Lyme, in infancy.

[64.]   4. HANNAH, b. March 10, 1712 ; m. William Clark Nov. 30, 1731, and d. in Derby, Conn.

[65.]   5. JOHN, (198) b. April 21, 1716 ; m. Catharine Lay and d. in Lyme, April 27, 1785.

[66.]   6. DAVID, (204) b. Feb. 15, 1721 ; m. Abigail Southworth, June 16, 1743, and is said to have d. in Lyme about 1810.

[67.]   7. NATHANIEL, (216) b. March 14, 1723 ; m. Lucy Mather, May 24, 1744 and d. in Lyme about 1784.

FIFTH GENERATION.

CHILDREN OF SAMUEL PECK (30) AND ELIZABETH, HIS WIFE,
ALL BORN IN GREENWICH, CONN.

[68.]   1. MARY, b. in 1716 ; was unm. and d. in Reading,
Conn. about 1737.

[69.]   2. JOHN, (222) b. in 1718 ; m. in 1741 Sarah Adams,
dau. of John Adams, and d. in Greenwich in Sept. 1771.   He
resided in Old Greenwich on a small farm near the shore of
Long Island Sound.   His wife d. in Clifton Park, N. Y., Jan.
11, 1814, aged 95 years, having, after about 1790, resided there
with her son, Abijah, (227) until her decease.

[70.]   3. SAMUEL, (230) b. in April, 1720, and m. Mary
Ferris, dau. of James Ferris, Nov. 7, 1745.   He resided in Old
Greenwich, was a man of great energy and decision of char-
acter, a valuable citizen, and for many years a Deacon of the
First Congregational church in Greenwich.   He d. there Jan.
29, 1793.   His wife d. there March 24, 1804, aged 76 years.

[71.]   4. RUTH, b. in Jan. 1724 ; m. Nehemiah Haight, Nov.
25, 1742 ; resided in Stanwich Society, in the town of Greenwich, and d. there Sept. 3, 1807.   She has a very numerous
posterity.

CHILDREN OF JEREMIAH PECK (31) AND MARY, HIS WIFE, ALL
BORN IN GREENWICH, CONN.

[72.]   1. MARY, m. Enos Reynolds, and d. in Greenwich
prior to 1764.

[73.]   2. JEREMIAH, was unm. and d. in Greenwich about
1803.

[74.]   3. JOSEPH, (239) b. in 1730 ; m. Elizabeth Peck (94)
and d. in Greenwich Dec. 4, 1822.

[75.]   4. HENRY, was unm. and d. in Greenwich in 1764.

[76.]   5. HANNAH, m. Japheth Ferris and d. in Stanwich
Society, Greenwich, about 1797.

[77.]   6. RUTH, m. Joseph Ferris and d. in Stanwich Society, Greenwich.

[78.]   7. ANNA, m. David Hoyt and d. at Long Ridge, Greenwich, about 1807.

[79.]   8. WILLIAM, (251) b. Aug. 24, 1741; m. Sarah Cable, Nov. 15, 1764, and d. in Westport, Conn., Dec. 23, 1800.   His wife b. June 6, 1746, d. at St. Johns, N. B., Aug. 9, 1785.

[80.]   9. MARTHA, m. George Linkletter, had two sons, George and another, and d. in Nova Scotia.

[81.]   10. ISAAC, (257) b. Oct. 10, 1745; m. Elizabeth Forman, Dec. 16, 1784, and d. in Greenwich, Aug. 20, 1827

[82.]   11. RACHEL, b. in 1747; m. John McKay and d. in Stanwich Society, Greenwich, Feb. 8, 1806.

[83.]   12. CATHARINE, b. in 1749; m. Samuel Peck (130) and d. in Bedford, N. Y., in June, 1825.

[84.]   13. THOMAS, (261) b. Sept. 1, 1750; m. Widow Mary Ferris and d. in Greenwich, in 1781.

CHILDREN OF DAVID PECK (33) AND ELIZABETH, HIS WIFE, SUPPOSED TO HAVE BEEN BORN IN GREENWICH, CONN.

[85.]   1. DAVID, was living in North Castle, N. Y., in 1772[1].

[86.]   2. JONAS, was living in North Castle, N. Y., in 1756[2].

CHILDREN OF NATHANIEL PECK (34) AND MARY, HIS WIFE, ALL BORN IN GREENWICH, CONN.

[87.]   1. ELIZABETH, b. June 19, 1724, and d. in Greenwich, July 1, 1724.

[88.]   2. NATHANIEL, (263) b. June 2, 1725; m. Jerusha Curtiss, Oct. 9, 1746, and d. in Greenwich in 1775.

[89.]   3. MARY, b. Dec. 12, 1727; m. Charles Belding Jan. 26, 1749, and d. in Stamford, Conn.

---

1. After much effort nothing further can be found as to him or his descendants, or whether there were any more children of David Peck (33.)

2. David Peck (85,) in 1772, resided in what is called Middle Patent, in the eastern part of the town of North Castle, N. Y., near the Connecticut line, and adjoining the town of Poundridge on the east.

[90.]   4. JOSHUA, (272) b. May 12, 1730 ; m. Sarah Mead, dau. of Benjamin Mead ; first settled in Greenwich, but about 1790 removed to Charlton, N. Y., and d. there in 1816.   His wife d. in Livonia, N. Y., Dec. 21, 1822, aged 88.

[91.]   5. ISAAC, b. Jan. 2, 1732, and d. in Greenwich Jan. 4, 1732.

[92.]   6. HEZEKIAH, b. Feb. 9, 1733, and d. in Greenwich in 1733.

[93.]   7. THANKFUL, b. Aug. 7, 1736 ; m. Daniel Lockwood and d. in Greenwich Sept. 3, 1798.

[94.]   8. ELIZABETH, again, b. Dec. 28, 1737 ; m. Joseph Peck (74) and d. in Greenwich, Oct. 29, 1815.

[95.]   9. YALE, b. Oct. 27, 1739, and d. in Greenwich in 1739,

[96.]   10. JONATHAN, (277) b. Sept. 23, 1740 ; m. Mehitable Blackman and d. in Stamford, Conn., in 1783.   His wife again m. Gen. John Mead, of Greenwich, and d. there about 1810.

[97.]   11. GEORGE, (281) b. Jan. 4, 1743 ; m. Mary Ferris and d. in Greenwich in 1797.   His wife d. there in 1820.

[98.]   12. SAMUEL, b. June 9, 1744, and d. in Greenwich in 1745.

CHILDREN OF ELIPHALET PECK (35) AND DEBORAH, HIS WIFE, ALL BORN IN GREENWICH, CONN.

[99.]   1. DEBORAH, b. April 30, 1733.

[100.]   2. ELIPHALET, b. April 28, 1734.

[101.]   3. ABIGAIL, b. April 6, 1736.

[102.]   4. JAMES, b. April 16, 1738.

[103.]   5. SUSANNAH, b. Feb. 28, 1739 ; m. Samuel Ferris.

[104.]   6. PHEBE, b. June 8, 1742; m. Jeduthan Ferris and d. in Greenwich Sept. 29, 1798, where her husband also d. June 23, 1809, aged 72.

[105.]   7. MARY, b. June 28, 1743 ; m. Josiah Ferris Nov. 3, 1762, and d. in New York city.

[106.] 8. CALEB, b. Sept. 30, 1745.[1]

CHILDREN OF THEOPHILUS PECK (36) AND ELIZABETH, HIS WIFE, ALL BORN IN GREENWICH, CONN.

[107.] 1. THEOPHILUS, (286) b. March 15, 1730 ; m. Rebecca Knapp, July 5, 1753, and d. in Greenwich, June 8, 1812.

[108.] 2. ELIZABETH, b. Nov. 21, 1731 ; m. Joseph Close, 3d, of Greenwich, and d. there Jan. 18, 1816, where her husband also d. Nov. 20, 1808, aged 79.

[109.] 3. SARAH, b. Oct. 29, 1733 ; m. 1. Nathaniel Close, son of Solomon Close, of North Salem, N. Y., about 1757, who d. there Feb. 6, 1773, aged 41 ; and m. 2. Thomas Paddock, of Southeast, N. Y., who d. Jan. 17, 1799, aged 77, and she d. in North Salem, Oct. 8, 1822.

[110.] 4. EUNICE, b. April 9, 1735 ; m. Joshua Knapp, of Greenwich, and d. there July 8, 1828.

[111.] 5. HANNAH, b. May 18, 1737 ; m. James Wallace, of North Salem, N. Y., Nov. 22, 1825, where her husband also d. Sept. 3, 1822.

[112.] 6. SAMUEL, (296) b. Jan. 22, 1739; m. Hannah Sherwood, April 29, 1762 ; resided in Greenwich, and d. there March 21, 1798. His wife d. there in 1811.

[113.] 7. BENJAMIN, (306) b. Oct 10, 1740; m. 1. Deborah Sackett, Nov. 11, 1766, who d. July 14, 1769 ; and m. 2. Hannah Reed, Aug. 12, 1772, who d. Nov. 30, 1783, aged 39. He resided in Greenwich, and d. there March 12, 1806.

[114.] 8. ABRAHAM, (312) b. Feb. 7, 1742; m. Hannah Purdy, dau. of Caleb Purdy, of Rye, N. Y., Dec. 6, 1770 ; resided in Greenwich, and d. there Feb. 3, 1792.

[115.] 9. RACHEL, b. Sept. 20, 1743 ; m. Benjamin Haight, of Somers, N. Y., May 6, 1778, and d. in Geneva, N. Y., May 7, 1820. He d. in Albany, N. Y., Nov. 13, 1805, aged 68.

---

1. Nothing further can be found relating to the children of Eliphalet Peck (35) or whether his sons had any descendants. It is said, however, that his daughter Mary (105) had several children.

[116.]   10. RUTH, b. Feb. 7, 1746 ; m. Caleb Purdy, Jr., and d. in Greenwich, Sept. 16, 1822.

[117.]   11. ISAAC, b. March 9, 1748 ; m. Hannah Fletcher ; resided in Greenwich, and d. there Sept. 24, 1838. He had no children.

[118.]   12. ISRAEL, (318) b. April 9, 1750 ; m. Lavina Purdy, dau. of Caleb Purdy, May 30, 1782 ; resided in Greenwich, and d. there Jan. 18, 1819.

CHILDREN OF PETER PECK (37) AND SARAH, HIS WIFE, ALL BORN IN GREENWICH, CONN.

[119.]   1. PETER, (325) b. in Jan. 1746 ; went from Greenwich to New Milford, Conn., with his mother ; m. Sarah Terrill, dau. of Paul Terrill, of New Milford, Dec. 7, 1768 ; resided in New Milford until 1786, when he removed to Queensbury, near Glen's Falls, N. Y., and resided there until his death, June 17, 1813, where his wife also d. Aug. 21, 1830, aged 81.

[120.]   2. SARAH, b. in 1748 and m. ——— Guernsey.

[121.]   3. JEMIMA, b. in 1750; m. Israel Newman, and d. at Glen's Falls, N. Y., in 1822.

[122.]   4. ENOS, (328) b. in 1752; m. 1. Anna Marsh, and m. 2. Lavina Wilcox, and, about 1789, removed from New Milford Conn., to New Haven, Vt., and from thence, about 1800, to Onondaga county, N. Y., and d. in Camillus in that county May 23, 1835.

[123.]   5. ELIZABETH, m. Benjamin Newman, brother of Israel Newman, and d. in the State of Michigan about 1830. It is said that her husband d. in Covington, N. Y.

[124.]   6. MARY, m. David Terrill, brother of the wife of her brother Peter, (119) and d. in Weybridge, Vt., aged 83.

CHILDREN OF ROBERT PECK (38) AND DEBORAH, HIS WIFE, ALL BORN IN GREENWICH, CONN.

[125.]   1. ROBERT, (338) b. June 30, 1739 ; m. Ann Reed, of Darien, Conn., Jan. 15, 1767, and settled and resided in Greenwich where he was a Deacon of the church, and d. July 25, 1827. His wife d. June 21, 1828, aged 85.

[126.] 2. AMY, b. in 1741 ; m. Henry Johnson and d. in Darien, Conn., July 11, 1824. Her husband had d. in Greenwich Sept. 26, 1801.

[127.] 3. EBENEZER, (347) b. March 12, 1743 ; m. Hannah Lockwood ; resided in Greenwich and d. there Sept. 8, 1833, where his wife had also d. April 19, 1830, aged 80.

[128.] 4. DEBORAH, b. May 14, 1746 ; m. Seth Palmer and d. in Greenwich July 18, 1837. He had d. there Jan. 26, 1831, aged 90.

[129.] 5. MERCY, b. in 1747 ; m. Moses Lockwood of Stamford, Conn., where they both died.

[130.] 6. SAMUEL, (355) b. in 1749 ; m. Catharine Peck (83) ; settled and resided in Bedford, N. Y., where he d. April 18, 1798.

CHILDREN OF JEREMIAH PECK (40) AND MERCY, HIS WIFE, ALL BORN IN WATERBURY, NORTHBURY SOCIETY, NOW THE TOWN OF PLYMOUTH, CONN.

[131.] 1. ESTHER, b. Nov. 3, 1740 ; was living in 1771 and probably d. unmarried.

[132.] 2. RUTH, b. Nov. 27, 1742 and d. unm. in Waterbury, now Plymouth, Conn., before Feb. 2, 1768.

[133.] 3. EUNICE, b. Feb 23, 1745 ; m. David Mansfield and d. in Harwinton, Conn., where he also d. in 1833, aged 90.

[134.] 4. RACHEL, b. Jan. 4, 1747 and d. in infancy in Waterbury, Conn.

[135.] 5. LEMUEL, b. Nov. 27, 1748 and d. in Waterbury, now Plymouth, Conn., in 1758.

By the death of Lemuel (135) the descendants in the male line of Jeremiah Peck (10) became extinct, and his brother Samuel (6) became the common ancestor of all the descendants in the male line, then living, of Rev. Jeremiah Peck (2).

CHILDREN OF SAMUEL PECK (50) AND MARY, HIS WIFE, ALL BORN IN WALLINGFORD, CONN.

[136.] 1. JOHN, (360) b. Nov. 5, 1727 ; m. 1. Patience Doolittle Nov. 16, 1752, who d. Sept. 14, 1753 ; and m. 2. Jerusha

Hall July 10, 1755 ; settled and resided in Cheshire, Conn., where he d. Jan. 15, 1799, and where his last wife d. Aug. 19 1817, aged 85.

[137.]   2. MARY, b. March 24, 1729 and d. same day in Wallingford.

[138.]   3. MARY, again, b. Feb. 1, 1730 and d. young in Wallingford.

[139.]   4. SUSANNA, b. Feb. 26, 1732 ; m. Benjamin Hall Jan. 24, 1754 and d. in Wallingford.

[140.]   5. SAMUEL, (369) b. Jan. 4, 1734 ; m. Susanna Doolittle Dec. 20, 1760 ; settled and resided in Wallingford and d. there Sept. 28, 1815, where his wife had also d. July 3. 1812, aged 72.

[141.]   6. CHARLES, (379) b. March 12, 1736 ; m. 1. Hannah Hull, of Wallingford, who d. April 10, 1760 ; and m. 2. Dorothy Hall, of Cheshire, Conn., who d. there Oct. 6, 1829. He d. at West Point, N. Y., Aug. 2, 1780, while in active service in the Revolutionary Army.

[142.]   7. MARY, again, b. Feb. 23, 1737 and d. same day at Wallingford.

[143.]   8. MARY, again, b. Sept. 25, 1738 and d. in Wallingford, May 23, 1745.

[144.]   9. JESSE, b. May 8, 1741 and d. unm. at Lake George, N. Y., in Sept. 1758, while in service in the old French war.

[145.]   10. ABIGAIL, b. Feb. 21, 1743 ; m. Tiriamus Collins April 13, 1759, who, about 1770, settled in Ballston, N. Y., where both probably died.

[146.]   11. NICHOLAS, (391) b. Feb. 22, 1745 ; m. Dinah Dowd Oct. 31, 1765 ; resided in Wallingford where he d. Dec. 30, 1820 and she d. Dec. 24, 1820, aged 73.

[147.]   12. JERUSHA, b. July 29, 1747 ; m. Samuel Mervin Nov. 18, 1764.

[148.]   13. JOEL, (395) b. April 23, 1750 ; m. 1. Mary Brooks March 25, 1773, who d. May 18, 1821 ; m. 2. Lucy Merriman, who d. March 6, 1822, and m. 3. Mary Bassett who d. Dec. 1, 1836. He settled and resided in Farmington, Conn., and d. there May 26, 1842.

CHILDREN OF SAMUEL PECK (53) AND ALICE, HIS WIFE, ALL BORN IN LYME, CONN.

[149.] 1. SAMUEL, (396) b. Sept. 7, 1729; m. Hannah Beckwith, dau. of Richard Beckwith, and d. in Lyme in 1776.

[150.] 2. ABNER, (404) b. Sept. 27, 1731; m. Caroline Reed Nov. 30, 1786 and d. in Lyme.

[151.] 3. DARIUS, (405) b. Sept. 11, 1733; m. Elizabeth Beckwith April 19,. 1757 and d. in Lyme in 1797.

[152.] 4. CARTER, b. June 23, 1737.

[153.] 5. ELISHA, b. Nov. 27, 1739 and d. unm. in Lyme.

[154.] 6. DANIEL, (415) b. March 27. 1742; m. Jerusha Yerrington Dec. 25, 1764 and d. in Lyme April 25, 1802.

CHILDREN OF WILLIAM PECK (54) AND JEMIMA, HIS WIFE, ALL BORN IN LYME, CONN.

[155.] 1. ELIZABETH, b. Dec. 11, 1736.

[156.] 2. LORUAMY, b. July 12, 1738.

[157.] 3. WILLIAM, b. Feb. 11, 1740, and d. in Lyme, April 20. 1749.

CHILDREN OF BENJAMIN PECK (55) AND SARAH, HIS WIFE, ALL BORN IN LYME, CONN.

[158.] 1. DAN, b. May 11, 1735, and d. in Lyme, Oct. 1, 1736.

[159.] 2. MEHITABLE, b. Jan, 12, 1738.

[160.] 3. BENJAMIN, b. April 26, 1740.

[161.] 4. DAN, b. April 1, 1742, and d. in Lyme, Conn., Oct. 30, 1746.

[162.] 5, ELIZABETH b. March 21, 1744.

[163.] 6. CYRUS, b. May 2, 1746.

[164.] 7. ELIAS, b, June 20, 1748.

[165.] 8. SARAH, b. Feb. 21, 1750, and d. unm. in Lyme. April 14, 1775.

[166.] 9. LEE, b. July 1, 1752, m. Elizabeth Marvin, Aug. 18, 1774, and d. in Lyme, Conn.

[167.] 10. ESTHER. b. Oct. 30, 1756.[1]

CHILDREN OF ELIJAH PECK (56) AND HEPSIBAH, HIS WIFE, ALL BORN IN LYME, CONN.

[168.] 1. MARY, b. May 14, 1738, and d. in Lyme, March 18, 1739.

[169.] 2. PETER, b. Feb. 1, 1740, and d. in Lyme, June 3, 1741.

[170.] 3. ELIJAH, b. May 28, 1742, and d. unm. in Lyme, March 31, 1766.

[171.] 4. PETER, again, b. March 22, 1744, and d. unm. in Lyme, Aug. 6, 1771. .

[172.] 5. HEPSIBAH, b. March 2, 1746 ; m. John Mather and d. in Lyme.

[173.] 6. JEDEDIAH, (422) b. Jan. 28, 1748 ; m. Tabitha Ely Nov. 5, 1772 ; served between three and four years in the Revolutionary Army, and about the year 1790 emigrated from Lyme, Conn., to Otsego county, N. Y., and settled in Burlington in that county. He soon became a very prominent man in that section of the State. He was an ardent and active politician in the Republican party of that period. For circulating petitions in Otsego county in 1798 against the alien and seditive laws he was indicted, arrested and taken from his family by an officer to the city of New York. It does not appear that he was ever tried, but it increased his popularity and did much for the Republican party. He was elected a Member of the Assembly from Otsego county in 1798, and annually thereafter until 1804, when he was elected a Senator of the western district of the State of New York, and remained in the Senate until 1808. He was, also, for many years a County Judge of Otsego county. He was a man of great native ability and influence. In 1799 he introduced a bill into the Legislature to abolish imprisonment for debt. He was the first projector and

---

1. After persistent effort nothing further as to this family or their descendants can be found.

persevering and efficient advocate of the common school sys-
tem of the State of New York, introducing into the Legislature,
in 1800, the first bill for its organization and establishment.   In
these and other important measures he exhibited much shrewd-
ness and sagacity, as well as benevolent and statesmanlike
qualities, not often witnessed in that early day.   He died in
Burlington, N. Y., Aug. 15, 1821.   His wife survived him and
d. there Jan. 14, 1858, aged 98 years.

[174.]   7. WILLIAM, b. March 22, 1750, and d. unm. in
Lyme, July 13, 1771.

[175.]   8. LUTHER, b. March 20, 1752, and d. unm. in Lyme,
Aug. 27, 1771.

[176.]   9. PARNEL, b. May 13, 1754; m. Roswell Clark and
d. in Lyme, March 12, 1813.

[177.]   10. ANNA, b. May 1 1756 ; m. Timothy Chittenden,
of Salisbury, Conn.. and d. there Oct. 10, 1837.   She had sons,
Moore, Samuel and Timothy, and one daughter, Julia.

[178.]   11. ELIZABETH, b. May 14, 1758, and d. in Lyme,
April 20, 1759.

[179.]   12. ELIZABETH, again, b. June 3, 1760; m. Stephen
Mather and d. in Chautauqua county, N. Y.

[180.]   13. ELISHA, (429) b. April 3, 1662; m. Olive Emmons, of E. Haddam, Conn. ; settled in Burlington, N. Y., in
1800, and d. in Victor, N. Y., July 15, 1829.   His wife d. in
Ypsilanti, Mich. April 29, 1847.

CHILDREN OF JEDEDIAH PECK (57) AND TABITHA, HIS WIFE, ALL
BORN IN LYME, CONN.

[181.]   1. PARNEL, b. about 1740, and d. in Lyme in 1754.

[182.]   2. MARY, m. 1. Daniel Murphy, in 1760, who d. in
1767 ; m. 2. ——— Lacy in 1771, and d. in Lyme in Dec.
1771.   She had an only child, Daniel Murphy, by her first
husband, b. in 1761, who was in the Revolutionary Army and
died in the service June 20, 1778.   He drew Military Lot No.
34 in Solon, N. Y., for his military services.

CHILDREN OF DANIEL PECK (58) AND ABIGAIL, HIS WIFE, ALL
BORN IN LYME, CONN.

[183.] 1. AHIJAH, b. Sept. 15, 1745.
[184.] 2. AZUBAH, b. Oct. 29, 1747.
[185.] 3. DANIEL, b. July 7, 1751.

CHILDREN OF SILAS PECK (59) AND ELIZABETH, HIS WIFE, ALL
BORN IN LYME, CONN., EXCEPT SAMUEL GRIFFIN,
WHO WAS BORN IN NOVA SCOTIA.

[186.] 1. SILAS, said to have been m. and had one dau.; was
in the service with his father in the Revolutionary War, and
d., while in such service, at Valley Forge, Penn., in the winter
of 1777–78.

[187.] 2. ELIZABETH, m. Zenas Huntley and d. in Otsego
Co., N. Y.

[188.] 3. MARTHA, b. in 1753; m. ——— Merchant, in
Nova Scotia, and d. in New Lyme, O., July 11, 1830.

[189.] 4. LOVISA, b. in 1756; m. Dan Huntley, and d. in
New Lyme, O., Aug. 6, 1828.

[190.] 5. DAN, (440) b. April 17, 1762; was in the service
in the Revolutionary War; m. Lovina Huntley April 19, 1786;
first settled in Lyme, Conn; removed to Ohio in 1811, and d.
in New Lyme, O., Jan. 16, 1839.

[191.] 6. SAMUEL GRIFFIN, (446] b. in Nova Scotia, Dec.
27, 1766; m. Zipporah DeWolf, April 3, 1790; first settled in
Lyme, Conn., whence, in the fall of 1811, he removed and settled in Ashtabula county, O., when it was yet an unbroken
wilderness, and d. in Colebrook, O., April 28, 1851.   His wife
had d. there May 18, 1846.

CHILDREN OF JASPER PECK (62) AND SARAH, HIS WIFE, ALL
BORN IN LYME, CONN.

[192.] 1. SARAH C., b. Dec. 24, 1732; m. Henry Champion,
and d. in Lyme about 1780.

[193.] 2. NATHANIEL, (456) b. March 11, 1735; m. 1.
——— Moore, and m. 2. her sister, Hannah Moore, and d.

ın Lyme, Conn., being accidentally killed, in 1785. After his death, his widow again m. Joseph Waite.

[194.] 3. JASPER, (464) b. Sept. 20, 1737 ; m. Phebe Dorr, Feb. 28, 1765 ; resided in Lyme and d. there Jan. 16, 1821.. His wife d. in West Bloomfield, N. Y., April 16, 1831. He was a soldier and Sergeant of his company in the French War of 1755–60, and served as such at the capture of Fort Frontenac by Col.. Bradstreet, in 1758, and was also in the service in the Revolutionary War.

[195.] 4. JUDITH, b. Jan. 22, 1740 ; m. 1. John Sears ; m. 2. Josiah Gates, and d. in Stafford, N. Y., Feb. 16, 1831.

[196.] 5. REYNOLD, (475) b. March 8, 1742 ; m. Deborah Beckwith, March 8, 1764, and d. in West Bloomfield, N. Y., Nov. 26, 1814.

[197.] 6. SUSANNA, b. Aug. 11, 1744 ; m. Ezra Marvin and d. in Granville, Mass., about 1810.

CHILDREN OF JOHN PECK (65) AND CATHARINE, HIS WIFE, ALL BORN IN LYME, CONN.

[198.] 1. LEBBEUS, (485) b. Aug. 10, 1736 ; m. Lydia Lee, June 17, 1784, and d. in Lyme, July 31, 1812.

[199.] 2. HEPSIBAH, b. Aug. 9, 1743 ; m. Peter Lay, June 13, 1765, and d. in Canajoharie, N. Y.

[200.] 3. PHEBE, b. April 28, 1746 ; m. Enoch Reed, and d. in Canajoharie, N. Y.

[201.] 4. JOHN, (489) b. Oct. 14, 1748; m. 1. Rebecca Smith, Nov. 3, 1774, who d. July 25, 1818, aged 64 ; and m. 2. Mary Mitchell, of Groton, Conn., in Nov. 1820, who d. Sept. 17, 1830, aged 79, and he d. in Lyme, Feb. 19, 1836.

[202.] 5. MARY, b. May 29, 1753 ; m. Martin Tinker, and d, in Westfield, Mass.

[203.] 6. JANE, b. Feb. 10, 1756 ; m. Benjamin Higgins, and d. in Westfield, Mass.

CHILDREN OF DAVID PECK (66) AND ABIGAIL, HIS WIFE, ALL
BORN IN LYME, CONN.

[204.]   1. ABIGAIL, b. Sept. 1, 1744 ; was unm. and d. in
Lyme.

[205.]   2. SAMUEL GILES, (496) b. Oct. 25, 1746, and lived
and d. in Lyme.

[206.]   3. EZRA, (497) b. Jan. 11, 1748, and lived and d. in
Lyme.

[207.]   4. DAVID, b. April 24, 1750, and d. in Lyme, May
11, 1750.

[208.]   5. DAVID, again, (498) b. June 28, 1751 ; m. 1. Eunice Lee and m. 2. Elizabeth Manwaring, Feb. 10, 1785 ; emigrated from Lyme and settled in Sand Lake, N. Y., in 1788,
and d. there June 3, 1839.   His last wife d. there July 15,
1828, aged 63.

[209.]   6. WILLIAM, (506) b. Jan. 6, 1754 ; m. Mrs. Judith
Marvin in 1779, and is said to have d. in Haverstraw, N. Y.

[210.]   7. JOSEPH, (510) b. June 10, 1756 ; m. Sarah Miller,
Dec. 21, 1780, and d. in Lyme, July 8, 1834.   His wife d. April
13, 1843, aged 83.

[211.]   8. HANANIAH, b. Nov. 14, 1758, and d. unm. in
Lyme about 1813.

[212.]   9. MISHAEL, b. June 6, 1761 ; d. in Lyme, said to
have been unmarried.

[213.]   10. AZARIAH, (515) b. Feb. 9, 1664 ; removed from
Lyme to Sharon, N. Y., about 1790, and d. in St. Lawrence
county, N. Y.

[214.]   11. DANIEL, (516) b. Oct. 18, 1766 ; m. Betsey Lee,
and d. in Lyme about 1830.

[215.]   12. ELIZABETH, b. May 1, 1770, and m. Reuben
Latimer.

CHILDREN OF NATHANIEL PECK (67) AND LUCY, HIS WIFE, ALL
BORN IN LYME, CONN.

[216.]   1. JOSEPH, b. Feb. 4, 1745, and d. young in Lyme.

[217.]   2. MATHER, (518) b. April 26, 1751 ; m. 1. Esther
Colt, April 25, 1771, who d. Sept. 1, 1786 ; m. 2. Ruama

Howell, Nov. 19, 1786, and m. 3. Azuba Watrous, Aug. 5, 1790, and d. in Lyme in June, 1819.

[218.] 3. WILLIAM, (530) b. Dec. 15, 1755 ; m. 1. Eunice Corlis, dau. of George Corlis, May 1, 1779, who d. April 28, 1784; and m. 2. Abigail Matthewson, dau. of Col. John Matthewson, Jan. 25, 1786, who d. May 10, 1832, and he d. at Providence, R. I., May 19, 1832. The following is extracted from the *Rhode Island American*, announcing his decease: "He graduated at Yale College in 1775, and soon after leaving college was appointed Adjutant of the 17th Regiment of foot, commanded by Col. Jedediah Huntington, of Conn., and first Lieutenant of one of the companies attached to that Regiment. In June 1776 he was appointed Brigade-Major in the Brigade commanded by General Spencer, and, in July 1776, was promoted to the rank of Major in the United States Army. In the summer of 1777 he was commissioned as Deputy Adjutant General to the forces stationed in Rhode Island and then under the command of Gen. Sullivan, and served in this capacity until the surrender of Cornwallis at Yorktown, in October, 1781. Upon the adoption of the Federal Constitution by Rhode Island, in 1790, Col. Peck was appointed by President Washington U. S. Marshal of Rhode Island, and for nearly twenty years he continued to discharge the duties of that office." He was a prominent member of the Society of Cincinnati, and intimate with the leading men and officers of the Revolutionary War, and his house in Providence, R. I., was the abode of a cheerful hospitality for his numerous friends and acquaintances, acquired in his long civil and military career.

[219.] 4. MEHITABLE, b. in 1758 ; m. Daniel Hall, and d. in Lyme in 1820. She had no children.

[220.] 5. MATTHEW, (536) b. in 1761; m. Polly King, of Oyster Bay, Long Island, N. Y., and died in Lima, N. Y., in 1815.

[221.] 6. RICHARD, (542) b. in 1764 ; m. Elizabeth Mather, March 13, 1783, and d. in Lyme, Sept. 16, 1786.

SIXTH GENERATION.

CHILDREN OF JOHN PECK (69) AND SARAH, HIS WIFE, ALL BORN
IN GREENWICH, CONN.

[222.]   1. JOHN, (544) b. Nov. 12, 1742; served as a soldier
in the French War; was in the campaign of 1759 and remained in the army until the treaty of peace in 1763; m. in Oct.
1764 Sarah Northrup, dau. of Nathan Northrup, of North
Salem, N. Y., and settled in his native town.   In 1772 he removed from Greenwich to that part of Great Nine Partners,
so called, which is now the town of Stanford, Dutchess County,
N. Y., from whence, late in the fall of 1780, he again removed
to that part of Little Nine Partners, so called, which is now
the town of Milan, in the same county, where he resided until
May, 1788, when he returned to Stanford.   In 1792 he removed from Stanford, west of the Hudson River, to what is now
known as the town of Hunter, Greene county, N. Y.[1]

The coldness and sterility of the soil, and the inaccessibility
of this location, induced him, in Feb. 1795, to emigrate with
his family to the fertile valley of the Chenango river, and he
settled in the town of Sherburne, Chenango County, N. Y.,
where, and in the adjoining town of Norwich, he resided until
his death in Sherburne, Sept. 19, 1819.   He had but little
school education, but superior natural talents, great firmness
and energy, and much knowledge derived from observation
and from intercouse with the public men of his day.   His
occupation, through life, was that of a farmer, being principally engaged in felling the forest and in the clearing up, sub-

---

1. His farm was about two miles southwesterly of the Catskill Mountain House,
and a short distance westerly of the Kaater's Kill falls.

It is a singular and remarkable fact that descendants of William Peck, (1) in the
sixth genenration from him, who also were descendants of his three sons, respectively,
should, about this time, have settled in Greene County, N. Y., within a few miles of
each other without, probably, any knowledge that they were kindred and descendants
in the same degree of a common ancestor. *Richard Peck*, (396) descended from
Joseph, (4) settled in Lexington in 1788; *Theophilus Peck* (371) and *Samuel Peck*
(372) descended from John, (3) settled in Lexington, in 1789, and *John Peck*, (222)
above named, descended from Jeremiah (2) settled in Hunter in 1792.

duing and cultivation of his land, in the new regions where he resided. Keeping, as he did, on the borders of civilization, after his removal from Greenwich in 1772, bearing himself and inuring his family to the hardships and labors of frontier life, he was one of the enterprising and valuable pioneers in the settlement of the State of New York. His wife was born in North Salem, N. Y., Oct. 28, 1746, and d. in Smyrna, N. Y., Nov. 11, 1830.

[223.] 2. HEATH, (554) b. in 1745 ; m. Rachel Roselle, and settled in Greenwich, in 1774. He was a soldier in the Revolutionary Army, but retired from the service, in the Summer of 1780, to look after his private affairs and provide for his family, which had suffered much from the calamities incident to the war. He was a bold and outspoken Whig ; and, after his return, was frequently in command of scouting parties, and a terror to the numerous Tories in that region who had become very vindictive against him. They burned his barn, stole his cattle and offered a reward for him. Nothing daunted, however, he continued to go out at the head of scouting parties, and while out with one of them, in October 1780, he stopped with his men at the house of Henry Hubbard, in the north part of the town of Greenwich, where he was shot from the outside through a window and instantly killed. There were well grounded suspicions as to who the perpetrator was, but from the troublous times and the want of sufficient evidence of identity, he was not convicted or punished. His widow, afterwards, again m. Ezra Weed, and d. in Mamaroneck, N. Y. She had a son, *Hiram*, by her second husband, who, in 1865, was living in Fairhaven, Conn.

[224.] 3. NATHAN, b. in 1747, and was unmarried. He was drowned in the Summer of 1775, while attempting to rescue several others, two of whom he had saved from a similar fate.

[225.] 4. SARAH, b. in 1749 ; m. Wilson Northrup, of Galway, N. Y., in 1789, and d. in Clifton Park, N. Y., Feb. 28, 1841, aged 92 years. She had no children.

[226.] 5. RUTH, b. July 11, 1751; m. William Kinch, of Greenwich, in 1755, who settled and resided there until 1806, and then removed to Hamden, N. Y., where he d. May 13, 1821, aged 72 years. She d. at Lodi, N. Y., May 12, 1841, aged 90 years. Her children were, *William, Abijah, Thomas,* and *Sarah*; also, *Nathan,* b. Dec. 25, 1788; *Heath P.,* b. Aug. 1, 1792, and *Lewis,* b. May 5, 1795.

[227.] 6. ABIJAH, (557) b. April 3, 1758; was a soldier in the Revolutionary War, entering the Continental Army in Jan., 1776; was under arms when the Declaration of Independence was read to the American Army, and one of the sentinels on duty when it evacuated the city of New York. He served in several campaigns, and was in the battle at White Plains. After the war, he resided in North Salem, N. Y., and there m., Nov. 18, 1784, Mindwell Close, dau. of Solomon Close, Jr., and shortly afterwards, removed to Galway, N. Y., where he resided until 1794, and then removed to, and resided in, Clifton Park, N. Y., until his decease there, Nov. 12, 1848. His wife, b. March 27, 1763, d. April 4, 1816, and he again, in Nov. 1821, m. Widow Lydia Montgomery, who d. Jan. 22, 1846. After his removal to Clifton Park he became a Baptist minister, and was ordained as such, March 12, 1801. He statedly preached to the Church in Clifton Park, with few intervals, and as his age permitted, until his death. He had a fluent diction, a strong and well balanced mind, and was a man of great influence and extensive usefulness, both as a citizen and christian minister.

[228.] 7. ABIGAIL, b. Sept. 30, 1760; m. Alexander Baird, of Greenwich, in 1787; resided in Greenwich until 1795, and then removed to Clifton Park, N. Y. Her husband was accidentally drowned in the Mohawk River, Nov. 12, 1807, and soon afterwards she removed with her children to Columbia, Herkimer County, N. Y., where she d. April 17, 1823. Her children were, *Sarah,* b. Oct. 1, 1788, m. David Hatch; *Samuel,* b. March 12, 1790; *Robert,* b. May 23, 1792; *Mary,* b. Nov. 25, 1794, m. Garret Welton; *Mindwell,* b. Aug. 23, 1796; *Wilson,*

b. July 13, 1798; and *Eliza*, b. Feb. 13, 1805, and m. Philip Lazelle.

[229.] 8. ELIZABETH, b. July 19, 1763; m. Joseph Youngs, of Stamford, Conn., Jan. 16, 1783, and resided in Stamford until Nov. 1784; then removed to Ballston, N. Y., and from thence to Amsterdam, N. Y., in 1789. In June 1807, she removed to what is now the town of Otego, N. Y., where she d. Nov. 16, 1820. Her husband d. at Smyrna, N. Y., Dec. 22, 1843. She had 16 children, 7 sons and 9 daughters, all of whom were m. and settled in Broome, Chenango and Otsego Counties, N. Y.

CHILDREN OF SAMUEL PECK (70) AND MARY, HIS WIFE, ALL BORN IN GREENWICH, CONN.

[230.] 1. SAMUEL, b. Jan. 7, 1747, and d. in Greenwich in 1763.

[231.] 2. MOSES, (565) b. in 1750; m. Hannah Reynolds and d. in Greenwich, March 11, 1828. His wife d. there, Oct. 11, 1828, aged 77.

[232.] 3. MARY, b. Nov. 13, 1752; m. Hezekiah Knapp, of Stamford, Conn., Sept. 7, 1775, and d. there Sept. 19, 1842. Her husband, b. Oct. 14, 1749, had d. in Stamford, Conn., Dec. 11, 1840.

[233.] 4. HANNAH, b. April 16, 1755, and d. in Greenwich in 1767.

[234.] 5. AARON, (567) b. May 3, 1757; m. Hannah Ferris, dau. of Japheth and Hannah (Peck) Ferris (76) and d. in Greenwich, Jan. 23, 1833.

[235.] 6. JAMES, b. in 1762, and d. unm., in Greenwich, Aug. 4, 1806.

[236.] 7. CALVIN, (572) b. Dec. 4, 1764; m. Betsey Parsons, dau. of Capt. Enoch Parsons, of Sharon, Conn. He resided in Sharon, was a Deacon of the Congregational Church in that town, and d. there Sept. 1, 1837.

[237.] 8. LUTHER, (581) b. Dec. 22, 1766; m. Rachel Peck (301) Sept. 19, 1797, and d. in Greenwich, Oct. 29, 1860, aged 94 years. His wife had d. April 21, 1855.

(238.) 9. GEORGE WHITFIELD, (585) b. in 1768 ; m. Mary Knapp, who d. Sept. 28. 1805, aged 29 years. He d. in Greenwich, Dec. 28, 1823.

CHILDREN OF JOSEPH PECK (74) AND ELIZABETH, HIS WIFE, ALL BORN IN GREENWICH, CONN.

[239.] 1. ELIZABETH, b. in 1760 ; m. John Johnson, and d. in Hanover, N. Y., Feb. 9, 1840.

[240.] 2. MARY,
[241.] 3. HENRY, } d. in Greenwich in infancy.
[242.] 4. CHARLES,

[243.] 5. JOSEPH, (591) b. March 16, 1767 ; m. Mary Palmer, and d. in Greenwich, Sept. 19, 1826. His wife d. there May 11, 1856.

[244.] 6. SOLOMON, (601) b. March 15, 1768 ; m. Mary Ferris, Dec. 29, 1799, and d. in Greenwich, June 2, 1816.

[245.[7. PREWY, b. in March, 1771 ; m. Solomon Close, son of Joseph Close, and d. at White Plains, N. Y., Dec. 14, 1850. Her husband had d. there Jan. 28, 1840, aged 80.

[246.] 8. JESSE, (605) b. March 30, 1772 ; m. Nancy Jessup; resided in Bedford, N. Y., and d. there Oct. 10, 1844.

[247.] 9. HEZEKIAH, d. unm., in New York city, about 1807.

[248.] 10. ALEXANDER, b, in 1781, and d. unm., on Staten Island, about 1800.

[249.] 11. CATHARINE, b. in 1783 ; m. Robert Barnard, and d. in Brookville, Ind., in 1844.

[250.] 12. MARY, again, b. in 1786 ; m. 1. Andrew Newman and m. 2. John Holmes Lockwood, and d. in Greenwich, Aug. 25, 1854.

CHILDREN OF WILLIAM PECK (79) AND SARAH, HIS WIFE, ALL BORN IN GERENWICH, CONN.

[251.] 1. HENRY, (609) b. Aug. 6, 1765 ; m. Sarah Freeman, June 15, 1779, and d. at Bedford, N. Y., May 18, 1825. His wife d. at Sing Sing, N. Y., March 11, 1858.

[252.] 2. ANNA, b. Oct, 6, 1767 ; m. John Clark, of New Brunswick, formerly of Rhode Island, and d. at St. Johns, N. B., in 1810.

[253.] 3. WILLIAM, (617) b. Oct. 29, 1769 ; m. Sarah Moore, and d. in New York city, July 8, 1804.

[254.] 4. SARAH, b. April 6, 1775 ; m. David Peck, (686) in Feb. 1800, and d. in Greenwich, Dec. 11, 1809.

[255.] 5. RHODA, b. March 19, 1777 ; m. Moses Judah, and d. in New York city in 1814.

[256.] 6. POLLY, b. Feb. 13, 1779 ; m. William Ray, and d. New York city, in March 1818.

CHILDREN OF ISAAC PECK (81) AND ELIZABETH, HIS WIFE, ALL BORN IN GREENWICH, CONN

[257.] 1. SANDS F., b. Dec. 7, 1785, and d. unm. in Greenwich, Aug. 20, 1826.

[258.] 2. ISAAC, (622) b. July 19, 1787 ; m. Harriet Mead, in 1814, and d. in Whitman, Ind., in 1865.

[259.] 3. DEBORAH, b. Sept. 29, 1789 ; m, Benjamin Sellick, and, in 1876, was living in Greenwich, Conn. Her husband had d. in Greenwich, April 16, 1846.

[260.] 4. STEPHEN, (623) b. Nov. 4, 1792, m. Catharine B. Walton, and d. in New York city, Dec. 13, 1820.

CHILDREN OF THOMAS PECK (84) AND MARY, HIS WIFE, ALL BORN IN GREENWICH, CONN.

[261.] 1. SUSANNA, b. June 19, 1778 ; m. Henry Waring, and d. in Brooklyn, N. Y., June 25, 1840.

[262.] 2. THOMAS, (627) b. March 30, 1780 ; m. Mary Mosher, and d. in Greenwich, March 5, 1854.

CHILDREN OF NATHANIEL PECK (88) AND JERUSHA, HIS WIFE, ALL BORN IN GREENWICH CONN.

[263.] 1. MARY, b. Aug. 6, 1767 ; m. Ezra Marshall, and d. in Greenwich, about 1800.

[264.]   2. NATHANIEL, (634) b. May 10, 1750 ; m. Experience Wood, and d. in Charleston, S. C., in Aug. 1803.

[265.]   3. HEZEKIAH, b. Sept. 26, 1752, and d. unm. in Greenwich, Aug. 31, 1774.

[266.]   4. EPHRAIM, (641) b. Jan. 5, 1755; m. 1. Sarah Classon and m. 2. Margaret Miner, and d. in Greenwich, June 15, 1806.

[267.]   5. ESTHER, b. July 12, 1756 ; m. Jeremiah Mead, Jr., and d. in Butler Co., O., in 1819.   Her husband d. there in 1831, aged 76.

[268.]   6. ELIZABETH, b. May 8, 1757, and d. unm. in Greenwich, Dec. 8, 1841.

[269.]   7. CHARLOTTE, b. Jan. 3, 1763, and d. in Greenwich, probably in infancy.

[270.]   8. ISAAC, (645) b. June 9, 1766 ; m. Rebecca Wardwell, and d. in New York city about 1803.   His wife d. there about 1840.

[271.]   9. JERUSHA, b. May 14, 1770 ; m. 1. John A. Graham, in 1787, who d. in May 1796 ; m. 2. Ebenezer Graham, in 1798, and m. 3. Nathaniel Ferris, in 1804, and d., in Greenwich, Sept. 8, 1815.

CHILDREN OF JOSHUA PECK (90) AND SARAH, HIS WIFE, ALL BORN
IN GREENWICH, CONN.

[272.]   1. EDWARD, b. in 1758, and d. unm. in New York city about 1783.

[273.]   2. BENJAMIN, (651) b. Jan. 26, 1760 ; m. Gertrude Van Epps, and d. in Charlton, N. Y., Nov. 17, 1817.

[274.]   3. SARAH, m. Hamlet Wright. and d. in Charlton, N. Y., Oct. 24, 1832.

[275.]   4. MARY, b. April 23, 1770 ; m. Seth Godfrey, and d. in Livonia, N. Y., May 14, 1842, where her husband also d., Aug. 30, 1851, aged 83.

[276.]   5. GIDEON, (652) b. Jan. 5, 1775 ; m. Phebe Wilkinson, and d. in Westfield, N. Y., Nov. 17, 1847.

CHILDREN OF JONATHAN PECK (96) AND MEHITABLE, HIS WIFE,
ALL BORN IN GREENWICH, CONN.

[277.] 1. JONATHAN RICHARD, (660) b. Dec. 7, 1768; m.
Theodosia Lockwood, of Greenwich, Oct. 8, 1784; removed
from Greenwich to Flushing, Long Island, N. Y., about 1790;
was the common ancestor of the numerous families of his surname in that locality, and d. there April 4, 1822. He was a
man of great business sagacity and enterprise.

[278.] 2. ABRAHAM, b. in 1771, and d. unm., in Greenwich, about 1810.

[279.] 3. CHARLES, (669) b. Aug. 23, 1773; m. Nancy
Hobby, dau. of Jabez M. Hobby, April 12, 1801, and d. in
Greenwich, Jan. 5, 1851. His wife had d. there March 10,
1823.

[280.] 4. SARAH, b. in 1776, and d. unm. in New York city
about 1836.

CHILDREN OF GEORGE PECK (97) AND MARY, HIS WIFE, ALL BORN
IN GREENWICH, CONN.

[281.] 1. GEORGE, b. in 1765, and d. unm., in Greenwich,
June 5, 1790.

[282.] 2. FREDERICK, [675] b. Dec. 6, 1767; m. Hannah
Lockwood and d. in Greenwich, Sept. 18, 1831.

[283.] 3. AUGUSTUS, (680) b. in 1769 and m. Jerusha Lockwood.

[284.] 4. MARY, b. June 6, 1771; m. Drake Lockwood, Dec.
4, 1791, and d. in Greenwich, in May 1841.

[285.] 5. CHARLOTTE, b. Aug. 20, 1779; Ethan Ferris in
March, 1799, and d. in Madison, N. J., June 19, 1838.

CHILDREN OF THEOPHILUS PECK (107) AND REBECCA, HIS WIFE,
ALL BORN IN GREENWICH, CONN.

[286.] 1. DAVID, (686) b. Feb. 1754; m. 1. Amy Rundell,
Aug. 10, 1773, who d. Jan. 31, 1793; and m. 2. Alathea Honey-
well, in 1794; resided in Greenwich where he was a farmer

and Baptist minister; and d. there April 23, 1835. His last wife d. May 14, 1850.

[287.] 2. GIDEON, (706) b. Sept. 3, 1756; m. 1. Eunice Close, Oct. 4, 1781, who d. April 12, 1801, and m. 2. Jerusha Lyon, Nov. 7, 1804. He d. in Greenwich, Jan. 7, 1813.

[288,] 3. THEOPHILUS, b. Dec. 8, 1758, and d. unm., in Greenwich, Jan. 15, 1777.

[289.] 4. THOMAS, (713) b. July 4, 1761; m. Tamizon Reynolds and settled in Poundridge, N. Y., where he d. May 5, 1829. His wife d. there Dec. 12, 1822.

[290.] 5. GILBERT, b. April 26, 1763; m. Deborah Rundell; resided in Greenwich and d. there July 13, 1832. His wife d. May 25, 1844. He had no children.

[291.] 6. SOLOMON, (719) b. Nov. 25, 1765; m. Mary Lyon, dau. of Caleb Lyon, and d. in Greenwich, Feb. 7, 1850.

[292.] 7. CHARLOTTE, b. Nov. 4, 1768; m. Gilbert Close, son of Odell Close, and d. in Greenwich, Sept. 26, 1806.

[293.] 8. REBECCA, b. Aug. 1, 1771; m. Thomas Purdy and d. in Bedford, N. Y., Oct. 13, 1838. Her husband d. Dec. 8, 1843.

[294.] 9. ELIPHALET, b. May 18, 1774; m. Rachel Lyon, dau. of Caleb Lyon, and d., in Greenwich, Sept. 11, 1851. He had no children.

[295.] 10. RUTH, b. Dec. 20, 1777; m. Luther Lyon and d. in Genoa, N. Y., June 28, 1843.

CHILDREN OF SAMUEL PECK (112) AND HANNAH, HIS WIFE, ALL
BORN IN GREENWICH, CONN.

[296.] 1. ELIZABETH, b. April 11, 1763; m. Thaddeus Reed, of Sharon, Conn., May 24, 1796, and d., in Sharon, May 26, 1823. Her husband d. there March 24, 1826.

[297.] 2. SAMUEL, (722) b. Dec. 22, 1765; m. Mary Mead, dau. of Benjamin Mead, 3d, Jan. 26, 1790, and d., in Greenwich, July 27, 1841. His wife b. Nov. 2, 1770, and d. there in April 1861.

[298.]   3. JABEZ, (731) b. May 12, 1768; m. Mary Mead, dau. Jehiel Mead, and d., in Greenwich, Sept. 25, 1831.

[289.]   4. HANNAH, b. June 8, 1770; m. Darius Mead and d., in Greenwich, May 5, 1836.   Her husband d. there Aug. 16, 1841, aged 74.

[300.]   5. JARED, (735) b. Feb. 27, 1773 ; m. Tamizon Adee and d., in Greenwich, in May 1842.

[301.]   6. RACHEL, b. May 19, 1775; m. Luther Peck (237) Sept. 19, 1797, and d., in Greenwich, April 21, 1855.

[302.]   7. ISAAC, (744) b. March 22, 1777; m. Sarah Knapp, Sept. 10, 1799; was a farmer, and resided at Round Hill, in Greenwich; represented that town in the Legislature of Connecticut, and d., in Greenwich, Aug. 1, 1859.   His wife d. there May 9, 1860.

[303.]   8. SARAH, b. March 25, 1779 ; m. Moses Husted, May 22, 1798, and d., in Greenwich, March 3, 1833.   Her husband d. there June 20, 1842.

[304.]   9. DANIEL, (745) b. Aug. 8, 1781; m. Hannah Mead, dau. of Platt Mead, and Deborah (306) Mead, May 25, 1814, and d., in Greenwich, Jan. 14, 1861.

[305.]   10. HULDAH, b. May 2, 1787; m. Benoni Peck (694) Dec. 2, 1812, and d. in Genoa, N. Y., April 7, 1865.

CHILDREN OF BENJAMIN PECK, (113) ALL BORN IN GREEN-
WICH, CONN.

[306.]   1. DEBORAH, b. Feb. 5, 1768; m. Platt Mead, son of Sylvanus Mead, July 24, 1790, and d., in Greenwich, Nov. 23, 1838.

[307.]   2. BENJAMIN, (749) b. May 20, 1773 ; m. Elizabeth Sherwood, July 28, 1810, and d., in New York city, Oct. 30, 1836.   His wife had d. Jan. 7, 1816.

[308.]   3. HANNAH, b. Feb. 21, 1775; m. James Peck (555) May 29, 1803, and d., at Bridgeport, Conn., Sept. 19, 1860.

[309.]   4. JAMES, (751) b. March 11, 1777; m. Mary Holmes, Feb. 8, 1804, and d., in Port Chester, N. Y., Sept. 22, 1835. His wife d. there Sept. 14, 1875, in her 94th year.

[310.]　5. ELIAS, (757) b. May 9, 1779; m. 1. Deborah Hobby, May 13, 1804; m. 2. Mary Haight, Oct. 31, 1820, and d., in Greenwich, May 14, 1846.

[311.]　6. NATHAN, (763) b. Jan. 17, 1781; m. Sarah Secor, Feb. 3, 1810, and d., in Greenwich, Sept. 21, 1860.

CHILDREN OF ABRAHAM PECK (114) AND ANNA, HIS WIFE, ALL BORN IN GREENWICH, CONN.

[312.]　1. ELIZABETH, b. Sept. 26, 1771, and d. in Greenwich, Oct. 31, 1772.

[313]　2. LAVINA, b. July 9, 1773; m. Robert Peck (340) and d., in Greenwich, about 1815.

[314.]　3. HANNAH, b. May 16, 1776; m. Jonathan Knapp, and d., in LaGrange, N. Y., about 1814.

[315.]　4. ABRAHAM, (774) b. April 30, 1779; m. Anna Peck (343) and d., in Lexington, Indiana, March 20, 1858. His wife d. there June 28, 1822.

[316.]　5. ANNA, b. Sept. 30, 1783; m. Silas Knapp, and d., in Washiugton, N. Y,, Jan. 4, 1860.

[317.]　6. ESTHER, b. Aug. 25, 1786; m. Seth Lawton, and d., in Washington, N. Y., Dec. 6, 1851.

CHILDREN OF ISRAEL PECK AND LAVINA, HIS WIFE, ALL BORN IN GREENWICH, CONN.

[318,]　1. ISRAEL, b. March 8, 1783, and d., in Greenwich, May 1, 1793.

[319.]　2. NEHEMIAH, (779) b. Dec. 2, 1784; m. Laviṇa Marshall, who d. Feb. 10, 1856. He d., in Greenwich, Dec. 13 1866.

[320.]　3. ELIZABETH, b. Dec. 5, 1786, and d., in Greenwich, Dec. 6, 1786.

[321.]　4. RACHEL, b. Oct. 28, 1787, and, in 1870, was living unm. in Port Chester, N. Y.

[322.]　5. LAVINA, b. March 20, 1791; m. Nathan Brown, of Rye, N. Y., Sept. 5, 1810, and was living there in 1870.

[323.] 6. ISRAEL, again, (789) b. Dec. 7, 1794; m. Dorinda Peck (731,) Oct. 20, 1819, and, in 1876, was living in Port Chester, N. Y.

[324.] 7. ELIZABETH, again, b. May 2, 1797, and d., in Greenwich, Jan. 14, 1808.

CHILDREN OF PETER PECK (119) AND SARAH, HIS WIFE, ALL BORN IN NEW MILFORD, CONN.

[325.] 1. REUBEN, (791) b. Feb. 8, 1772; m. 1. Tryphena Bishop, in 1799, and m. 2. Jane Haight, who d. in Aug. 1869. He d., at Glen's Falls, N. Y., May 6, 1851.

[326.] 2. DANIEL, (796) b. Jan. 22, 1775; m. Content Sisson, Sept. 23, 1806, and d., at Glen's Falls, N. Y., Aug. 12, 1836. His wife was living there in 1869.

[327.] 3. EDMUND, (806) b. Nov. 21, 1778; m. Sarah Ranger, of East Hampton, N. Y., and d., at Glen's Falls, N. Y., March 14, 1852, where his wife also died.

CHILDREN OF ENOS PECK, (122) ALL BORN IN NEW HAVEN, VT., EXCEPT THE LAST THREE, WHO WERE BORN IN POMPEY, N. Y.

[328.] 1. ELIHU, (808) b. Jan. 1, 1775; m. Ruana Farnham and d., in Camillus, N.. Y., March 7, 1841.

[329.] 2. PHEBE, b. May 4, 1777; m. Daniel Thomas and d., in Pompey, N. Y., Oct. 11, 1850.

[330.] 3. MARTHA, b. May 9, 1781; m. Jonathan Farnham and d., in Pompey, N. Y., May 12, 1836.

[331.] 4. PETER, (819) b. Sept. 8, 1783; m. Eunice Beckwith. who d. in Jan., 1844. He d., in Van Buren, N. Y., Jan. 3, 1871.

[332.] 5. ANNA, b. Jan. 6, 1785; m. Joel Hall and, in 1870, was living in Marion, N. Y.

[333.] 6. ENOS, (824) b. Aug. 14, 1790; m. Annis Hopkins and, in 1875, was living in Camillus, N. Y.

[334.] 7. ISAAC, (828) b. April 4, 1793; m. 1. Rachel Knapp, m. 2. Hannah Coats and m. 3. Susan Cheney, and d., in Van Buren, N. Y., April 24, 1864.

[335.]   8. RACHEL, b. Feb. 14, 1796 ; m. Holden Hart and d., in Belleview, Penn., about 1863.

[336.]   9. CHLOE, b. June 11, 1799 ; m. Eleazer Waterman and, in 1875, was living in Van Buren, N. Y.

[337.]   10. ALMOND, (839) b. Oct. 16, 1801 ; m. Fidelia Dewey and, in 1875, was living in Lysander, N. Y.

CHILDREN OF ROBERT PECK (125) AND ANN, HIS WIFE, ALL BORN IN GREENWICH, CONN.

[338.]   1. NATHAN, b. Dec. 12, 1767, and d., in Greenwich, Dec. 16, 1767.

[339.]   2. MOLLY, b. Dec. 21, 1768 ; m. Samuel Whiting, of Darien, Conn., June 20, 1789, and d., in Darien, May 28, 1829.

[340.]   3. ROBERT, (845) b. Nov. 1, 1771 ; m. Lavina Peck (313) and d., in Greenwich, April 30, 1799, being killed by the fall of a tree.

[341.]   4. NATHAN, again, b. Feb. 18, 1774, and d., in Greenwich, Nov. 2, 1775.

[342.]   5. URIAH, b. Jan. 22, 1777, and d., in Greenwich, Oct. 20, 1777.

[343.]   6. ANNA, b. June 21, 1779 ; m. Abraham Peck (315) and d., in Lexington, Ind., June 28, 1822.

[344.]   7. PHINEAS, b. May 15, 1782, and d., in Greenwich, Feb. 13, 1789.

[345.]   8. ELIAS, (847) b. Jan. 5, 1785 ; m. Eunice Wilson, Oct. 11, 1812, and d., in La Salle, Ill., Aug. 10, 1867.   His wife had d., in Stamford, Conn., April 26, 1865.

[346.]   9. LEWIS, (854) b. Dec. 15, 1787 ; m. Sally Peck (575) Oct. 18, 1808, and d., in Sharon, Conn., Dec. 12, 1857.

CHILDREN OF EBENEZER PECK (127) AND HANNAH, HIS WIFE, ALL BORN IN GREENWICH, CONN.

[347.]   1. EBENEZER, (859) b. March 22, 1771 ; m. Elizabeth Raymond, of Norwalk, Conn., Nov. 8, 1799, and d., in Stamford, Conn., Nov. 9, 1837, and she d. March 16, 1848.

[348.] 2. HANNAH, b. Feb. 28, 1774 ; m. Ezra Lockwood, of Watertown, Conn., and d. there July 15, 1854.

[349.] 3. ELIZABETH, b. July 7, 1776 ; m. Augustus Lockwood, of Stamford, Conn., Jan. 1, 1800, and d. there Nov. 27, 1865.

[350.] 4. DEBORAH, b, July 13, 1779 ; m. Elias Raymond, of Norwalk, Conn., Jan. 7, 1802, and d. there June 8, 1855.

[351.] 5. RUFUS, (864) b. March 22, 1782; m. Letitia Lockwood, of Greenwich, July 8, 1816, and d., in Greenwich, July 8, 1856.

[352.] 6. EDMOND, b. May 11, 1787, and d,, in Greenwich, May 26, 1802.

[353.] 7. ANN, b. Nov. 6, 1790 ; m. James Schofield, of Stamford, Conn., in Nov. 1844, and d., in Sharon, Conn., May 12, 1864.

[354.] 8. MARY, b. Nov. 6, 1790 ; m. Enoch P. Peck (573) Nov. 7, 1815, and d., in Sharon, Conn., March 28, 1866.

CHILDREN OF SAMUEL PECK (130) AND CATHARINE, HIS WIFE, ALL BORN IN BEDFORD, N. Y.

[355.] 1. ANN, b. April 1, 1785 ; m. Stephen Schofield, of Bedford, N. Y., and d. there April 10, 1812.

[356.] 2. DEBORAH, b. July 17, 1787 ; m. Stephen Westcott, of Bedford, N. Y., and d. there July 5, 1819.

[357.] 3. CATHARINE, b. June 17, 1790 ; m. David D Smith, of Bedford, N. Y., and d., in Groton, N. Y., Aug. 30, 1867.

[358.] 4. POLLY, b. June 14, 1794 ; m. Jeremiah Miller, of Bedford, N. Y., and d. there about 1847.

[359.] 5. SALLY, b. March 1, 1797 ; m. Robert Quintard, of Greenwich, Sept. 23, 1817, and d., in Greenwich, in 1869.

CHILDREN OF JOHN PECK (136) AND JERUSHA, HIS WIFE, ALL BORN IN WALLINGFORD, CONN., EXCEPT ROXANA (367) AND SAMUEL (368) WHO WERE BORN IN CHESHIRE, CONN.

[360.] 1. SAMUEL, b. April 10, 1756 ; was in the Revolutionary Army, where he d. of disease, unm., Oct, 13, 1776.

[361.] 2. PATIENCE, b. March 28, 1758; m. Samuel Atwater, Dec. 6, 1781, and d., in Cheshire, Conn., Jan. 22, 1837.
Her husband d. there Jan. 12, 1848.

[362.] 3. JERUSHA, b. June 8, 1760; m. Warren Benham,
Feb. 22, 1786, and d., in Cheshire, April 16, 1833. Her husband
had d. there Jan. 16, 1829.

[363.] 4. JOHN, (867) b. April 9, 1762; m. Merab Moss,
Feb. 22, 1786, and d., in Cheshire, March 12, 1813. His wife
d. there Feb. 15, 1835.

[364.] 5. MARY, b. June 13, 1764; m. Jesse Thompson and
d., in Cheshire, Dec. 1, 1826.

[365.] 6. ASA, (873) b. March 10, 1767; m. Betsey Hall,
Feb. 4, 1789, and d., in Cheshire, Aug. 9, 1839. His wife d.
there May 28, 1851.

[366.] 7. LEVI, (881) b. Feb. 21, 1770; m. Esther L. Ives
May 27, 1799, and d., in Cheshire, Feb. 16, 1813. His wife d.
there Nov. 22, 1847.

[367.] 8. ROXANA, b. Feb. 1, 1774, and d., in Cheshire
Jan. 15, 1775.

[368.] 9. SAMUEL, again, (884) b. May 23, 1777; m. 1.
Elizabeth Brooks, Feb. 22, 1801, who d. Sept. 2, 1807; m. 2.
Lydia Tyler, Feb. 1, 1809, who d. Jan. 17, 1821, and m. 3.
Harriet Brocket, Nov. 13, 1822. He settled in Cheshire, Conn.,
and resided there until 1827, and afterward, until 1835, in the
town of Prospect, Conn. He was a Captain in the war of
1812, and subseqently a Major and Lieut.-Colonel in the Connecticut Militia, a Deacon, for several years, of the Congregational Church, of Prospect, and a Justice of the Peace for more
than twenty years, successively, in the towns of Cheshire and
Prospect, both of which towns he represented in the State
Legislature. His superior and well cultivated mind, genial
temperament and popular and agreeable manners secured him
the respect, esteem and affection of all who knew him. In
1835 he emigrated from Prospect to East Bloomfield, N. Y.,
where he d. April 21, 1848. His last wife, in 1862, was living
in Greenville, Mich.

CHILDREN OF SAMUEL PECK (140) AND SUSANNA, HIS WIFE, ALL
BORN IN WALLINGFORD, CONN.

[369.]   1. SARAH, b. Oct. 16, 1761; m. Ebenezer Johnson
and d. in Lexington, now the town of Jewett, N. Y., June 19,
1830.

[370.]   2. LUCY, b. Feb. 26, 1763; m. Chester Hull, of Wallingford, and d. in Lexington, now the town of Jewett, N. Y.,
July 4, 1829.   Her husband d. there Jan. 10, 1847.

[371.]   3. THEOPHILUS, (897) b. Sept. 2, 1764; m. Mary
Hull, of Wallingford, and, in 1789, emigrated from Wallingford to Lexington, now the town of Jewett, N. Y., where he
settled and d. Dec. 22, 1839.   His wife d. there March 29, 1849.

[372.]   4. SAMUEL, (900) b. July 20. 1766; m. Abigail Hall
and removed with his brother, Theophilus, from Wallingford
to Lexington, now the town of Jewett, N. Y., in 1789, where
he settled and d. March 9, 1834; and where, also, his wife d.
July 23, 1856.

[373.]   5. JOHN, (911) b. Aug. 23, 1768; m. Eunice Hall
and d., in Farmington, Conn., Jan. 21, 1811.   His wife d. there
in 1812.

[374.]   6. ISAAC, (919) b. Jan. 15, 1771; m. Miriam Rice,
Dec. 22, 1799; lived on the homestead of his ancestors, in Wallingford, and d. there Feb. 24, 1847, as did his wife Jan. 3,
1861.

[375.]   7. PATTY, b. May 7. 1773; m. Jesse Peck (395) and
d., in Farmington, Conn., Feb. 10, 1826.

[376.]   8. LUCINA, b. Jan. 8, 1775; m. Samuel Gillett, of
Bloomfield, Conn., and d., in Farmington, Conn.. May 1, 1844.

[377.]   9. AMOS, (925) b. July 27, 1777; m. Sybil Parker,
Sept. 22, 1799; settled in Lexington, now the town of Jewett,
N. Y., and d. there Feb. 26, 1854.   His wife d. there April 11,
1845.

[378.]   10. SUSANNAH. b. April 6, 1779; m, Levi Hull, of
Wallingford, in 1803, and d., in Wallingford, December 30,
1805.

CHILDREN OF CHARLES PECK, (141) JEHIEL AND HANNAH BORN
IN WALLINGFORD, AND THE OTHERS IN CHESHIRE, CONN.

[379.]   1. JEHIEL, b. Dec. 24, 1757, and was a soldier in the
Revolutionary Army.   In the latter part of his life he settled
in the State of Maryland, and d., in Rockville, in that State,
about 1830.   It is said that he was twice married and that he
had several children, but very little can be ascertained in relation to them or their descendants.[1]

[380.]   2. HANNAH, b. April 5, 1760 ; m. 1. Stephen Yale,
of Wallingford, and m. 2. Elihu Thompson, and d. in Wallingford.

[381.]   3. JESSE, (934) b. Nov. 21, 1761 ; m. 1. Mary Raymond, of Cheshire, and m. 2. Sarah Dean, and d., in Farmington, O., May 11, 1832.   His last wife d. Oct. 14, 1838.

[382.]   4. DOROTHY, b. March 16, 1763 ; m. Caleb Parker
Nov. 1, 1783, and d., in Cheshire, May 12, 1806.   Her husband
d. there Dec. 31, 1800.

[383.]   5. ABIGAIL, b. Nov. 10, 1764, and d., unm., in
Cheshire, Jan. 10, 1844.

[384.]   6. CHARLES, b. July 10, 1766, and d., in Wallingford, in March 1767.

[385.]   7. ABIAH, b. March 16, 1768, and d., in Wallingford,
Sept. 25, 1773.

[386.]   8. BENJAMIN, b. April 11, 1770 ; entered the Revolutionary Army as a drummer boy, in 1780, and served until
the close of the war ; was present at the execution of Major
Andre and at the surrender of Cornwallis ; m. 1. a Widow Dodge,
and m. 2., in 1823, Sarah Wilson Cutter, and d., in Fall River,
Mass., Oct. 3, 1854.   His last wife d., in Providence R. I., Dec.
24, 1844.   He had no children.

[387.]   9. CHARLES, again, (943) b. Aug. 14. 1772 ; m.
Nancy Fanning, in 1793, who d. April 8, 1836, and m. 2.

---

1. *Henry*, a son of his, about eighty years of age, residing in Baltimore, Md., very
strangely declined to give any account of his father, or of his father's descendants, and
all other attempts to gain similar information from other sources (except as to a
daughter, *Clarissa*, who m. Webb Hart and d., in Meriden Conn., about 1851,) have
proved ineffectual.

Emeline Ormsbee, in Sept. 1840, and d., in Shaftsbury, Vt., May 4, 1857.

[388.] 10. JOEL, (951) b. Oct. 15, 1774 ; m. Abigail Tuttle, June 9, 1804, and d., in Scott, N. Y., Oct. 31, 1851.

[389.] 11. EUNICE, b. Oct. 5, 1776 ; m. Stephen Seymour and d., in Windsor, N. Y , in March 1852. He d. in April 1850.

[390.] 12. JOHN, (957) b. Sept. 28, 1780 ; m. Lucinda Johnson and d., in Bristol, Conn., Nov. 24, 1863. His wife had d. there April 20, 1863.

CHILDREN OF NICHOLAS PECK (146) AND DINAH, HIS WIFE, ALL BORN IN WALLINGFORD, CONN.

[391.] 1. OLIVE, b. Oct. 29, 1766, and d., in Wallingford, Aug. 8, 1770.

[392.] 2. JESSE S., (966) b. April 15, 1769 ; m. Sally Barnes, of Middletown, Conn., and d., in Buffalo, N. Y., March 3, 1845.

[393.] 3. MILES, (972) b. May 15, 1771 ; m. Eunice Hall, of Wallingford. and d. there March 27, 1832. His wife d. there April 5, 1842.

[394.] 4. OLIVE, again, b. Aug. 9, 1773 ; m. Bilious B. Newton, of Pittsburgh, Penn., and d. there Oct. 19, 1854. He d., at Braceville, O., June 25, 1834.

ONLY CHILD OF JOEL PECK (148) AND MARY, HIS WIFE, BORN IN FARMINGTON, CONN.

[395.] 1. JESSE, (976) b. May 4, 1778 ; m. 1. Patty Peck (375) who d. Feb. 10, 1826, and m. 2. Margaret Baldwin, and he d., in Farmington, Conn., June 23, 1856.

CHILDREN OF SAMUEL PECK (149) AND HANNAH, HIS WIFE, ALL BORN IN LYME, CONN.

[396.] 1. RICHARD, (979) b. Aug. 5, 1753; m. 1. Sarah Tennant, in 1775, and m. 2. Elizabeth Chamberlin ; removed from Lyme, in 1788, and settled in Lexington, N. Y., and d., in Durham, N. Y., Oct. 24, 1837.

[397.]   2. SAMUEL, (991) m. 1. Lucretia Ingraham, Oct. 18, 1781, and m. 2. Elizabeth Conklin, and d. in Lyme in the Fall of 1837.

[398.]   3. ELIFF, b. about 1757 ; m. William Fellows and d. in Watertown, N. Y.,

[399.]   4. HANNAH, b. May 27, 1759 ; m. Silas Robbins, Dec. 13, 1782, nnd d., in Lyme, Jan. 1, 1840.

[400.]   5. ABNER, (997) b. May 4, 1761 ; 'm. Hannah Tinker, Nov. 30, 1786, and d., iu Shelburne, Mass., June 4, 1842.   He was a soldier in the Revolutionary war, and one of the guards around the gallows at the execution of Major Andre.

[401.]   6. PHEBE, b. Sept. 5, 1764 ; m. Solomon Fellows and d., in Albion, N. Y , March 12, 1840.

[402.]   7. JASON, (1003) b. June 5, 1769 ; m. Rhoda Whitcomb, Nov. 27, 1794, and d., in Reading, N. Y., Oct. 2, 1845. He had settled in Reading in 1808.

[403.]   8. DORCAS, b. Jan. 5, 1772 ; m. Benjamin Farnsworth and d., in Charlemont, Mass., Oct. 23, 1858.

CHILD OF ABNER PECK (150) AND CAROLINE, HIS WIFE, BORN IN LYME, CONN.

[404]   1. NATHANIEL, b. Sept. 28, 1788.[1]

CHILDREN OF DARIUS PECK (151) AND ELIZABETH HIS WIFE, ALL BORN IN LYME, CONN.

[405.]   1. MARTIN, (1011) b. Oct. 8, 1759 ; m. 1. Lucy Sennet, who d. Aug. 19, 1805, and m. 2. Frances Seburn, who d., April 7, 1853, and he d., at Hector, N. Y., Sept. 30, 1808, where he had settled about the year 1800.

[406.]   2. ELIZABETH, b. Dec. 10, 1761, and m. Simeon Holton, of Montague, Mass.

[407.]   3. DARIUS, (1020) b. Feb. 2, 1764 ; Lydia Mack, July 20, 1786, and d., iu Phelps, N. Y., July 31, 1814.   He

---

1. There were probably other children, but none are found on the Lyme town records, and long and persistent effort to obtain information from other sources has been unavailing.

removed from Lyme to Conway, Mass., in 1789, and from Conway to Phelps, N. Y., in 1804.

[408.] 4. SIMEON, b. Jan. 3, 1766 ; said to have m. ——— Lamphere, and to have lived and d. in Deerfield, Mass.

[409.] 5. ANDREW, b. Feb. 2, 1768 ; said to have been m. and to have d. in one of the Western States.

[410.] 6. JOHN MOORE, (1031) b. Feb. 1, 1770 ; m. Abigail Pratt, about 1797, and d., in Bethany, N. Y., in Sept. 1831, to which place he had removed from Lyme, in 1830.

[411.] 7. HULDAH, b. Aug. 31, 1772; m. Elisha Rice and had daughters, *Phebe* and *Betsey.*

[412.] 8. WILLIAM, b. July 18, 1774, and d., unm., in Lyme, about 1794.

[413.] 9, ELISHA, b. May 16, 1777, and d., unm., in Lyme, about 1820.

[414.] 10. TIMOTHY, (1045) b. Aug. 15, 1779 ; m. 1. Catharine Smith, Sept. 18, 1805, who d. April 30, 1833 ; m. 2. Mehitable Smith, who d. March 19, 1843, and m. 3. Betsey Brockway, who d. Nov. 6, 1845. He was for 30 or 40 years a Deacon of the Church in Lyme, and d. there March 14, 1851.

CHILDREN OF DANIEL PECK (154) AND JERUSHA, HIS WIFE, ALL BORN IN LYME, CONN.

[415.] 1. ELISHA, b. Feb. 3, 1766, and d., unm., in Lyme, Sept. 7. 1774.

[416.] 2. JERUSHA, b. Jan. 1, 1768 ; m. Benjamin Crosby and d., in Ellington, Conn., March 8, 1852.

[417.] 3. DANIEL, (1059) b. Oct. 21, 1769 ; m. Persis Ladd, of Stafford, Conn., was a physician and d., in Stafford, Conn., April 20, 1828.

[418.] 4. RUTH, b. Sept. 19, 1771 ; m. William Crowell and d., in Rome, O., June 16, 1856.

[419.] 5. EZEKIEL, (1065) b. Dec. 11, 1773 ; m. Lucina Clark and d., in East Haddam, Conn., Dec. 24, 1831. His wife d. Jan. 13, 1867, aged 85.

[420.]   6. ASENATH, b. Aug. 7, 1777 ; m. Eliel Parker and d., in East Haddam, Conn., Sept. 5, 1817.

[421.]   7. CLARISSA, b. Jan. 12, 1780, and d., unm., in Stafford, Conn., Nov. 27, 1825.

CHILDREN OF JEDEDIAH PECK (173) AND TABITHA, HIS WIFE, ALL BORN IN LYME, CONN.

[422.]   1. HEPSIBAH, b. June 27, 1774; m. Abel Sill, March 9, 1796, and d., in Burlington, N. Y., Jan. 19, 1860.

[423.]   2. POLLY, b. Nov. 6, 1776 ; m. David Willard, Jan. 7, 1802, and d., in Otisco, N. Y., June, 22, 1856.

[424.]   3. ELIJAH, b. Aug. 29, 1780, and d., in Lyme, Conn., Sept. 20, 1780.

[425.]   4. ELIJAH, again, (1076) b. Oct. 1, 1781 ; m. Clarissa Bates, Jan. 22, 1807, and d., in Sheffield, O., June 7, 1840.

[426.]   5. PETER, (1084) b. Nov. 12, 1783 ; m. Sarah Colgrove, March 5, 1809, and d., in Monroe, O., April 8, 1826.

[427.]   6. ANNA, b. May 27, 1786, and d., unm., in Burlington, N. Y., Aug. 8, 1815.

[428.]   7. JEDEDIAH, (1090) b. May 19, 1788 ; m. Sarah Peck, widow of his brother, Peter, and d., in Frederick, O., March 8, 1844.

CHILDREN OF ELISHA PECK (180) AND OLIVE, HIS WIFE.

[429.]   1. WILLIAM E., (1091) b. in East Haddam, Conn., Sept. 5, 1786 ; m. Ruamah Huntley, Feb. 22, 1809, and, in 1865, was living in Spring Prairie, Wis.

[430.]   2. LUTHER P., b. in East Haddam, Conn., June 19, 1788, and d., unm., in Ypsilanti, Mich., Feb. 19, 1851.

[431.]   3. JOSEPH H., (1100) b. in East Haddam, Conn., Aug. 5, 1790 ; m. Sophara Churchill, in 1821, and d., in Ypsilanti, Mich., Feb. 15, 1849.

[432.]   4. ANNA G., b. in East Haddam, Conn., Sept. 15, 1792 ; m. Amos Graham, in 1812, and d., in Tully, N. Y., July 23, 1827.

[433.] 5. ELIZABETH L., b. in East Haddam, Conn., March 9, 1795, and d., unm., in Burlington, N. Y., March 15, 1813.

[434.] 6. OLIVE L., b. in East Haddam, Conn., July 7, 1797; m. Ephraim Huntington, in 1828, and d., in Burlington, Wis., Jan. 17, 1861.

[435.] 7. ELISHA, (1102) b. in Canaan, Conn , Oct. 3, 1800; m. Olive Bailey, Nov. 6, 1826, and, in 1869, was living in Victor, N. Y.

[436.] 8. BENJAMIN, (1105) b. in Canaan, N. Y., Feb. 28, 1803; m. Mary Alby, in 1826, and, in 1865, was living in Delaware, O.

[437.] 9. LOIS, b. in Burlington, N. Y., May 21, 1805; m. Isaac N. Green, in Oct. 1832, and, in 1861, was living in London, Mich.

[438.] 10. ASA, b. in Burlington, N. Y., Feb. 8, 1808, and d., unm., in Ypsilanti, Mich., Jan. 17, 1842.

[439.] 11. SILAS, (1113) b. in Burlington, N. Y., June 10, 1811; m. Mary Rappler, Dec. 29, 1833, and d., in Burlington, Wis., April 23, 1865.

CHILDREN OF DAN PECK (190) AND LOVINA, HIS WIFE, ALL BORN IN LYME, CONN.

[440.] 1. LEMUEL, b. Oct. 29, 1787, and d., in Lyme, June 17, 1788.

[441.] 2. SILAS, (1118) b. May 8, 1789; m. Abby Cutting, Oct. 28, 1810, who d. March 10, 1865; settled in Pittsfield, N. Y., and d. there Sept. 7, 1864.

[442.] 3. EDWARD C., (1127) b. Oct. 20, 1790; m. Lovisa Chapin, Jan. 11, 1818; settled in New Lyme, O., and d. there Dec. 20, 1866.

[443.] 4. ANSEL, b. Sept. 23, 1792, and probably d. many years since unm., in the western part of the State of Ohio.

[444.] 5. POLLY, b. June 15, 1801; m. Elias Brockway, and, in 1870, was living in the State of Michigan.

[445.] 6. LYMAN, (1134) b. June 18, 1803; m. Laura E. Brown, Nov. 2, 1830, and, in 1870, was living in New Lyme, O.

CHILDREN OF SAMUEL GRIFFIN PECK (191) AND ZIPPORAH, HIS
WIFE, ALL BORN IN LYME, CONN.

[446.] 1. WILLIAM D., (1136) b. Sept. 11, 1791; m. Zipporah Minor, Sept. 12, 1816, who d. Oct. 3, 1863, and, in 1870,
was living in Fairfield, Iowa.

[447.] 2. JOSIAH J., (1145) b. Jan. 31, 1793; m. Betsey
Bogul, who d. Oct. 14, 1863.   He had d. in Colebrook, O., Oct.
25, 1849.

[448.] 3. SUSANNAH, b. Aug. 17, 1794; m. Calvin Knowlton, May 28, 1812, and, in 1870, was living in Morgan, O.

[449.] 4. BETSEY, b. March 27, 1796; m. Eli Andrews,
and, in 1870, was living in Bloomingdale, Mich.   .

[450.] 5. LOVISA, b. July 5, 1798; m. Selden Huntley and
d., in Beaver, Iowa, May 18, 1868.

[451.] 6. ELIJAH, (1149) b. March 26, 1800; m. Parny
Hubbard, March 27, 1822, and, in 1870, was living in New
Lyme, O.

[452.] 7. SAMUEL G., (1159) b. Feb. 2, 1802; m. Nancy
E. Canfield, Sept. 7, 1826, and, in 1875, was living in New
Lyme, O.   His wife d., in Rome, O., Feb. 21, 1872.

[453.] 8. SILAS, (1164) b. Feb. 19, 1804; m. 1. Angeline
Dee, Feb. 19, 1832; m. 2. Phebe Foreman and, in 1870, was
living in New Lyme, O.

[454.] 9. ZIPPORAH, b. Dec. 29, 1805, and d., unm., in
New Lyme, O., Dec. 24, 1828.

[455.] 10. MARY ANN, b. Feb. 1, 1808; m. Stephen Archer
and, in 1870, was living in New Hartford, Butler Co., Iowa.

CHILDREN OF NATHANIEL PECK, (193), SON OF JASPER PECK,
(62) ALL BORN IN LYME, CONN.

[456.] 1. ABNER, early emigrated to Muskingum, O., where
he settled and d. many years since.   Nothing further can be
ascertained about him, or whether he had any descendants.

[457.] 2. LOT, (1167) b. in 1760; m. Mrs. Polly Kent, May
13, 1787; first settled in Lyme, Conn., whence, in 1806, he
emigrated to what is now West Bloomfield, N. Y., and from

thence, in 1822, removed to Tonawanda, N. Y., where he d. in 1837.   His wife d. in West Bloomfield, in May 1816, aged 57.

The christian names of two daughters, next in the order of birth, cannot be ascertained.   One m. ———— Latimer, and first settled in Lyme, Conn.   The other m. Saddens Miller, and settled and d. in Alstead, N. H.

[458.]   5. SUSANNAH, b. Jan. 22, 1770 ; m. Gurdon Lamphere, and settled in Sullivan Co., N. H., whence, in 1815, they emigrated to Mendon, N. Y., where he died.   She d. in West Bloomfield, N. Y., April 28, 1849.

[459.]   6. JOHN, b. in 1772 ; m. Temperance Thompson ; emigrated from Lyme, Conn., and settled in Clarence, N. Y., about 1808, where his wife d. April 15, 1820, aged 36, and where he d. in Aug. 1843.   He had three sons, viz. : *Erastus*, b. in 1808 ; *John*, b. in Feb. 1810, and *William*, all of whom were unm. and d. some years before the death of their father. He had three daughters, one b. April 14, 1816, and d. in eight days, and *Caroline* and *Adeline*, twins, b. Aug. 11, 1819.   *Caroline* d. July 18, 1831.   *Adeline*, in 1836, m. Benjamin Driggs, who d. March 17, 1838, and she d., in Tonawanda, N. Y., April 8, 1847, having had, and leaving her surviving, but one child, *Leander B. Driggs*, b., in Tonawanda, Feb. 15, 1837, who, in 1871, was living in Virginia City, Montana Territory, and supposed to be unm., being the only survivor of the posterity of the above named John Peck.

[460.]   7. PHEBE, b. in 1774 ; m. John Haynes about 1796, and d., at Hoosick Falls, Rensselaer Co., N. Y., Oct. 19, 1850.

[461.]   8. PEGGY, b. in 1777 ; m. Linus Curtiss, of Granville, Mass., and d., in Charlestown, O., in 1833.

[462.]   9. HARRIS, (1174) b. Oct. 28, 1779 ; left Lyme, Conn., about 1795, accompanying the early settlers of West Bloomfield, N. Y., where he also settled and resided until 1834, when he removed and settled in Wellington, O., and d. there Feb. 16, 1836.   He was thrice married.   He m. 1. Jerusha Gates, in West Bloomfield, who d. there Dec. 21, 1811, aged 33 ; m. 2. Mary Willes, in West Bloomfield, who d. there

Jan. 22, 1813, aged 23, and m. 3. Joanah Beckwith, in Lyme, Conn., who, in 1871, was living in Wellington, O.

[463.]· 10. WAITSTILL, b. July 11, 1785; m. Joseph Leavens, Sept. 6, 1801, and d., in Lansingburgh, N. Y., Aug, 22, 1851. Her son, *Josephus P. Leavens*, was living there in 1869.

CHILDREN OF JASPER PECK (194) AND PHEBE, HIS WIFE, ALL BORN IN LYME, CONN.

[464.] 1. PALMER, b. Dec. 18, 1765, and d., in Lyme, May 5, 1768.

[465.] 2. CLARK, (1185) b. Jan. 7, 1767 ; m. Caroline Hall Jan. 18. 1797, and d., in West Bloomfield, N. Y., Jan. 27, 1825, where he had settled in 1790.   His wife d., in West Bloomfield, May 11, 1870, aged 90.

[466.] 3. PALMER, again, (1192) b. March 27, 1768 ; m. Clarissa Douglass, who d. March 20, 1825.   He d., in West Bloomfield, N. Y., Nov. 20, 1843.

[467.] 4. JASPER, b. Aug. 5, 1769, and d., unm., in West Bloomfield, N. Y., in 1849.

[468.] 5. DUDLEY, b. Nov. 30, 1770, and d., in Lyme, Conn., July 26, 1785.

[469.] 6. OLIVER, (1200) b. July 20, 1774 ; m. Amy Lee, Aug. 29, 1797, and d., in Lyme, Conn., May 8, 1815.   His wife d., in Sheffield, Mass., March 20, 1854.

[470.] 7. PHEBE, b. Aug. 28, 1778 ; m. Joseph Chadwick, June 13, 1799, and d., in West Bloomfield, N. Y., April 18, 1865.

[471.] 8. ELIZABETH, b. Oct. 21, 1780 ; m. James Gillett, in Nov. 1798, and d., in West Bloomfield, N. Y., Sept. 9, 1846.

[472.] 9. MATTHEW, (1201) b. June 4, 1783; m. Lois Hall, Sept. 18, 1808, and d., in New York city, Feb. 17, 1829.

[473.] 10. RICHARD SEARS, (1207) b. Sept. 22, 1784; m. Phebe Hunting, June 24, 1812; was a physician and d., in Chatham, N. Y., July 3, 1827.

[474.] 11. ANN, b. Dec. 20, 1788 ; m. Gurdon Clark, Aug. 2, 1809, and d., in West Bloomfield, N. Y., Sept. 5, 1868.

CHILDREN OF REYNOLD PECK (196) AND DEBORAH, HIS WIFE,
ALL BORN IN LYME, CONN.

[475.] 1. ANNIE, b. Jan. 24, 1765; m. Gurdon Lewis, in
1785; resided in Marlow, N. H., where she d. May 28, 1858.

[476.] 2. HANNAH, b. April 13, 1767; m. Allen Smith and
d., in West Bloomfield, N. Y., Jan. 25, 1863.

[477.] 3. JOHN SEARS, (1210) b. May 13, 1769; m. Betsey Rice and settled in West Bloomfield, in 1792, where he d.
Oct. 23, 1813.

[478.] 4. BETTIE, b. Dec. 26, 1771; m. 1. Shadrach Gillett,
and m. 2. Joseph King, and d., in Detroit, Mich., Nov. 15, 1817.

[479.] 5. THOMAS, (1215) b. May 23, 1774; m. Sarah Dem-
ing and d., in Lima, N. Y., Sept. 28, 1843.

[480.] 6. WATROUS, (1224) b. April 14, 1777; m. 1. Betsey
Ball, Sept. 3, 1804; m. 2. Paulina Rexford, in Sept. 1829; removed from Lyme, Conn., to West Bloomfield, in 1799, where
he settled and d. March 23, 1862.

[481.] 7. GEORGE, (1232) b. March 26, 1780; m. Martha
Dimion and d., in West Bloomfield, N. Y., April 25, 1849.

[482.] 8. ABNER, (1238) b. Oct. 15, 1782; m. Maria Taft
and d., in West Bloomfield, N. Y., May 20, 1843.

[483.] 9. SARAH, b. Aug. 21, 1786; m. 1. Isaac Champlin,
Feb. 20, 1805; m. 2. Erastus Bennett, Feb. 20, 1817, and d., in
Batavia, N. Y., Oct. 19, 1867.

[484.] 10. REYNOLD, (1241) b. Nov. 7, 1790; m. Nancy
Wheelock and d., in Canandaigua, N. Y., Nov. 20, 1849. In
1840 he was a representative of Ontario county, in the Legislature of the State of New York.

CHILDREN OF LEBBEUS PECK (198) AND LYDIA, HIS WIFE, ALL
BORN IN LYME, CONN.

[485.] 1. CATHARINE, b. April 20, 1785; m. Dan Tinker,
of Lyme, Conn., and d. there Aug. 14, 1832.

[486.] 2. MARY, b. Feb. 4, 1787; m. David Caulkins, of
Waterford, Conn., Jan. 1, 1806, and d., in Lyme, Conn., Aug.
21, 1828.

[487.]   3. STEPHEN L., (1251) b. Feb. 14, 1791; m. Diana McIntyre, of Springfield, Mass., Nov. 29, 1829, and d., in Lyme, Conn., Oct. 13, 1857.   She d., in Saybrook, Ill., Aug. 21, 1873.

[488.]   4. MEHITABLE, b. Feb. 14, 1791, and d., unm., in Lyme, Conn., Nov. 13, 1839.

CHILDREN OF JOHN PECK (201) AND REBECCA, HIS WIFE, ALL BORN IN LYME, CONN.

[489.]   1. STEPHEN, b. Dec. 20, 1775; m. 1. Elizabeth Johnson, Aug. 23, 1801, who d. Nov. 3, 1803; m. 2. Ann W. Green, May 15, 1806, and d., in Brooklyn, N. Y., July 5, 1847.   He had no children.

[490.]   2. LUCY, b. Aug. 10, 1778; m. 1. Jeremiah Osborn, May 4, 1802; m. 2. Rev. Lathrop Rockwell, in Oct. 1820, and m. 3. Epenetus Reed, Oct. 23, 1832, and d., in Coxsackie, N. Y., July 29, 1863.

[491.]   3. ELISHA, b. Feb. 25, 1781; and d., unm., in Kingston, Jamaica, Jan. 29, 1802.

[492.]   4. CLARINE, b. March 9, 1785; m. Anthony Van Bergen, of Coxsackie, N. Y., April 19, 1806, and d. there Oct. 30, 1872.

[493.]   5. JOHN, (1255) b. Aug. 8, 1787; m. 1. Mary Lee Harriman, July 13, 1814; m. 2. Mary Gold, in Oct. 1821, and d., in Brooklyn, N. Y., Oct. 20, 1856.

[494.]   6. SETH S., (1260) b. Aug. 23, 1790; m. Sarah Lay, in Sept. 1814, and d., in St. Augustine, Florida, July 5, 1841.

[495.]   7. CHARLES L., (1265) b. June 22, 1794; m. Hannah Augusta Mitchell, of Groton, Conn., June 30, 1819.   He d., in Lyme, Conn., Jan. 16, 1877, residing and having resided upon the same premises which were the homestead of his ancestor, Joseph Peck, (4) more than two centuries ago.

CHILDREN OF SAMUEL GILES PECK, (205) ALL BORN IN LYME, CONN.

[496.]   Nothing is found on the Lyme town records relating to the descendants of Samuel Giles Peck, (205) and persistent effort to gain definite information from his kindred and other sources has been unavailing. It is said that he had children whose names were *Lucinda, Mary, Fannie, Samuel, Frasier* and *Peter*.

CHILDREN OF EZRA PECK (206).

[497.] The Lyme town records furnish no account of the descendants of Ezra Peck (206). He is said to have had children whose names were *Mary, Eleazer, Ann,* who m. Stephen Sawyer, *Curtis,* who m. —— Bramble, two sons, *Charles* and *Thomas J.*, residing in Lyme; also a son, *Peter,* and daughters, *Betsey* who m. Andrew Peck, *Phebe* and *Lois*. Many attempts to acquire further information have proved ineffectual.

CHILDREN OF DAVID PECK (208) AND EUNICE, HIS WIFE, ALL EXCEPT THE OLDEST BORN AT SAND LAKE, N. Y.

[498.] 1. ELISHA, b. in Lyme, Conn., Jan. 28, 1787, and d., unm., at Sand Lake, Jan. 24, 1811.

[499.] 2. DANIEL, b. Sept. 29, 1788, and d., unm., at Sand Lake, Aug. 20, 1834.

[500.] 3. DAVID, b. Oct. 7, 1791, and in 1877 was living unm. in Albany, N. Y.

[501.] 4. ELIZABETH, b. Sept. 9, 1793, and d., unm., at Sand Lake, Sept. 29, 1810.

[502.] 5. EUNICE, b. Nov. 24, 1795, and d., unm., at Sand Lake, March 25, 1841.

[503.] 6. SAMUEL, b. Oct. 9, 1798, and d., unm., at Sand Lake, March 12, 1813.

[504.] 7. ABIGAIL, b. Aug. 26, 1801, and d., unm., at Sand Lake, in July, 1851.

[505.] 8. JOHN M., (1271) b. June 28, 1808; m. Adaline Adelia Tucker Feb. 4, 1830, and, in 1877, was living in Albany, N. Y.

CHILDREN OF WILLIAM PECK (209) AND JUDITH, HIS WIFE,
ALL BORN IN LYME, CONN.

[506.] 1. REYNOLD M., b. March 21, 1780, and is said to have d., unm., in 1815, in Saratoga, N. Y.

507.] 2. FRANKLIN, b. Aug. 3, 1781; m. Bridget Sisson Sept. 15, 1805, and, soon afterwards, settled in Onondaga Valley, N. Y., where he d., about 1854 or 1855. His children, all born in Onondaga Valley, N. Y., were 1. *Morgan,* who m. and settled at or near Rock Island, Ill., and d. there in 1853; 2. *Nathaniel;* 3. *William,* who at one time resided in Syracuse, N. Y.; 4. *Hannah.* b. March 4, 1811, m. Rev. Abner Morse, Oct. 15, 1836, and d., at Onondaga Valley, Aug. 29, 1842; 5. *Emeline,* b. in 1806, m. 1. Albert Field, of Salina, N. Y., and m. 2. John Sherman, and in 1874 resided in Homer, Cortland Co., N. Y.; and 6. *James,* residing at Ottumwa, Iowa.

The children of Hannah, all born in Onondaga Valley, N. Y., were *Elijah A. Morse,* now of Canton, Mass.; *Albert F. Morse,* of Sharon, Mass., and *Abner L. Morse,* now of Salt Lake City, Utah.

[508.] 3. JUDITH, b. Dec. 6, 1782; m. Reuben Smith, who resided in Ontario Co., N. Y.

[509.] 4. NATHANIEL, b. Oct. 14, 1787

CHILDREN OF JOSEPH PECK (210) AND SARAH, HIS WIFE, ALL BORN IN LYME, CONN.

[510.] 1. PHEBE, b. July 26, 1781, and d., in Lyme, in infancy.

[511.] 2. EZRA M., (1278) b. July 4, 1784; m. Eunice Clark, in May 1808, and d., in New York city, Sept. 5, 1839.

[512.] 3. JOSEPH, (1284) b. July 23, 1790; m. Ann Gilbert, June 13, 1824, and d., in Lyme, in 1825.

[513.] 4. WILLIAM, b. Oct. 16, 1792, and d., in Lyme, Sept. 3, 1794.

[514.] 5. FANNY, b. April 16, 1795; m. Thomas Chadwick, Oct. 17, 1861, and in 1870 was living in Lyme, Conn.

CHILDREN OF AZARIAH PECK (213).

[515] 1. DANIEL, (1285) b. in 1792, in Sharon, N. Y., was a physician, and d., in Jackson, Mich., Jan. 19, 1859.

It is said that Azariah Peck (213) had two other sons, *William* and *Joseph*, and seven daughters, *Polly, Electa, Rebecca, Elizabeth, Lucretia, Lucinda*, and *Jerusha*, but all efforts to obtain further information concerning them or their descendants have been unsuccessful, except that his daughter *Polly* m. Dexter Peck, who, in 1807, settled in Harrisburgh, Lewis Co., N. Y.

CHLDREN OF DANIEL PECK (214) AND BETSEY, HIS WIFE, ALL BORN IN LYME, CONN.

[516.] 1. WILLIAM.

[517.] 2. DANIEL.

It is said that one of these sons died young, and that the other was last heard of many years since as residing in the western part of the State of New York.

CHILDREN OF MATHER PECK (217) ALL BORN IN LYME, CONN.

[518.] 1. LUCY, b. May 5, 1772 ; m. Martin Smith, and d., in Big Flats, N. Y.

[519.] 2. POLLY, b. March 12, 1774, and d. unm., in West Bloomfield, N. Y., in 1859.

[520.] 3. JOSEPH, (1286) b. April 26, 1776 ; m. Anna Reed, Feb. 7, 1799, and d., in Lyme, July 4, 1838.

[521.] 4. ESTHER, b. Oct. 17, 1778, and d., unm., in Lyme, in 1806.

[522.] 5. ABBY, b. Feb. 4, 1781 ; m. Jesse Taft, and d., in W. Bloomfield, in 1855.

[523.] 6. MIRIAM, b. Sept. 9, 1783 ; m. Joel Godfrey, and d., in W. Bloomfield, in 1819.

[524.] 7. MATHER, (1288) b. Jan. 12, 1786 ; m. Julia Ann Comstock, Sept. 20, 1813. He settled in Bethany, N. Y., in 1806, where he d. March 16, 1872.

[525.]   8. DAVID H., (1296) b. Aug. 20, 1787 ; m. Hannah S. Caulkins, of New London, Conn.   He emigrated from Lyme in 1812, and d., in Middletown, O., July 18, 1870.   His wife had d. there, Aug. 14, 1869, aged 73.

[526.]   9. JERUSHA, b. June 1, 1791, and d., unm., in Bethany, N. Y., in 1824.

[527.]   10. JESSE, (1308) b. Feb. 6, 1794 ; m. Asenath Huntley in 1819, and d., in Lyme, Oct 28, 1859.

[528.]   11. NANCY, b. in Dec., 1798, and d., in Lyme, in Jan., 1801.

[529.]   12. RUAMA, b. July 12, 1800 ; m. John Marvin, and d., in Bethany, N. Y., Oct. 15, 1826.

R. J.

CHILDREN OF WILLIAM PECK (218) ALL BORN IN PROVIDENCE, N. J.

[530.]   1. GEORGE C., b. Feb. 13, 1780, and d. at sea unmarried.

[531.]   2. WILLIAM, b. Dec. 22, 1781 ; m. Betsey Philips, and d., in Providence, R. I., Feb. 9, 1832.

[532.]   3. ELIZA, b. Nov. 16, 1783, and d., unm., in Providence, R. I., Jan. 15, 1856.

[533.]   4. PASCAL P., b. Oct. 13, 1786, and d., unm., at sea, off Sandy Hook, by casualty, while on board of the brig Nimrod, April 5, 1812.   He was in the U. S. Navy during the war with Tripoli, and was one of the select few who crossed the desert of Lybia in company with Gen. Eaton, and attacked and captured the city of Derne.

[534.]   5. JOHN M., b Nov. 5, 1788, and d., unm., in New York city, Jan. 12, 1823.

[535.]   6. ABBY ELIZABETH, b. Dec. 15, 1790, and d., unm., in Providence, R. I., Sept. 30, 1875.

CHILDERN OF MATTHEW PECK (220) AND POLLY, HIS WIFE, ALL BORN IN LYME, CONN.

[536.]   1. MEHITABLE, b. Sept. 22, 1783 ; m. Nathaniel Clark, May 28. 1802, and d., in Lima, N. Y., Oct. 10 1862.

[537.] 2. MARY, b. in 1785, and d., unm., in Lima, N. Y., in 1844.

[538.] 3. BENJAMIN K., (1315) b. Dec. 6, 1788; m. 1. Anna Griffin, in 1810, and m. 2. Emily Reed, in Sept. 1833, and d. in Rochester, N. Y., in Dec. 1855.

[539.] 4. LUCY, b. Aug. 12, 1790, and d., in Lyme, May 1, 1800.

[540.] 5. WILLIAM, (1324) b. Jan. 14, 1792; m. Marietta Hall, July 8, 1827, and d., in W. Bloomfield, N. Y., Oct. 16, 1850.

[541.] 6. HENRY, b. in Aug., 1794, and d., in Saratoga, N. Y., in Aug., 1803.

CHILDREN OF RICHARD PECK (221) AND ELIZABETH, HIS WIFE, ALL BORN IN LYME, CONN.

[542.] 1. NATHANIEL, b. Jan. 24, 1784; m. Martha Chadwick, and d., in Bethany, N. Y., Dec. 15, 1812. He had no children.

[543.] 2. RICHARD, (1332) b. Feb. 5, 1786; m. Catharine Hope Comstock, who d. July 8, 1861, and he d., in Bethany, May 10, 1857. He removed from Lyme and settled in Bethany N. Y., in 1808.

SEVENTH GENERATION.

CHILDREN OF JOHN PECK (222) AND SARAH, HIS WIFE.

[544.] 1. SAMUEL, b. in Greenwich, Conn., in 1765, and d. there in 1768.

[545.] 2. JOEL, (1343) b. in Greenwich, Conn., Dec. 2, 1767; m. 1. Huldah Munger, who d. in 1807; m. 2. Mercy Couch, April 23, 1808; was one of the earliest settlers, as a farmer, in Norwich, Chenango Co., N. Y., in 1792, and d. there Feb. 16, 1852. His second wife d. there Aug. 9, 1855.

[546.]   3. SARAH, b. in Greenwich, Conn., Dec. 1, 1769;
m. 1. Daniel Fisher, of Amenia, N. Y., April 15, 1788, and, in
1796, emigrated from Amenia to Norwich, N. Y.   He died in
the adjoining town of Plymouth, N. Y., Dec. 20, 1820, and
July 8, 1828, she m. 2. William Yerrington ; and, he having
d., she, Aug. 20, 1839, m. 3. Peter Cole, and d. in Plymouth,
Aug. 20, 1847.   Her children, all by her first husband, were
1. *Polly*, b. Aug. 13, 1789; m. Lyman Cook ; 2. *Thompson G.*,
b. Nov. 26, 1792; 3. *Rachel*, b. Aug. 3, 1795, and m. Ira
Rider; 4. *Phebe*, b. Aug. 15, 1798; m. Benjamin Phelps ; 5.
Calvin, b. May 14, 1801 ; 6. *John*, b. March 20, 1804 ; 7. *Wilbur*, b. Dec. 7, 1807, and 8. *Sally Maria*, b. Dec. 7, 1813, who
m. William Walker, and who resided in Sherburne, Chenango
Co., N. Y.

[547.]   4. MARY, b. in Greenwich, Conn., Oct. 28, 1771; m.
David Wilbur, Dec. 16, 1790, and d., in Smyrna, N. Y., Sept.
14, 1862.   Her husband, born Nov. 12, 1771, d. there Feb. 2,
1865.   She had children, 1. *Thompson*, b. Feb. 13, 1792 ; 2.
Sally, b. July 31, 1794 ; m. 1. David Calkins, and m. 2. John
Miller ; 3. *Smyth*, b. Feb. 17, 1797 ; 4. *Maria*, b. July 8, 1799,
and m. Elizur Graves ; 5. *German*, b. Dec. 20, 1801 ; 6.
Lyman, b. May 12, 1804 ; 7. *Cynthia*, b. March 26, 1812, and
m. Sidney Purdy ; 8. *Platt*, b. Feb. 27, 1815, and 9. *Miles*, b.
July 17, 1818.

[548.]   5. PHEBE, b. in Stanford, N. Y., Aug. 16, 1774 ;
m. Job Loper, Oct. 2, 1796, and d. in Smyrna, N. Y., July 31,
1857.   She had children, 1. *Sarah*, b. Aug. 24, 1797, and d. in
infancy ; 2. *Phebe*, b. March 19, 1799, and m. Dudley Bennett;
3. *Joel*, b. Aug. 29, 1804, and 4. *Betsey K.*, b. March 31, 1814,
and m. Tunis Blanberry.

[549.]   6. STEPHEN, b. in Stanford, N. Y.. in Oct. 1776,
and d. there in Dec. 1777.

[550.]   7. STEPHEN NORTHRUP, (1353) b. in Stanford,
N. Y., May 14, 1778; m. 1. Lydia Philips, Dec. 4, 1800, and
m. 2. Clarissa Hobart, Oct. 3, 1849 ; was a farmer, and one of

the first settlers of the town of Solon, N. Y., about the year 1800, and d. there Aug. 17, 1874, in the 97th year of his age. His excellent judgment, cheerful and genial characteristics, strong common sense, and agreeable manners, secured the special respect and esteem of all who knew him.

[551.] 8. JOHN, (1363) b. in Stanford, N. Y., Sept. 11, 1780; went with his father to the Chenango Valley, in 1795, and there m. Sarah Ferris, dau. of Israel Ferris, Aug. 20, 1801. He early commenced preaching, and, in 1804, settled in Cazenovia, N. Y., as a Baptist Minister, and resided there until his decease. A commemorative notice of him, and a brief account of his ministerial career, will be found in Vol. VI, 431 to 438 of Sprague's Annals of the American Pulpit. He was a distinguished minister of his denomination, among the foremost in its religious and benevolent enterprises, and eminent for his devotion to pastoral duty, his fervid eloquence, and his conservative theological tendencies. His wife, b. May 7, 1784, d., in Cazenovia, Sept. 21, 1847, and he d. Dec. 15, 1849, in New York city, being there on a temporary visit.

[552.] 9. NATHAN, (1369) b. in Milan, N. Y., Jan. 27, 1783; m. Sally Beebe, dau. of Ephraim Beebe, Feb. 29, 1804; first settled in Chenango County, whither he went with his father in 1795, and was ordained as a Baptist minister in July, 1814. Though devoting considerable attention to farming, he discharged his official duties for many years with much ability and acceptance. His wife d., at South Bend, Ind., April 8, 856, and he d., at Cortlandville, N. Y., April 6, 1872.

[553.] 10. BETSEY, b. in Milan, N. Y., April 1, 1786; m. John Nash, June 4, 1804, who d. in Sherburne, N. Y., July 2, 1820, aged 39, and she d., in the adjoining town of Smyrna N. Y., Nov. 4, 1825. She had children, 1. *Celina*, b. June 22, 1806; d., unm., in 1843; 2. *Northrup*, b. April 2, 1808; d., at Elizabeth, Ill., in 1854; 3. *Phebe*, b. April 16, 1810; m. Franklin Crosby, and d., in Rockford, Ill., in 1841; 4. *Darius A.*, b. March 4, 1812; m. Ann Rebecca Peck (1567), and d., in Des

Moines, Iowa, about 1868 ; 5. *Sally Ann*, b. March 14, 1814 · m. Nathan P. Colwell, and, in 1876, was living in Republic, O.; 6. *John*, b. July 11, 1815, and, in 1876, was living in Des Moines, Iowa ; 7. *Almira*, b. April 18, 1817 ; m. James Sisson, and d., at Rockford, Ill., in 1842, and 8. *Juliaette*, b. July 2, 1819 ; m. Charles W. Page, and, in 1876, was living in Omaha, Nebraska.

CHILDREN OF HEATH PECK (233) AND RACHEL, HIS WIFE, ALL BORN IN GREENWICH, CONN.

[554.] 1. SARAH, b. in 1775 ; m. 1. Lewis Jones ; m. 2. Zebediah Taylor, and d., in Yonkers, N. Y., Aug. 17, 1854.

[555.] 2. JAMES, (1380) b. Dec. 13, 1777 ; m. Hannah Peck (308), May 29, 1803, and d., in New Haven, Conn., Dec. 8, 1864.

[556.] 3. HEATH, (1384) b. in April, 1779 ; m. Sally Kinch, May 25, 1801, and d., in Schoharie, N. Y., Sept. 8, 1829.

CHILDREN OF ABIJAH PECK (227) AND MINDWELL, HIS WIFE, THE FIRST FOUR BORN IN GALWAY, N. Y., THE OTHERS IN CLIFTON PARK, N. Y.

[557.] 1. ABIGAIL, b. Nov. 28, 1785 ; m. William Higby, and d., in Penfield, N. Y., in June, 1848.

[558.] 2. RUTH, b. March 10, 1788; m. Andrew Evans, and d., in Clifton Park, March 6, 1873.

[559.] 3. NATHAN, (1386) b. Dec. 10, 1791 ; m. Nancy Kennedy, and d., in Watervliet, N. Y., Aug. 26, 1836.

[560.] 4. SOLOMON C., (1389) b. Sept. 12, 1793; m. 1. Lydia Schauber, and m. 2. Mary Terpening, and, in 1877, was living in Clifton Park, N. Y.

[561.] 5. SARAH, b. Feb. 28, 1796 ; m. Richard Smith, and d., in Clifton Park, April 12, 1842.

[562.] 6. ABIJAH, (1398) b. May 29, 1798 ; m. 1. Caroline Vanderburgh, and m. 2. Jane Reed, and d., in Clifton Park, Feb. 22, 1859.   He was a representative from Saratoga County in the New York Legislature in 1841.

[563.] 7. ELIZABETH, b. Oct. 13, 1800; m. Nehemiah G. Philo, and d., in Half Moon, N. Y., Sept. 26, 1836.

[564.] 8. JOHN (1403) b. July 31, 1803; m. Maria Montgomery, and d., in Clifton Park, Nov. 25, 1861. His widow in 1875, was living, and resided at Saratoga Springs, N. Y.

CHILDREN OF MOSES PECK (231) AND HANNAH, HIS WIFE, ALL BORN IN GREENWICH, CONN.

[565.] 1. SAMUEL, (1411) b. in 1774; m. Abigail Reynolds who d. April 21, 1827, aged 51; and he d. in Greenwich, Nov. 17, 1814.

[566.] 2. SYLVANUS, b. in 1776, and d., unm., in Greenwich, April 20, 1818.

CHILDREN OF AARON PECK (234) AND HANNAH, HIS WIFE, ALL BORN IN GREENWICH, CONN.

[567.] 1. DEBORAH, b. Feb. 9, 1782; m. Solomon Ferris, Jr., and d., in Greenwich, Sept. 15, 1861.

[568.] 2. PRISCILLA, b. Jan. 20, 1783; m. John Henning, June 11, 1806, being his first wife, and d., in New York city, June 16, 1814.

[569.] 3. HANNAH, b. July 29, 1785; m. John Chapel, and, in 1870, was living in New York city, and has probably d. there.

[570] 4. SAMUEL, (1419) b. Nov. 11, 1786; m. Sarah Brundage and d., in North Castle, N. Y., March 2, 1829.

[571.] 5. HENRY, b. March 4, 1800, and d. unm., in Greenwich, Aug. 20, 1823.

CHILDREN OF CALVIN PECK (236) AND BETSEY, HIS WIFE, THE FIRST TWO BORN IN GREENWICH, AND THE OTHERS IN SHARON, CONN.

[572.] 1. POLLY, b. Aug. 18, 1785; m. Luther Chaffee, of Sharon, April 14, 1811, and d., in Sharon, Conn., April 5, 1866.

[573.] 2. ENOCH P., (1425) b. Nov. 14, 1787; m. Mary Peck, (354) Nov. 7, 1815, and d., in Sharon, Aug. 24, 1858. His wife d. there March 28, 1866.

[574.] 3. GEORGE W., (1429) b. Dec. 5, 1789 ; m. Hannah Lockwood, of Watertown, Conn., July 2, 1818, who d. June 23, 1844, and he d. in Greenwich, Conn., Jan. 25, 1870.

[575.] 4. SALLY, b. Oct. 7' 1791 ; m. Lewis Peck, (346) Oct. 18, 1808, and d., in Sharon, Conn., Sept. 10, 1871.

[576.] 5. AMARILLIS, b. Dec. 10, 1794, and d. unm., in Sharon, Conn., Nov. 8, 1828.

[577.] 6. BETSEY, b. Jan. 29, 1797 ; m. John Wells, of Amsterdam, N. Y., Jan. 18, 1818, and was living there in 1877.

[578.] 7. LAURA, b. Dec. 19, 1798 ; m. John Henning, Nov. 6, 1844, being his third wife, and d., in Sharon, Conn., Aug. 29, 1871.

[579.] 8. JOHN C., (1435) b. Oct. 14, 1800 ; m. Sarah Van Loan, of Athens, N. Y., Sept. 3, 1833, and d., in Catskill, N. Y., Dec. 17, 1846.

[580.] 9. SAMUEL F., (1437) b. Dec. 7, 1802 ; m. Laura Ann Parsons, of Sharon, Conn., Oct. 9, 1831, and d. there Sept. 3, 1864.

CHILDREN OF LUTHER PECK (237) AND RACHEL, HIS WIFE, ALL BORN IN GREENWICH, CONN.

[581.] 1. SAMUEL, (1438) b. March 25, 1799 ; m. Eliza Robbins who d. Jan. 17, 1875. He was living in New York city in 1876.

[582.] 2. HULDAH, b. April 29, 1802 ; m. Isaac Weed, of Greenwich, Conn., and was living there in 1875.

[583.] 3. WILLIAM, (1446) b. May 4, 1804 ; m. Lydia A. Lockwood, and, in 1875, was living in Norwalk, Conn.

[584.] 4. EDWIN, (1457) b. Jan. 24, 1810 ; m. Martha H. Vail and d., in New York city, Sept. 14, 1861.

CHILDREN OF GEORGE WHITFIELD PECK, (238) ALL BORN IN GREENWICH, CONN.

[585.] 1. MARY R., b. Nov. 12, 1794, and d. in Greenwich, Jan. 19, 1802.

[586.]   2. DAVID, b. Jan. 15, 1796 ; m. Mary Peck, widow of his brother, Enos K., (590) and d., in Madison, Ga., in the Fall of 1841.   He had no children.

[587.]   3. SALLY L., b. Sept. 28, 1798 ; m. George Ferris, May 22, 1818, and, in 1870, was living in Greenwich, Conn.

[588.]   4. CHARLES, b. Aug. 11, 1800 ; m. Maria Volk, Dec. 25, 1821 ; his children d. young ; and he d., in Pennsylvania, about 1830.

[589.]   5. RHODA K., b. Dec. 1, 1802; m. George P. Ferris, son of Deborah Ferris, (567) Feb. 9, 1829, and, in 1870, was living in Greenwich, Conn.

[590.]   6. ENOS K., (1461) b. April 15, 1805; m. Mary Waterbury and d., in Madison, Ga., Sept. 18, 1837.   His widow afterwards m. David Peck (586) and, after his death, she again m. Lester Markham.

CHILDREN OF JOSEPH PECK (243) AND MARY, HIS WIFE, ALL BORN IN GREENWICH, CONN.

[591.]   1. ELIZABETH, b. Jan. 20, 1793 ; and, in 1870, was living unm. in Greenwich, Conn.

[592.]   2. HANNAH, b. Sept. 30, 1795 ; m. William Banks and d., in Greenwich, Oct. 21. 1826.

[593.]   3. JERUSHA, b. Feb. 7, 1797 ; and, in 1870, was living unm. in Greenwich, Conn.

[594.]   4. ALEXANDER, b. Dec. 27, 1799, and d. unm., in Greenwich, Oct. 21, 1826.

[595.]   5. MARY, b. Oct. 27, 1801 ; m. James Lyon and d., in Greenwich, Sept. 22, 1834.

[596.]   6. CHARLES. b. April 14, 1803, and d., in Greenwich, Dec. 4, 1809.

[597.]   7. CHARLOTTE, b. March 2, 1805, and, in 1870, was living unm. in Greenwich, Conn.

[598.] 8. JARED WILLIAM, b. April 4, 1807, and d., in Brooklyn, N. Y., Sept. 19, 1826.

[599.]   9. DARIUS, b. Jan. 14, 1811, and d., in Greenwich, Oct. 15, 1826.

[600.]   10. GEORGE A., (1464) b. Nov. 28, 1813; m. Eliza Valentine, and, in 1870, was living in Greenwich, Conn.

CHILDREN OF SOLOMON PECK (244) AND MARY, HIS WIFE, ALL BORN IN GREENWICH, CONN.

[601.]   1. SOLOMON, (1472) b. Dec. 31, 1802; m. Caroline Sellick, July 15, 1829, and d., in Greenwich, Conn., in May 1861.

[602.]   2. EMELINE, b. Dec. 29, 1805; m. Lemuel Wells, Jan. 3, 1829, and d., in St. Catharine's, Brazil, Dec. 18, 1839.

[603.]   3. JEDUTHAN, (1477) b. March 17, 1811; m. Mary Jessup, Nov. 23, 1845, and, in 1870, was living in Greenwich, Conn.

[604.]   4. JOHN FERRIS, b. Nov. 6, 1814; and d. unm., in Greenwich, Feb. 5, 1839.

CHILDREN OF JESSE PECK (246) AND NANCY, HIS WIFE, THE OLDEST BORN IN GREENWICH, CONN., THE OTHERS IN BEDFORD, N. Y.

[605.]   1. MARY, b. Oct. 28, 1798; m. 1. Enoch Miller, and m. 2. Abijah Harris, and, in 1861, was living in Bedford, N. Y.

[606.]   2. BELINDA, b. Jan. 1, 1800; m. Allen Teed and d., in Somers, N. Y., Sept. 16, 1853.

[606 1-2.]   3. ALEXANDER, b. April 15, 1804, and, in 1860, was living unm. in Bedford, N. Y.

[607.]   4. JESSE, (1481) b. Oct. 15, 1806; m. Rosena Finch and, in 1861, was living in Bedford, N. Y

[608.]   5. JULIA, b. March 3, 1816; m. Uriah Harris and d., in Chicago, Ill., Sept. 27, 1849.

CHILDREN OF HENRY PECK (251) AND SARAH, HIS WIFE.

[609.]   1. WILLIAM H., (1482) b. in Fairfield, Conn., Nov. 29, 1795; m. Jane S. Coutant and d., in Sing Sing, N. Y., June 27, 1871.

[610.]   2 CHARLES, b. in New York city, Feb. 18, 1798, and d. there, unm., June 25, 1828.

[611.]　3. JULIA ANN, b. in New York city, May 4, 1800 ; m. Thomas George and d., in Philadelphia, Penn., in Dec. 1853.

[612.]　4. MARY, b. in Westport, Conn., March 7, 1802 ; m. James Spencer and d., in New York city, Sept. 20, 1821.

[613.]　5. STEPHEN F., b. in Westport, Conn., May 26, 1804, and d. unm., in New York city, in Aug. 1839.

[614.]　6. DAVID J., b. in New York city, Sept. 4, 1806, and d. there Oct. 4, 1807.

[615.]　7. SARAH E., b. in New York city in Feb. 1812 ; m. Thomas Smull and d., in New York city, Nov 25, 1866. Her husband had d. there Nov. 28, 1866.

[616.]　8. EDMUND, (1490) b. in New York city, Feb. 10, 1814 ; m. Mary Girvan, July 3, 1843, and d., in Carbon county, near White Haven, Luzerne county, Penn., Oct. 23, 1859.

CHILDREN OF WILLIAM PECK (253) AND SARAH, HIS WIFE, ALL BORN IN NEW YORK CITY.

[617.]　1. WILLIAM M., b. in Oct. 1795, and d. unm., in New York city, in 1825.

[618.]　2. MARIA, b. in 1797 ; m. Peter Smith, of New York city, and d. there in 1813.

[619.]　3. CAROLINE, b. in New York city in 1799, and d. there the same year.

[620.]　4. CAROLINE, again, b. Nov. 18, 1800, and d. unm., in Newtown, Long Island, N. Y., Aug. 9, 1858.

[621.]　5. SARAH, b. in 1802, and was said to be living, in 1873, in Otsego, N. Y.

ONLY CHILD OF ISAAC PECK (258) AND HARRIET, HIS WIFE, BORN IN GREENWICH, CONN.

[622.]　WILLIAM JACKSON, b. March 12, 1815 ; m. 1. Mary Ann Hackleman, April 7, 1844, who d. Oct. 6, 1856, and m. 2. Sarah Caroline Roberts, March 4, 1858, and, in 1870, was living in Brookville, Ind. He was a physician and had no children.

CHILDREN OF STEPHEN PECK (257) AND CATHARINE, HIS WIFE.

[623.] 1. CHARLES H., (1494) b. in New York city Sept. 21, 1817; m. Rebecca Adams, of Frankford, Penn., and, in 1876, was living in St. Louis, Mo.

[624.] 2. JOHN WALTER, (1503) b. Dec. 30, 1818, in New York city; m. 1. Ann S. Boswell, and m. 2. Mary Jane Ramsay, and, in 1876, was living in St. Louis, Mo.

[625.] 3. STEPHEN S., b. in Freehold, N. J., May 1, 1820, and d. there July 15, 1822.

[626.] 4. CHARLOTTE, b. in Freehold, N. J., Aug. 20, 1821, and d. there July 16, 1822.

CHILDREN OF THOMAS PECK (262) AND MARY, HIS WIFE, ALL
BORN IN GREENWICH, CONN.

[627.] 1. ANN, b. Jan. 4, 1804; m. Alexander S. Newman aed d. in Greenwich, April 22, 1851.

[628.] 2. ELIZA, b. Sept. 15, 1806, and, in 1870, was living unm. in Greenwich, Conn.

[629.] 3. WILLIAM H., (1507) b. Jan. 30, 1811; m. Mary Ferris, dau. of George Ferris, and d., in Greenwich, in 1862.

[630.] 4. SUSAN, b. March 9, 1814, and d., in Greenwich, Aug. 11, 1824.

[631.] 5. CHARLES, b. Nov. 22, 1817; m. Phebe A. Broadway, and, in 1870, was living in New York city. He has no children.

[632.] 6. STEPHEN, (1510) b. Oct. 10, 1819; m. Susan A. Doty, Dec. 18, 1847, and d., in Greenwich, in 1862.

[633.] 7. JOHN ALBERT, (1512) b. Sept. 28, 1824; m. Jane A. Hobby, Oct. 31, 1847, and, in 1870, was living in Stamford, Conn.

CHILDREN OF NATHANIEL PECK (264) AND EXPERIENCE, HIS WIFE,
ALL BORN IN GREENWICH, CONN.

[634.] 1. WALTER, (1514) b. Jan. 22, 1779; m. Catharine Dally, dau. of Abraham Dally, of New York city, and d., in

New York city, March 11, 1836. His wife d., in Greenwich, Nov. 8, 1869, aged 85.

[635.] 2. MARY, b. March 8, 1782 ; m. Lewis Webb, and d., in New York city, March 9, 1835.

[636.] 3. HANNAH, b. March 31, 1784, and d. unm., in Greenwich, Conn., Feb. 27, 1869.

[637.] 4. CHARLOTTE, b. Feb. 16, 1787, and d. unm., in Aug. 1856, at Greenwich, Conn.

[638.] 5. ELIZA, b. Dec. 30, 1790 ; m. Alvan Mead, of Greenwich, Dec. 24, 1821, and d, there Sept. 22, 1864.

[639.] 6. EBENEZER, b. Sept. 20, 1793, and d. young, at Greenwich, Conn.

[640.] 7. RALPH, (1529) b. Dec. 23, 1796 ; m. 1. Elizabeth E. Barker, Jan. 24, 1826, who d. Nov. 20, 1833, and m. 2. Sarah M. Brown, Oct. 6, 1835, and, in 1877, was living at Mianus, Fairfield county, Conn.

CHILDREN OF EPHRAIM PECK, (266) ALL BORN IN GREEN-
WICH, CONN.

[641.] 1. FANNY, who m. —— Green.

[642.] 2. MATILDA, who m. Thomas Mead, and d., in Greenwich, in Dec. 1810. Her husband d. there in July, 1827.

[643.] 3. CLARISSA, b. in 1783 ; m. Walter Avery, and d., in Bridgeport, Conn., May 17, 1857.

[644.] 4. WILLIAM, (1533) b. Aug. 24, 1784 ; m. 1. Margaret Foster, and m. 2. Isabella Foster, and d., in New York city, in 1834.

CHILDREN OF ISAAC PECK (270) AND REBECCA, HIS WIFE.

[645.] 1. WILLIAM, b. in Stamford, Conn., Feb. 9, 1796, and d. there unm., about 1862.

[646.] 2. MARIA, b. in Greenwich, Conn. ; m. Peter Grant and d., in New York city, in March 1831.

[647.] 3. CHARLES, d. unm., in New Orleans, La., about 1842.

[648.] 4. SARAH ANN, m. James C. Everett and d., in New York city, about 1842.

[649.] 5. HENRY, m. but had no children, and d., in New York city, about 1850.

[650.] 6. EPHRAIM, d. unm. in Wilmington, N. C.

ONLY CHILD OF BENJAMIN PECK (273) AND PHBEE, HIS WIFE, BORN IN GLENVILLE, N. Y.

[651.] ABRAHAM, (1537) b. Aug. 21, 1813 ; m. Margaret Ann Swart, and, in 1877, was living in Amsterdam, N. Y.

CHILDREN OF GIDEON PECK (276) AND PHEBE, HIS WIFE, ALL BORN IN MAYFIELD, N. Y.

[652.] 1. PHEBE W., b. April 11, 1802 ; m. Jacob Purcell, and, in 1861, was living in Carroll, N. Y.

[653.] 2. EDWARD, (1539) b. Nov. 13, 1804 ; m. 1. Mary Ann Richmond, and m. 2. Cornelia Merrill, and, in 1861, was living in Westfield, N. Y.

[654.] 3. ISABELLA T., b. April 6, 1807 ; m. William F. Gornea, and, in 1861, was living in Ottowa, Ill.

[655.] 4. MARY, b. Feb. 29, 1812 ; m. John A. Stetson, and, in 1861, was living in Northeast, Penn.

[656.] 5. SAMUEL, b. Feb. 12, 1814, and d., in Mayfield, N. Y., March 22, 1821.

[657.] 6. HARVEY, (1547) b. Jan. 6, 1816 ; m. Minerva C. Taylor, and, in 1861, was living in Westfield, N. Y.

[658.] 7. GEORGE, b. June 25, 1818, and d., in Mayfield, N. Y., Oct. 28, 1819.

[659.] 8. SALLY, b. Aug. 25, 1822, and d., in Mayfield, N. Y., July 4, 1826.

CHILDREN OF JONATHAN RICHARD PECK (277) AND THEODOSIA, HIS WIFE, THE OLDEST THREE BORN IN GREENWICH, CONN., AND THE OTHERS IN FLUSHING, N. Y.

[660.] 1. JONATHAN, (1552) b. Jan. 26, 1786 ; m. Caroline Cornell, of Flushing, N. Y., and d., in New York city, Sept. 19, 1833.

[661.] 2. CURTIS, (1563) b. March 30, 1787 ; m. 1. Hannah Lowere, of Flushing, N. Y., and m. 2. Anna Maria Cannon, of Bridgeport, Conn., and d., in Flushing, N. Y., Aug. 11, 1851.

[662.] 3. CHARLES, (1576) b. April 1, 1789 ; m. 1. Elizabeth Thorne, of New York city, and m. 2. Mrs. Amanda Smith of New Haven, Conn., and d., in Hartford, Conn., March 17, 1857.

[663.] 4. ISAAC, (1583) b. Feb. 13, 1791 ; m. Agnes Polhemus, of New York city, and d., in Flushing, N. Y., Dec. 27, 1859.

[664.] 5. ELIJAH, (1589) b. Sept. 30, 1793 ; m. 1. Margaret Cornell, of Flushing, N. Y. ; m. 2. Ann Cornell, of Flushing, N. Y., and m. 3. Amelia Lewis, of Litchfield, Conn., and d.. in Flushing, N. Y., May 21, 1863.

[665.] 6. ALEXANDER, (1593) b. Sept. 8, 1795 ; m. Rebecca Albertson, and d., in Flushing, N. Y., Sept. 29, 1817

[666.] 7. WILLIAM, (1594) b. April 27, 1798 ; m. Lydia Ann Odell, of Shrewsbury, N. J., and d., in New York city, Feb. 5, 1848.

[667.] 8. RICHARD, (1600) b. Aug. 8, 1800 ; m. Harriet Keith ; was an Episcopal clergyman and d., in Sheldon, Vt., July 3, 1846.

[668.] 9. JENNETT, b. April 1, 1805 ; m. John Horton, of Madrid, N. Y., and, in 1860, was living in Flushing, N. Y.

CHILDREN OF CHARLES PECK (279) AND NANCY, HIS WIFE, ALL BORN IN GREENWICH, CONN.

[669.] 1. ABIGAIL JANE H., b. Oct. 18, 1803 ; m. David Fowler, of Newburgh, N. Y., March 3, 1823, and d. there May 17, 1824.

[670.] 2. MEHITABLE, b. Jan. 27, 1805, and d., in Greenwich, Feb. 18, 1805.

[671.] 3. THOMAS H., b. May 4, 1807 ; m. Diadamia Congar, and d., in Detroit, Mich., in 1845. His wife had d. there in 1837.

[672.] 4. MEHITABLE, again, b. Sept. 17, 1809; m. Thomas M. Lyon, Oct. 29, 1806, who d., in New York city, June 10, 1853. She was living in Norwalk Conn., in 1870.

[673.] 5. CHARLES E., (1604) b. April 17, 1812; m. Mary Thompson, of Newburgh, N. Y., and, in 1875, was living in New York city.

[674.] 6. THEODOSIA, b. Oct. 18, 1814, and d., in New York city, March 10, 1823.

CHILDREN OF FREDERICK PECK (282) AND HANNAH, HIS WIFE, ALL BORN IN GREENWICH, CONN.

[675.] 1. SARAH, b. Sept. 10, 1795; m. Abijah Smith, and, in 1861, was living in Mt. Blanchard, O.

[676.] 2. HANNAH, b. May 8, 1797; m. Jesse Sherwood and d., in New Rochelle, N. Y., May 30, 1825.

[677.] 3. FREDERICK, (1612) b. March 1, 1803; m. Sarah Hoyt, Sept. 25, 1831, and, in 1861, was living in Stamford, Conn.

[678.] 4. WILLIAM H., (1615) b. Oct. 28, 1804; m. Mary Lyon, of New York city, and was living there in 1860.

[679.] 5. MARY, b. Sept. 25, 1809, and, in 1861, was living in Stamford, Conn.

CHILDREN OF AUGUSTUS PECK (283) AND JERUSHA, HIS WIFE, ALL BORN IN GREENWICH, CONN.

[680.] 1. MARIA, b. about 1799; m. Peter V. Sang, and, in 1861, was living in Lamartine, Wis.

[681.] 2. JULIA, b. about 1803; m. Ebenezer Heard, and, in 1870, was living in Greenwich, Conn.

[682.] 3. GEORGE, b. about 1809; m. Sarah Jane Crabb, March 2, 1840, and, in 1870, was living in Greenwich, Conn. He had no children.

[683.] 4. ANTOINETTE, b. about 1811; m. James Hickman, and, in 1861, was living in Philadelphia, Penn.

[684.] 5. JOHN, b. about 1813, and, in 1870, was living unm. in Greenwich, Conn.

[685.] 6. ISAAC, (1621) b. July 5, 1815; m. Margaret Wood and d., in New York city, Oct. 3, 1854.

CHILDREN OF DAVID PECK, (286) ALL BORN IN GREENWICH, CONN.

[686.] 1. DAVID, (1625) b. May 13, 1775 ; m. Sarah Peck, (254) in Feb. 1800 ; was a physician, and resided in Newbern, N. C., and d. there May 26, 1802.

[687.] 2. AMY, b. Aug. 12, 1777 ; m. Caleb Lyon, and d., in Genoa, N. Y., Jan. 30, 1843, where her husband also d. July 1, 1856.

[688.] 3. MARY, b. Sept. 9, 1799 ; m. David Scofield, and d., in Greenwich, July 5, 1844.

[689.] 4. ESTHER, b. Nov. 25, 1781 ; m. Joseph Lyon, Feb. 18, 1801, and d., in Genoa, N. Y., Jan. 7, 1832. Her husband d. there in 1856.

[690.] 5. THEOPHILUS, b. Jan 24, 1784, and d., in Greenwich, June 6, 1784.

[691.] 6. ANNA, b. April 30, 1785; m. Charles Wilson, of Greenwich, Oct. 31, 1804, and, in 1870, was living in Greenwich, Conn.

[692.] 7. THEOPHILUS, again, b. Aug. 10, 1787, and d., in Greenwich, Sept. 19, 1787.

[693.] 8. DEBORAH, b. Sept. 15, 1788, and, in 1870, was living unm. in Greenwich, Conn.

[694.] 9. BENONI, (1627) b. Nov. 5, 1790 ; m. Huldah Peck (305) Dec. 12, 1812 ; removed from Greenwich and settled in Genoa, N. Y., in 1838, and d. there July 8, 1859.

[695.] 10. CHARLOTTE, b. Jan. 21, 1793 ; m. Benjamin W. Drake, Sept. 1, 1836, and, in 1870, was living in Genoa, N. Y.

[696.] 11. REBECCA, b. Jan. 21, 1793, and d., in Bedford, N. Y., Jan. 11, 1837.

[697.] 12. PHEBE, b. Oct. 14, 1795 ; m. John Bretett, and d., Dec. 2, 1863, in Quincy, Ill.

[698.] 13. MARILDA, b. May 7, 1796 ; m. David Banks, May 10, 1821, and, in 1870, was living in Greenwich, Conn.

[699.]   14. ZILLA, b. March 1, 1798; m. John Purdy, in 1845, and d., in New York city, Aug. 9, 1858.

[700.]   15. RUTH, b. Oct. 21, 1799 ; m. William Johnson in 1836, and was living in New York city in 1861.

[701.]   16. ELIPHALET, (1635) b. June 24, 1801; m. 1. Deborah M. Peck, (732) and m. 2. Sarah Hatfield, and d., in Port Chester, N. Y., Jan. 4, 1865.

[702.]   17. ALATHEA, b. May 15, 1803; m. Gilbert P. Finch, April 8, 1827, and, in 1870, was living in Greenwich, Conn.

[703.]   18. DAVID, again, (1640) b. March 16, 1805; m. Mary B. Miller, March 11, 1829, and, in 1870, was living in Greenwich, Conn.

[704.]   19. DELILA, b. March 4, 1807; m. Jotham Sherwood, in 1839, and, in 1861, was living in Montrose, Penn.

[705.]   20. JARED, b. June 14, 1811, and d. unm., in New York city, Aug. 7, 1837.

CHILDREN OF GIDEON PECK (287) AND EUNICE, HIS WIFE, ALL BORN IN GREENWICH, CONN.

[706.]   1. CLARA, b. May 29, 1783; m. Elias Purdy, and d., in Greenwich, Nov. 3, 1850.   Her husband had d. Dec. 5, 1828.

[707.]   2. FRANCES, b. June 23, 1785 ; m. Samuel Brown and d., in Greenwich, Ohio, July 26, 1861.

[708.]   3. MARY, b. Sept. 6, 1787 ; m. Thomas Purdy, and was living in New York city, in 1861.

[709.]   4. GIDEON, (1650) b. Nov. 23, 1791 ; m. Phœbe W. Merritt, Sept. 19, 1813, who d. Oct. 31, 1856 ; and he was living in New York city, in 1861.

[710.]   5. ELIZABETH, b. June 20, 1793 ; m. Noah Mead, and, in 1861, was living in Greenwich, Conn.

[711.]   6. EUNICE, b. June 20, 1793 ; m. Justus Sackett and d., in Greenwich, in 1857.

[712.]   7. THEOPHILUS, (1661) b. April 6, 1795 ; m. Sarah Hobby and d., in New York city, Aug. 19, 1856.

CHILDREN OF THOMAS PECK (289) AND TAMIZON, HIS WIFE, THE
OLDEST THREE BORN IN NORTH SALEM, N. Y., AND
THE OTHERS IN POUNDRIDGE, N. Y.

[713.] 1. NANCY, b. May 29, 1792, and, in 1870, was living
unm. in Poundridge, N. Y.

[714.] 2. OBADIAH, b. May 11, 1794, and d., in North
Salem, N. Y., in 1798.

[715.] 3. THOMAS, (1665) b. Oct. 28, 1795; m. Jane Bishop
in 1845, and d., in Lewisboro, N. Y., April 10, 1870.

[716.] 4. RUFUS, b. Jan. 8, 1805, and, in 1870, was living
unm. in Poundridge, N. Y.

[717.] 5. EZRA R., (1669) b. Jan. 8, 1807; m. Catharine
Hobby in 1834, and, in 1870, was living in Stamford, Conn.

[718.] 6. DELILA, b. July 5, 1810; m. Samuel Hobby in
1837, and, in 1870, was living in Poundridge, N. Y.

CHILDREN OF SOLOMON PECK (291) AND MARY, HIS WIFE, ALL
BORN IN GREENWICH, CONN.

[719.] 1. ARAD, (1674) b. April 16, 1791; m. Eliza Stephens, Sept. 3, 1833, who d. about 1838. He d., in Greenwich,
Dec. 16, 1874.

[720.] 2. RACHEL, b. June 8, 1795, and d. unm., in Greenwich, Feb. 28, 1821.

[721.] 3. MARY, b. Nov. 25, 1797; m. Allen P. Carpenter,
and, in 1870, was living in Rye, N. Y.

CHILDREN OF SAMUEL PECK (297) AND MARY, HIS WIFE, ALL
BORN IN GREENWICH, CONN.

[722.] 1. ALLEN, b. Sept. 3, 1791, and d. unm., in New
Rochelle, N. Y., Nov. 20, 1835.

[723.] 2. OBADIAH, (1675) b. Dec. 17, 1793; m. Lizetta
Mead, dau. of Calvin Mead, and d., in Brooklyn, N. Y., June
30, 1864.

[724.] 3. MARIA, b. April 6, 1796, and d. unm., in Greenwich, May 14, 1840.

[725.]   4. ANNA M., b. Aug. 25, 1800, and, in 1870, was living unm. in Greenwich, Conn.

[726.]   5. SAMUEL, b. Nov. 29, 1804, and d. unm., in Greenwich, Conn., May 18, 1841.

[727.]   6. JANE, b. May 18, 1806, and, in 1870, was living unm. in Greenwich, Conn.

[728.]   7. SOPHIA, b. Dec. 4, 1809, and d. unm., in Greenwich, May 16, 1841.

[729.]   8. ISAAC, (1680) b. April 12, 1812; m. Julia Mead, dau. of Zenas Mead, and d., in Greenwich, Conn., March 8, 1876.

[730.]   9. WHITMAN, (1682) b. May 16, 1815; graduated at Yale College in 1838 ; m. Ruth Maria Keeler; is a Presbyterian minister, and, in 1869, resided in Ridgefield, Conn.

CHILDREN OF JABEZ PECK (298) AND MARY, HIS WIFE, ALL BORN
IN GREENWICH, CONN.

[731.]   1. DORINDA, b. Feb. 20, 1796 ; m. Israel Peck, (323) Oct. 20, 1819, and, in 1870, was living in Port Chester, N. Y.

[732.]   2. DEBORAH M., b. Feb. 25, 1800 ; m. Eliphalet Peck, (701) June 25, 1824, and d., in Greenwich, May 15, 1851.

[733.]   3. JEHIEL M., b. March 10, 1811, and d., in Greenwich, Jan. 7, 1812.

[734.]   4. ABIGAIL, b. Oct. 1, 1812, and, in 1861, was living unm., at Tuscarora, N. Y., as missionary to the Indians.

CHILDREN OF JARED PECK (300) AND TAMIZON, HIS WIFE, ALL
BORN IN RYE, N. Y.

[735.]   1. WILLIAM, (1685) b. July 19, 1797 ; m. Nancy Sniffen, of Rye, N. Y., and d., in New York city, July 26, 1825.

[736.]   2. JAMES HERVEY, (1688) b. Feb. 20, 1800 ; m. Phebe C. Moseman, of Rye, N. Y., Oct. 10, 1839, and d., in Port Chester, N. Y., April 22, 1872.

[737.]   3. CAROLINE, b. May 6, 1802, and d. unm., in Rye, N. Y., March 19, 1845.

[738.]   4. CHARLES A., (1696) b. July 6, 1804; m. Mary H. Bloodgood, of Rye, N. Y., Oct. 18, 1827, and, in 1875, was living in New York city.

[739.]   5. HENRY A., b. March 10, 1806, and d. unm., in Port Chester, N. Y., Aug. 21, 1861.

[740.]   6. GEORGE T., b. Sept. 16, 1809, and d. unm., in Rye, N. Y., Jan. 3, 1830.

[741.]   7. SARAH E., b. June 2, 1812, and, in 1873, was living unm. in Rye, N. Y.

[742.]   8. JARED V., (1703) b. Sept. 21, 1816; m. Phebe Bergen, of New Jersey, April 3, 1856; was representative in the New York Legislature, in 1848, and in Congress, from Westchester county, N. Y., in 1853 to 1855, and, in 1873, was living in Rye, N. Y.

[743.]   9. MARY P., b. Jan. 13, 1819, and, in 1873, was living unm. in Rye, N. Y.

ONLY CHILD OF ISAAC PECK (302) AND SARAH, HIS WIFE, BORN IN GREENWICH, CONN.

[744.]   ISAAC, (1709) b. Aug. 7, 1802; graduated at Yale College in 1821; became an Episcopal clergyman; m. Catharine Cornelia Jones, of New York city, Oct. 5, 1841, and, in 1875, was living at Round Hill, in Greenwich, Conn.

CHILDREN OF DANIEL PECK (304) AND HANNAH, HIS WIFE, ALL BORN IN GREENWICH, CONN.

[745.]   1. HARRIET M., b. March 30, 1816, and d. unm., in Greenwich, Nov. 12, 1842.

[746.]   2. ELIZABETH, b. Dec. 20, 1820, and d. unm., in Greenwich, Dec. 23, 1842.

[747.]   3. SAMUEL, (1713) b. Oct. 11, 1829; m. Anna Augusta Peck, (1642) Dec. 17, 1855, and, in 1861, was living in Bridgport, Conn.

[748.]   4. DANIEL, b. Sept. 25, 1833, and, in 1861, was living in Greenwich, Conn.

CHILDREN OF BENJAMIN PECK (307) AND ELIZABETH, HIS WIFE,
ALL BORN IN GREENWICH, CONN.

[749.] 1. HANNAH REED, b. May 1, 1811 ; m. Isadore
Vallier, Oct. 6, 1828, and, in 1861, was living in Keyport, N. J.

[750.] 2. PRUELLA, b. July 21, 1813, and d., in Greenwich,
June 5, 1814.

CHILDREN OF JAMES PECK (309) AND MARY, HIS WIFE, ALL BORN
IN GREENWICH, CONN.

[751.] 1. REED, b. Dec. 10, 1804 ; m. Susan D. Moore,
July 8, 1832, and d., in Port Chester, N. Y., Feb. 6, 1863.   His
wife d. there June 19, 1872.   He had no children.

[752.] 2. BENJAMIN, (1714) b. Oct. 3, 1806 ; m. 1. Lavina
Smith, who d. March 17, 1836 ; m. 2. Nancy Weed, who d.
Aug. 20, 1845, and m. 3. Priscilla Lyon, and d., in Greenwich,
July 14, 1870.

[753.] 3. ANN, b. Oct. 9, 1808 ; m. Henry Smith, in 1836,
and, in 1861, was living in New York city.

[754.] 4. EBENEZER, (1718) b. Aug. 27, 1810 ; m. Eliza R.
Reynolds, in 1837, and, in 1861, was living in Perth Amboy,
N. J.

[755.] 5. CHARLOTTE, b. June 3, 1813, and d. unm., in
New York city, March 27, 1854.

[756.] 6. MARY, b. Oct. 14, 1815 ; m. James E. Johnson, in
1842, and, in 1861, was living in New York city.

[757.] 7. HANNAH, b. March 4, 1818, and d. unm., in
Greenwich, March 7, 1860.

[758.] 8. DEBORAH, b. July 12, 1821 ; m. James Holden,
in 1848, and d., in Brooklyn, N. Y., March 27, 1848.

[759.] 9. ELIAS, (1729) b. June 14, 1823 ; m. Ellen E.
Rogers, May 15, 1850, and, in 1861, was living in New London,
Conn.

CHILDREN OF ELIAS PECK (310) AND DEBORAH, HIS WIFE, ALL
BORN IN GREENWICH, CONN.

[760.] 1. ALBERT N. (1736) b. March 10, 1805 ; m. 1.
Elizabeth C. Mead, dau. of Titus Mead, 2d, June 13, 1832, who
d. June 13, 1835, and m. 2. Ann Callender, Sept. 20, 1849, and,
in 1874, was living in New York city.

[761.] 2. MARY M., b. Feb. 17, 1807 ; m. Isaac Holley, in
1854, and, in 1861, was living in Greenwich, Conn.

[762.] 3. WILLIAM, (1740) b. Nov. 6, 1809 ; m. Caroline
Sherwood, June 2, 1838, and, in 1861, was living in Greenwich,
Conn.

[763.] 4. HARRIET H., b. Jan. 22, 1812, and, in 1861, was
living unm. in Greenwich, Conn.

[764.] 5. JOHN, (1747) b. July 30, 1814 ; graduated at
Western Reserve College, Ohio, in 1842; became a Presbyterian minister; m. Sarah N. Bremner, of New York city, in
1849, and, in 1861, was living in Traverse des Sioux, Minn.

[765.] 6. ABRAHAM H., (1750) b. July 27, 1816 ; m. Susan
Peck (770) and d., in Greenwich, Conn., March 8, 1855. His
widow was living in New York city, in 1861.

CHILDREN OF NATHAN PECK (311) AND SARAH, HIS WIFE, THE
OLDEST TWO BORN IN GREENWICH, CONN., THE
OTHERS IN NEW YORK CITY.

[766.] 1. ANN SECOR, b. Oct. 19, 1810 ; m. Asahel A.
Denman, June 6, 1832, and d., in New York city, Nov. 11, 1861.

[767.] 2. MARY CLARK, b. July 28, 1812 ; m. Reuben
Bettis May 18, 1839, and, in 1861, was living in Camden, N. Y.

[768.] 3. NATHAN REED, b. Aug. 13, 1815, and d., in
New York city, Sept. 9, 1833.

[769.] 4. ELIZABETH, b. Dec. 9, 1817 ; m. Rev. James B.
Ramsay, April 1, 1846, and d., in Choctaw Nation, July 17,
1849.

[770.] 5. SUSAN, b. April 9, 1820 ; m. 1. Abraham H. Peck
(765) Sept. 8, 1847, and m. 2. Bornt S. La Forge, Feb. 26, 1861,
and, in 1870, was living in Greenwich, Conn.

[771.] 6. WILLIAM J., (1753) b. June 6, 1822; m. 1. Ann C. Gedney, April 23, 1844, who d. Feb. 19, 1851, and m. 2. Catharine A. McLaughlin, Dec. 20, 1854; was President of the Board of Aldermen of New York city, and d. there Oct. 31, 1869. His widow was living there in 1874.

[772.] 7. JOSHUA S., (1759) b. Nov. 28, 1824; m. Sarah King, May 23, 1847, and, in 1875, was living in New York city.

[773.] 8. SARAH L., b. July 9, 1827; m. William A. Hubbard, Dec. 15, 1847, and was living in Rochester, N. Y., in 1861.

CHILDREN OF ABRAHAM PECK (315) AND ANNA, HIS WIFE, ALL BORN IN WARWICK, N. Y., EXCEPT ABRAHAM B., WHO WAS BORN IN ADAMS COUNTY, OHIO.

[774.] 1. MARIA, b. April 20, 1801; m. Alphonso Brooks and d., in Lexington, Ky., Aug. 10, 1839.

[775.] 2. ANN ELIZA, b. June 20, 1804, and d., in West Union, Adams county, Ohio, in June 1818.

[776.] 3. ELIAS, (1764) b. Nov. 10, 1806; m. Catharine Isabella Millard, of New York city, May 4, 1834; was a physician and resided in Newburgh, N. Y., and d. there July 11, 1865. His wife had d. there April 21, 1862.

[777.] 4. CLARISSA W., b. July 25, 1814, and was living unm. in New York city, in 1873.

[778.] 5. ABRAHAM B., Jan. 25, 1818; m. Mary Ann Van Vliet, and d., in Newburgh, N. Y., May 2, 1852. He had no children.

CHILDREN OF NEHEMIAH PECK (319) AND LAVINA, HIS WIFE, ALL BORN IN GREENWICH, CONN.

[779.] 1. ELIZA, b. March 9, 1808, and, in 1870, was living unm. in Greenwich, Conn.

[780.] 2. HENRY, b. April 23, 1810; m. Isabella Peters, and, in 1874, was living in New York city.

[781.] 3. ZACHARY, b. Dec. 27, 1811; m. Sarah H. Avery, Dec. 26, 1835, and was living in New York city in 1875. He has no children.

[782.] 4. ISRAEL, (1769) b. Dec. 17, 1814; m. Nancy H. Glover, Nov. 8, 1817, and, in 1870, was living in Southold, N. Y.

[783.] 5. LAVINA, b. Dec. 13, 1816 ; m. Nathaniel Wilson, and, in 1860, was living in Greenwich, Conn.

[784.] 6. ORPHA, b. Sept. 18, 1819, and d. unm., in Greenwich, Nov. 26, 1859.

[785.] 7. NEHEMIAH, (1776) b. Jan. 8, 1822 ; m. Mary Dunham, July 1, 1846, and d., in New York city, Jan. 7, 1867.

[786.] 8. ALPHEUS, (1777) b. Oct. 3, 1824 ; m. Louisa A. Steitz, Oct. 1, 1851, and, in 1861, was living in New York city.

[787.]. 9. ANDREW JACKSON, b. July 31, 1827, and, in 1870, was living in Greenwich, Conn.

[788.] 10. EMILY, b. July 22, 1829 ; m. William E. Peck (1639) April 16, 1860, and, in 1870, was living in Greenwich, Conn.

CHILDREN OF ISRAEL PECK (323) AND DORINDA, HIS WIFE, ALL BORN IN GREENWICH, CONN.

[789.] 1. MARY, b. July 12' 1820 ; m. Gilbert Shute, Oct. 28, 1846, and d., in Greenwich, March 24, 1867.

[790.] 2. JABEZ, b. April 12, 1822, and d. unm., in Greenwich, April 9, 1847.

CHILDREN OF REUBEN PECK, (325) ALL BORN AT GLEN'S FALLS, N. Y.

[791.] 1. HERMON, (1779) b. April 18, 1800 ; m. 1. Nancy Quin, in 1825, and m. 2. Martha Kenworthy, in 1830, and d., at Glen's Falls, July 27, 1865.

[792.] 2. DANIEL B., b. April 15, 1803 ; m. Maria Philo, in 1826, and d., at Glen's Falls, Oct. 28, 1828. He had no children.

[793.] 3. BETSEY, b. Sept. 23, 1805 ; m. Elmore Platt, in 1826, and was living at Glen's Falls, in 1869.

[794.] 4. NOBLE, b. March 6, 1811; m. Diadamia S. Beach, May 23, 1834, and d., at Glen's Falls, May 24, 1862. He had no children.

[795.] 5. PETER, b. Nov. 13, 1813 ; m. Ann Moon, in 1834, and was living in Queensbury, N. Y., in 1869. He has no children.

CHILDREN OF DANIEL PECK (326) AND CONTENT, HIS WIFE, ALL BORN AT GLEN'S FALLS, N. Y.

[796.] 1. AMANDA, b. Sept. 8, 1807, and d. unm., at Glen's Falls, June 21, 1832.

[797.] 2. SARAH, b. May 9, 1809, and d., at Glen's Falls, April 12, 1812.

[798.] 3. WILLIAM, (1786) b. Sept. 14, 1810 ; m. Hannah Newman, Dec. 1, 1836, and d., at Glen's Falls, Sept. 11, 1862.

[799.] 4. DANIEL, b. Feb. 22, 1812, and d., at Glen's Falls, March 8, 1812.

[800.] 5. GEORGE, b. Feb. 24, 1813, and d., at Glen's Falls, April 27, 1818.

[801.] 6. BENJAMIN, (1790) b. May 19, 1815 ; m. Sarah H. Button, Oct. 7, 1840, and was living in Queensbury, N. Y., in 1869.

[802.] 7. NATHANIEL S., (1793) b. June 23, 1817 ; m. Harriet E. Baker, March 29, 1856, and, in 1870, was living in Conneautville, Penn.

[803.] 8. CHARLES, (1800) b. Aug. 10, 1819 ; m. 1. Charlotte A. Elmore, May 13, 1848, who d. Oct. 27, 1857, and m. 2. Frances A. Philips, Nov. 9, 1858, and d., at Glen's Falls, Jan. 4, 1866.

[804.] 9. DELIA, b. Nov. 27, 1821 ; m. William Otis, Jan. 20, 1841, and d., in Danby, Vt., July 28, 1848.

[805.] 10. SARAH G., b. Feb. 20, 1824 ; m. Orange Newman, Dec. 14, 1843, and was living in Queensbury, N. Y., in 1869.

CHILDREN OF EDMUND PECK (327) AND SARAH, HIS WIFE, ALL BORN AT GLEN'S FALLS, N. Y.

[806.] 1. DARIUS, (1802) b. July 30, 1805 ; m. Mary S. Smith, Oct. 22, 1829, and, in 1873, was living in Newark, N. J.

[807.] 2. EMELINE, b. Aug. 30, 1812, and, in 1869, was living unm. at Glen's Falls. N. Y.

CHILDREN OF ELIHU PECK (328) AND RUANA, HIS WIFE.

[808.] 1. CALVIN, b. in Pompey, N. Y., Oct. 23, 1798, and d. unm., in Van Buren, N. Y., m 1860.

[809.] 2. MARTHA, b. in Pompey, N. Y., July 24, 1800; m. Nathaniel Cornell, and, in 1875, was living in Van Buren, N. Y.

[810.] 3. PHILO, (1808) b. in Pompey, N. Y., Dec. 23, 1802; m. 1. Emeline Barnes, and m. 2. Miranda Dewey, and d., in 1873, in Van Buren, N. Y.

[811.] 4. AURILLA, b. in Pompey, N. Y., Feb. 2, 1804; m. Harvey Tuttle, and, in 1875, was living in Camillus, N. Y.

[812.] 5. EUNICE, b. in Cato, N. Y., Sept. 5, 1808; m. Richmond Janes and, in 1870, was living in Hannibal, N. Y.

[813.] 6. RUANA, b. in Cato, N. Y., Oct. 22, 1810; m. Damon Barnes, and d., in Van Buren, N. Y., in 1861.

[814.] 7. EMILY, b. in Cato, N. Y., Aug. 24, 1813; m. Daniel Abrams, and, in 1875, was living in Camillus, N. Y.

[815.] 8. ETHAN, (1811) b. in Camillus, N. Y., Oct. 19, 1814; m. Alma Davis, and, in 1870, was living in Lansing, Mich.

[816.] 9. ANN, b. in Camillus, N. Y., April 21, 1816; m. Ira Hinsdale, and, in 1875, was living in Camillus, N. Y.

[817.] 10. LYMAN, (1821) b. in Camillus, N. Y., Dec. 29, 1820; m. Tira McCracken, and, in 1875, was living in Camillus, N. Y.

[818.] 11. ELIHU, (1826) b. in Camillus, N. Y., June 14, 1824; m. Agnes Bryant, and, in 1875, was living in Lansing, Mich.

CHILDREN OF PETER PECK (331) AND EMMA, HIS WIFE, ALL BORN IN CAMILLUS, N. Y.

[819.] 1. LYDIA, b. May 10, 1815; m. Joel Foster, and, in 1875, was living in Van Buren, N. Y.

[820.] 2. HARRIET, b. Sept. 10, 1818; m. William Davis, and d., in Camillus, N. Y., in 1875.

[821.] 3. BETSEY, b. May 15, 1822; m. Asahel K. Clark and, in 1875, was living in Van Buren, N. Y.

[822.] 4. DANIEL, (1829) b. July 2, 1826; m. Betsey Foster, and, in 1875, was living in Van Buren, N. Y.

[823.] 5. WILLIAM, (1830) b. Oct. 23, 1830; m. Matilda Lamerson, and, in 1875, was living in Van Buren, N. Y.

CHILDREN OF ENOS PECK (333) AND ANNIS, HIS WIFE, ALL BORN IN CAMILLUS, N. Y.

[824.] 1. ISAAC, (1837) b. July 28, 1817; m. Tammy Lamerson, and, in 1875, was living in Camillus, N. Y.

[825.] 2. AARON, (1838) b. July 28, 1817; m. Caroline Austin, and, in 1875, was living in Camillus, N. Y.

[826.] 3. JANE, b. May 28, 1820; m. William Mack, and, in 1875, was living in Davenport, Iowa.

[827.] 4. EDWIN, (1841) b. May 3, 1826; m. 1. Sarah Marble, and m. 2. Ann Sherwood, and, in 1875, was living in Camillus, N. Y.

CHILDREN OF ISAAC PECK, (334) ALL BORN IN CAMILLUS, N. Y., EXCEPT THE LAST THREE, WHO WERE BORN IN VAN BUREN, N. Y.

[828.] 1. RICHARD, (1844) b. about 1820; m. Mary Ann Miller, and, in 1875, was living in Cayutaville, Schuyler county N. Y.

[829.] 2. LEONARD, (1851) b. about 1822; m. Susan Sullen, and, in 1875, was living in Groton, N. Y.

[830.] 3. ENOS, (1854) b. in 1824; m. Esther St. John, and, in 1875, was living in Camillus, N. Y.

[831.] 4. CORNELIA, b. in 1826; m. John Clapper and d. in Van Buren, N. Y.

[832.] 5. CORDELIA, b. in 1828; m. Andrew Craver, and d., in Camillus, N. Y., in Oct. 1862.

[833.] 6. ELAM, b. in 1830 ; was m. and, in 1875, was living in the State of Michigan.

[834.] 7. HORACE, (1856) b. in 1832; was m. and d., Oct. 15, 1863, in the State of Michigan.

[835.] 8. AARON, b. in 1833 ; m. Mary Colburn, and, in 1875, was living in Elbridge, N. Y.

[836.] 9. EMILY, b. Dec. 27, 1847, and, in 1875, was living unm. in Van Buren, N. Y.

[837.] 10. IRVIN, b. May 11, 1848 ; m. Esther E. Tibbits, and, in 1875, was living in Pompey, N. Y.

[838.] 11. DUANE, b. Aug. 22, 1850, and, in 1875, was living unm. in Van Buren, N. Y.

CHILDREN OF ALMOND PECK (337) AND FIDELIA, HIS WIFE.

[839.] 1. LANSING, b. in Camillus, N. Y., Oct. 16, 1823, and d. unm., in Lysander, N. Y., July 16, 1848.

[840.] 2. TRUMAN, b. in Camillus, N. Y., April 22, 1825 ; m. Margaret Decker, and, in 1875, was living in Lysander, N. Y. He has no children.

[841.] 3. AMANDA, b. in Hannibal, N. Y., Aug. 20, 1828 ; m. Frank Avery, and, in 1875, was living in Lysander, N. Y.

[842.] 4. ALELIA, b. in Hannibal, N. Y., May 10, 1832; m. Comly A. Teal, and, in 1875, was living in Lysander, N. Y.

[843.] 5. ALMIRA, b. in Hannibal, N. Y., April 22, 1833 ; m. Edwin Van Dorn, and, in 1875, was living in Lysander, N. Y.

[844.] 6. ANN, b. in Hannibal, N. Y., March 20, 1835 ; m. James E. Decker, and, in 1875, was living in Lysander, N. Y.

CHILDREN OF ROBERT PECK (340) AND LAVINA, HIS WIFE, ALL BORN IN GREENWICH, CONN.

[845.] 1. ROBERT, (1859) b. June 7, 1795 ; m. Sarah Elizabeth Fletcher, July 9, 1817, and d., in Washington, N. Y., Sept. 8, 1830.

[846.]   3. ANNA, b. Nov. 15, 1797 ; m. Alfred Carhart, of New York city, June 5, 1818, and d. there Sept. 7, 1843.

CHILDREN OF ELIAS PECK (345) AND EUNICE, HIS WIFE, ALL BORN IN GREENWICH, CONN.

[847.]   1. WILSON, (1865) b. Aug. 11, 1813 ; m. Phebe Alward, Jan. 9, 1845, and, in 1872, was living in Henry, Marshall county, Ill.

[848.]   2. ELIAS REED, (1872) b. July 27, 1815 ; m. Elizabeth G. S. Bohanan, Sept. 24, 1839, and, in 1872, was living in Prarie City, Iowa.

[849.]   3. SALLY ANN, b. Jan. 10, 1818, and d., in Greenwich, Nov. 24, 1821.

[850.]   4. JONATHAN, (1882) b. Aug. 13, 1821 ; m. Frances S. Garfield, and, in 1872, was living in La Salle, Ill.

[851.]   5. JOHN, b. June 7, 1825, and d., the same day, in Greenwich, Conn.

[852.]   6. JOSEPHUS, (1883) b. June 7, 1825 ; m. Amy Jane Dingee, in 1848, and, in 1872, was living in Stamford, Conn.

[853.]   7. LUCRETIA, b. May 21, 1829 ; m. Edward H Taylor, and, in 1872, was living in Port Chester, N. Y.

CHILDREN OF LEWIS PECK (346) AND SALLY, HIS WIFE, ALL BORN IN SHARON, CONN.

[854.]   1. WILLIAM R., (1888) b. April 29, 1810 ; m. 1. Lucretia Louisa Woodward, Jan. 5, 1832, who d. Jan. 25, 1853, and m. 2. Lucia M. Tuttle, of Syracuse, N. Y., March 3, 1854 ; was a physician and d., in Bowling Green, O., in April, 1867.

[855.]   2. MARY A., b. April 23, 1813 ; m. 1. George Peck, of Sharon, Conn., in Dec. 1831, and m. 2. F. A. Lockwood, July 19, 1857, and d., in Sharon, Oct. 8, 1861.

[856.]   3. CALVIN F., (1894) b. Oct. 9, 1816 ; m. Mary L. Hoyt, of Cornwall, Conn., Dec. 11, 1842, and d., in Sharon, Sept. 28, 1861.

[857.]   4. FREDERICK L., b. Nov. 21, 1821, and d. unm., in Sharon, March 29, 1843.

[858.]   5. CHARLES H., (1896) b. July 21, 1830 ; m. Fannie M. Blakeman, of Albany, N. Y., Sept. 21, 1852, and d., in Camden, S. C., June 19, 1864.

CHILDREN OF EBENEZER PECK (347) AND ELIZABETH, HIS WIFE, ALL BORN IN STAMFORD, CONN.

[859.]   1. NANCY, b. Oct. 9, 1800 ; m. Edwin Lounsbury, Feb. 12, 1823, and d., in Greenwich, Conn., March 30, 1867.

[860.]   2. CAROLINE, b. Aug. 5, 1802, and d., Jan. 8, 1804.

[861]   3. JULIA A., b. April 10, 1805 ; m. 1. William A. Lockwood, and m. 2. Hiram Raymond, and, in 1870, was living in Stamford, Conn.

[862.]   4. ELIZABETH, b. May 2, 1808, and d., the same day, in Stamford, Conn.

[863.]   5. EDMOND, b. May 9. 1812, and d., July 30, 1821 in Stamford, Conn.

CHILDREN OF RUFUS PECK (351) AND LETITIA, HIS WIFE, ALL BORN IN GREENWICH, CONN.

[864.]   1. EDMOND, (1899) b. June 10, 1817 ; m. 1. Charlotte A. Peck, (1437) and m. 2. Elizabeth Smith, in March 1863, and, in 1870, was living in West Haven, Conn.

[865.]   2. CHARLES, b. Aug. 30, 1820 ; and, in 1870, was living unm. in Greenwich, Conn.

[866.]   3. SANFORD, (1902) b. Aug. 30, 1820 ; m. Emily Peck, (1431) and d., in Norwalk, Conn., April 9, 1867.   His widow again m. John Trowbridge, of Bethlem, Conn., Sept. 21, 1869.

CHILDREN OF JOHN PECK (363) AND MERAB, HIS WIFE, ALL BORN IN CHESHIRE, CONN.

[867.]   1. WILLIAM, (1903) b. Dec. 9, 1788 ; m. Mary Ann Atwater, Nov. 2, 1814, and, in 1861, was living in Cheshire, Conn.

[868.]   2. ALTIMIRA, b. July 2, 1790 ; m. John Smith, of Cheshire, and, in 1861, was living in Wellsboro, Pa.

[869.]   3. ROXANA, b. April 28, 1792 ; m. John Barnes, of Cheshire, and d. there Aug. 1, 1829.

[870.]   4. MELISSA, b. March 24, 1794; m. Russell Foster, of Cheshire, and, in 1861, was living in Cheshire, Conn.

[871.]   5. MERAB. b. Jan. 20, 1799 ; m. Ambrose R. Barnes, of Cheshire, and, in 1861, was living in New Haven, Conn.

[872.]   6. BURTON, (1906) b. Aug. 24, 1803 ; m. Caroline Merriman, of Cheshire, and d., in McHenry, Ill., Dec. 17, 1858.

CHILDREN OF ASA PECK (365) AND BETSEY, HIS WIFE, ALL BORN IN CHESHIRE, CONN.

[873.]   1. CLEMENT, (1916) b. Feb. 6, 1791 ; m. Damaris B. Brooks, Dec. 20, 1814, and, in 1861, was living in Cheshire, Conn.

[874.]   2. CHAUNCEY, (1921) b. June 18, 1793 ; m. 1. Rebecca Brooks, Nov. 15, 1815, who d. May 19, 1816, and m. 2. Martha Ives, May 20, 1818, and d., in Cheshire, April 17, 1839.

[875.]   3. ASA, (1925) b. Feb. 10, 1795 ; m. 1. Eliza Hough, July 19, 1819, who d. Aug. 2, 1819, and m. 2. Patience W. Saunders, Dec. 19, 1822, and d., in Leesburgh, Va., Nov. 21, 1839.

[876.]   4. AUGUSTUS, b. Jan. 10, 1797 ; m. Maria A. Hall Nov. 20, 1822, and, in 1861, was living in Milford, Conn.   He had no children.

[877.]   5. JOHN, (1933) b. July 4, 1799 ; m. 1. Ruth Tuttle, Aug. 28, 1822, who d. Sept. 17, 1829, and m. 2. Mary Thompson, April 23, 1830, and d., in Cheshire, Sept. 20, 1854.

[878.]   6. BETSEY, b. April 2, 1802. and d., in Cheshire, Oct. 5, 1814.

[879.]   7. CHARLOTTE, b. Aug. 1, 1805 ; m. Jared Ives, who d. June 28, 1861, and she d., in Cheshire, July 2, 1860.

[880.]   8. JUSTUS, (1937) b. March 1, 1807 ; m. Marietta Moss, Jan. 21, 1834, who d. Aug. 23, 1835, and m. 2. Jane French, April 11, 1839.   He is said to have been living in Bethany, Conn., in 1861.

CHILDREN OF LEVI PECK (366) AND ESTHER, HIS WIFE, ALL
BORN IN CHESHIRE, CONN.

[881.] 1. ESTHER LOIS, b. March 10, 1800; m. Wyllys
Todd, and d., in Northford, Conn., April 16, 1853.

[882.] 2. GEORGE, (1941) b. May 28, 1802; m. Lydia Hall,
April 24, 1823, who d. Feb. 17, 1857, and, in 1861, he was liv
ing in Cheshire.

[883.] 3. LEVI, (1946) b. May 20, 1808; m. Esther Lavina
Todd, and d., in Cheshire, June 28, 1855.

CHILDREN OF SAMUEL PECK, (368) THE FIRST FOUR BORN IN
CHESHIRE, AND THE OTHERS, EXCEPT CHAUNCEY
H., IN PROSPECT, CONN.

[884.] 1. CAROLINE, b. Nov. 22, 1801; m. Amos Bronson,
and, in 1861, was living in Olean, N. Y.

[885.] 2. EDWARD, (1953) b. June 1, 1803; m. Persis S.
Stanton, March 13, 1838, and d., in Warsaw, N. Y., June 16,
1854.

[886.] 3. SAMUEL B., (1960) b. Feb. 22, 1805; m. Dency
Cooke, April 22, 1833, and, in 1861, was living in Muskegon,
Mich.

[887.] 4. EMILY, b. April 24, 1807, and d. unm., in Olean,
N. Y., Jan. 29, 1856.

[888.] 5. ENOS T., (1963) b. Nov. 19, 1809; m. Harriet
Hurd, in 1835, who d. April 29, 1861. He d., in Greenville,
Mich., Feb. 23, 1856.

[889.] 6. FREDERICK, b. Dec. 29, 1811, and d., in Prospect, Conn., April 29' 1812.

[890.] 7. ELIZABETH B., b. May 12, 1813, and, in 1861,
was living unm. in Canandaigua, N. Y.

[891.] 8. SOLON B., b. Dec. 31, 1814, and, in 1861, was
living in Virginia City, Nevada.

[892.] 9. FREDERICK B., (1969) b. Nov. 11, 1823; m.
Sophia S. Fitch, April 17, 1851, and, in 1861, was living in
East Bloomfield, N. Y.

[893.]   10. FRANK S., (1970) b. Nov. 17, 1825 ; m. Caroline Bronson, in Nov. 1858, and, in 1861, was living in Greenville, Mich.

[894.]   11. PHILANDER A., b. March 23, 1829, and, in 1861, was living unm., in Greenville, Mich.

[895.]   12. JOHN A., (1972) b. June 16, 1831 ; m. Imogen L. Sanford, Sept. 17, 1857, and, in 1861, was living in Muske-gon, Mich.

[896.]   13. CHAUNCEY H., b. Nov. 12, 1840, in East Bloom-field, N. Y., and, in 1861, was living unm. in Greenville, Mich.

CHILDREN OF THEOPHILUS PECK (371) AND MARY, HIS WIFE.

[897.]   1. ELECTA, b. in Wallingford, Conn., about 1787, and d. unm., in Lexington, now Jewett, N. Y., in the Spring of 1830.

[898.]   2. CHARLES, (1974) b. in Lexington, now Jewett, N. Y., Oct. 26, 1789 ; m. Sarah Goslee and d., in Jewett, N. Y., Jan. 6, 1866.   His wife d. there in 1874.

[899.]   3. JOEL, (1986) b. in Lexington, now Jewett, N. Y., May 13, 1792 ; m. Elizabeth Arnold, and, in 1874, was living in Jaynesville, Iowa.   His wife was dead in 1874.

CHILDREN OF SAMUEL PECK (372) AND ABIGAIL, HIS WIFE, ALL
    BORN IN LEXINGTON, NOW THE TOWN OF JEWETT, N. Y.
        EXCEPT THE OLDEST, BORN IN WALLINGFORD, CONN.

[900.]   1. CLARISSA, b. Feb. 13, 1790 ; m. Ira Whitcomb, and, in 1861, was living in Middletown, N. Y., and has since died.

[901.]   2. LOWLY, b. April 28, 1792 ; m. Ransom Wolcott, and d., in Webster, N. Y., May 11, 1848.

[902.]   3. CHAUNCEY, (1995) b. Oct. 31. 1793 ; m. Minerva Goslee, and d., in Middletown, N. Y., in March 1860.

[903.]   4. GEORGE, b. Feb. 22, 1796 ; m. Clorinda Gunn, who was living in Catskill, N. Y., in 1876, and he d. there Dec. 13, 1860.   He had no children.

[904.] 5. ESTHER, b. May 6, 1798 ; m. Jesse Barker, and d., in Jewett, N. Y., in 1869.

[905.] 6. PHILO, b. June 8, 1800, and, in 1876, was living unm. in Catskill, N. Y.

[906.] 7. LUCY, b. Aug. 5, 1802 ; m. Jesse Barker, and d., in Jewett, N. Y., Sept. 29, 1823.

[907.] 8. JOHN, (2002) b. March 2, 1805 ; m. Jane Hosford, and, in 1876, was living in Catskill, N. Y.

[908.] 9. SUSAN, b. April 26, 1807 ; m. Edward Squire, May 4, 1828, and d., in Milan, O., March 12, 1846.

[909.] 10. ALMIRA, b. May 13, 1810 ; m. Chauncey Rice, Nov. 28, 1832, and d., Oct. 13, 1850, in Utica, Mich.

[910.] 11. DENNIS, d. in infancy, in Lexington, now Jewett, N. Y.

CHILDREN OF JOHN PECK (373) AND EUNICE, HIS WIFE, ALL BORN
IN FARMINGTON, CONN., EXCEPT THE OLDEST,
BORN IN WALLINGFORD, CONN.

[911.] 1. IRA, (2005) b. Nov. 15, 1790 ; m. Penelope Keyes, of Ashford, Conn., Feb. 22, 1823, and d., in Hartford, Conn., July 4, 1870.

[912.] 2. GEORGE, (2014) b. Feb. 10, 1793 ; m. Pamelia Clark, Nov. 27, 1814, and d., in West Avon, Conn., May 28, 1865.

[913.] 3. CALEB, (2018) b. Aug. 12, 1795 ; m. Lucy Dutton, and d., in Jewett, N. Y., April 14, 1864.

[914.] 4. DAMARIS, b. May 4, 1798 ; m. Nathaniel Hull, and d., in Jewett, N. Y., March 24, 1834.

[915.] 5. JOHN, b. June 8, 1800, and d. unm., in Marion, Ga., Oct. 3, 1825.

[916.] 6. CHAUNCEY, (2020) b. March 4, 1803 ; m. Lura Merwin, and, in 1870, was living in Windham, N. Y.

[917.] 7. AMANDA, b. Feb. 9, 1806 ; m. Remas Merwin, and d., in Jewett, N. Y.

[918.]   8. BENJAMIN, b. July 29, 1808 ; m. Elizabeth Lester, of Stewart Co., Ga., and d., in Lumpkin, Ga., Dec. 24, 1839. He had no children.

CHILDREN OF ISAAC PECK AND MIRIAM, HIS WIFE, ALL BORN IN WALLINGFORD, CONN.

[919.]   1. PAMELIA, b. Jan. 10, 1801, and, in 1875, was living unm. in Wallingford, Conn.

[920.]   2. JOEL, (2027) b. March 22, 1803 ; m. Ann E. Carrington, May 12, 1840, and d., April 15, 1869, in Wallingford, Conn.

[921.]   3. MARTHA, b. Nov. 5, 1805, and, in 1875, was living unm., in Wallingford, Conn.

[922.]   4. SAMUEL, (2029) b. March 22, 1808 ; m. Eliza Munson, Dec. 21, 1843, and, in 1875, was living in Wallingford, Conn.

[923.]   5. MARY, b. Dec. 12, 1811, and d. unm., in Wallingford, Conn., about 1865.

[924.]   6. CHESTER, b. June 28, 1815, and d. unm., in Wallingford, Jan. 16, 1838.

CHILDREN OF AMOS PECK (377) AND SYBIL, HIS WIFE, ALL BORN IN LEXINGTON, NOW JEWETT, N. Y., EXCEPT THE OLDEST FOUR, WHO WERE BORN IN WALLINGFORD, CONN.

[925.]   1. HARRIET, b. April 13, 1800 ; m. Luther Ford, and d., in Lexington, now Jewett, N. Y., April 21, 1821.

[926.]   2. ORRIN, (2030) b. Feb. 4, 1802 ; m. 1. Volutia Coe ; m. 2. Lucinda Goslee, and, in 1875, was living in Harpersfield, N. Y.

[927.]   3. LEVI, (2035) b. Dec. 27, 1803 ; m. Mary Coe and d., in Jewett, N. Y., in the Spring of 1869.

[928.]   4. SAMUEL, d. in infancy at Wallingford, Conn.

[929.]   5. MARY, b. Sept. 7, 1809 ; m. Nathaniel Hull, and d., in Jewett, N. Y., Oct. 10, 1865.

[930.]   6. CHARLES B., (2041) b. Jan. 11, 1811 ; m. 1. Stata Coe, and, in 1875, was living in Jewett, N. Y.

[931.] 7. JANE, b. May 6, 1815 ; m. Alfred Peck (1974) and d., in Jewett, N. Y., May 22, 1850.

[932.] 8. LYDIA B., b. Feb. 15, 1818 ; m. Alfred Peck (1974) and, in 1876, was living in Great Barrington, Mass.

[933.] 9. MUNSON, (2048) b. Nov. 18, 1820 ; m. Mary Peck (1977) and, in 1876, was living in South Egremont, Mass.

CHILDREN OF JESSE PECK, (381.)

[934.] 1. DOLLY, b. in Cheshire, Conn., April 15, 1789 ; m. Wait P. Green, March 9, 1812, and d. in Burlington, Iowa.

[935.] 2. SAMUEL, m. Hannah Manly, of Marcellus, N. Y., and d. in the State of Ohio.

[936.] 3. JOHN, nothing is known of him ; was last heard from on the Mississippi river, so his brother Charles says.

[937.] 4. EUNICE, b. in Cheshire, Conn., in 1797 ; m. Hiram Whitman, Jan. 1, 1818, and d., in Detroit, Mich., in 1828.

[938.] 5. CHARLOTTE, b. in Cheshire, Conn., and d. young, in Marcellus. N. Y.

[939.] 6. JOEL, (2051) b. in Pompey, N. Y., Dec. 22, 1801 ; m. Eliza Hyde, Jan. 23, 1822. He d. in Farmington, O., in Oct. 1869.

[940.] 7. MARY, b. in Pompey, N. Y., Feb. 27, 1803 ; m. Rev. Russell Downing, Jan. 22, 1821, and d., in Windsor, O., Aug. 2, 1838.

[941.] 8. BENJAMIN H., (2055) b. in Marcellus, N. Y., Dec. 17, 1804 ; m. Julia Graves, March 9, 1825, and d., in Uniontown, Ind., June 18 1854.

[942.] 9. CHARLES, (2054) b. in Marcellus, N. Y., July 16, 1808 ; m. 1. Assenett Jordan, in 1833, who d. June 10, 1862, and m. 2. Eliza Alice Barnes, Feb. 9, 1863, and, in 1870, was living in Orwell, O. He has no children.

CHILDREN OF CHARLES PECK, (387) ALL SUPPOSED TO HAVE BEEN BORN IN CHESHIRE, CONN., EXCEPT THE LAST TWO, WHO WERE BORN IN SHAFTSBURY, VT.

[943.] 1. ELIZA SAMANTHA, b. Nov. 5, 1794, and d. unm. April 8, 1825.

[944.] 2. HARRIET MARIA, b. Nov. 15, 1797 ; m. Jonathan B. Norton, July 18, 1819, who d. Nov. 16, 1831, and, in 1862, was living in Bennington, Vt.

[945.] 3. ADELINE, b. in Nov. 1800, and d. in 1801.

[946.] 4. NANCY, b. Oct. 6, 1802 ; m. Dexter Damon, in Dec. 1825, and, in 1862, was living in Bennington, Vt.

[947.] 5. LAURA ANN, b. Nov. 30, 1805 ; m. David F. Squires, Nov. 30, 1830, and, in 1862, was living in Bennington, Vt.

[948.] 6. CAROLINE AMELIA, b. March 21, 1809 ; m. Abel H. Wills, April 20, 1829, and, in 1862, was living in Bennington, Vt.

[949.] 7. CATHARINE E., b. Oct. 8, 1842, and, in 1862, was living unm. in Shaftsbury, Vt.

[950.] 8. MARY E., b. Oct. 31, 1846, and, in 1862, was living unm. in Shaftsbury, Vt.

CHILDREN OF JOEL PECK (388) AND ABIGAIL, HIS WIFE.

[951.] 1. CORNELIA, b. in Cheshire, Conn., Feb. 21, 1806, and, in 1861, was living unm. in Scott, N. Y.

[952.] 2. MATILDA, b. in Cheshire, Conn,, March 9, 1809 ; m. William M. Elston, and, in 1861, was living in Scott, N. Y.

[953.] 3. ARABELLA, b. in Cheshire, Conn., Feb. 18, 1812; m. Josiah P. Fuller, and, in 1861, was living in Scott, N. Y.

[954.] 4. JULIA A., b. in Marcellus, N. Y., Jan. 9, 1815 ; m. John H. Gillett, and, in 1861, was living in Scott, N. Y.

[955.] 5. EDWARD, b. in Marcellus, N. Y., Feb. 4, 1818 ; m. Julia A. Miller, and, in 1861, was living in West Hawley, Mass. Had no children, except one who d. three days old.

[956.] 6. AUGUSTUS T., b. in Scott, N. Y., Aug. 27, 1821, and, in 1861, was living unm. in Scott, N. Y.

CHILDREN OF JOHN PECK (390) AND LUCINDA, HIS WIFE.

[957.] 1. HENRY, (2063) b. in Cheshire, Conn., Dec. 22 1806 ; m. Laura Olds, and d., in Bristol, Conn., Oct. 17, 1873.

[958.] 2. GEORGE, (2067) b. in Cheshire, Conn., June 23, 1809 ; m. Jane DeMunn and d., in Hinsdale, N. Y., Jan. 22, 1846.

[959.] 3. LOUISA, b. in Marcellus, N. Y., March 17, 1813 ; m. Charles Bailey, and, in 1872, was living in Bristol, Conn.

[960.] 4. ADELINE, b. in Bristol, Conn., Feb. 5, 1816 ; m. Elisha Thompson, and, in 1872, was living in Bristol, Conn.

[961.] 5. RICHARD, b. in Bristol, Conn., April 4, 1820, and d. there Nov. 4, 1827.

[962.] 6. JOHN, (2071) b. in Bristol, Conn., Sept. 22, 1822 ; m. Maria Jacocks, and, in 1872, was living in West Meriden, Conn.

[963.] 7. CHARLES, (2074) b. in Bristol, Conn., May 22, 1824 ; m. Lucia Lane, of Plymouth, Conn., and, in 1872, was living in Bristol, Conn.

[964.] 8. JULIUS, b. in Bristol, Conn., June 13, 1830 ; m. 1. Phebe Allen, who d. in 1865   He again m., and, in 1872, was living in Belmond, Iowa.   He had no children.

[965.] 9. JANE, b. in Bristol, Conn., May 20, 1832 ; m. William H. Alvord, and, in 1872, was living in Brooklyn, N. Y.

CHILDREN OF JESSE S. PECK (392) AND SALLY, HIS WIFE.

[966.] 1. OLIVE, b. in Middletown, Conn., Feb. 15, 1793 ; m. 1. John Beers, of New Haven, Conn., and m. 2. John Winn, of Kingston, C. W., and, in 1862, was living in Racine, Wis.

[967.] 2. JESSE, (2078) b. in Middletown, Conn., Oct. 9, 1795 ; m. Mary Ann Seagreaves, of Allentown, Penn., and, in 1872, was living in Buffalo, N. Y.

[968.] 3. CHARLES, (2086) b. in Middletown, Conn., Aug. 22, 1797 ; m Mary Beach, of Henderson, Ky., and d. there.

[969.] 4. SARAH, b. in New York city, July 3, 1799 : m. Jonathan Buddington, of New Haven, in Jan. 1824, and was living in Dunkirk, N. Y., in 1862.

[970.] 5. JOHN B., b. in New Hampshire, July 8, 1801 ; was m. and d. in Indiana, in Oct. 1821.   He had no children.

[971.]   6. b. HIRAM, b. in Eaton, C. W., Jan. 1, 1804; m. 1. Amanda Doan, and m. 2ʳ Mary Nichols, and d., in Auburn, N. Y., Jan. 10, 1845.   He had no children.

CHILDREN OF MILES PECK (393) AND EUNICE, HIS WIFE.

[972.]   1. SALINA, b. in Wallingford, Conn., Sept. 17, 1797; m. Jonah Curtiss and d., in Wallingford, Conn., Sept. 28, 1829.

[973.]   2. EUNICE, b. in Wallingford, Conn., Dec. 25, 1804; m. Miles Ives and d., in Wallingford, Conn., Oct. 13, 1855.

[974.]   3. MILES, (2096) b. in Montreal, C. W., Dec. 2, 1810; m. Emily Steele, of Berlin, Conn., and, in 1862, was living in Kansas.

[975.]   4. HARRIET M., b. in Wallingford, Conn., Oct. 7, 1814; m. Myron Tuttle, and, in 1862, was living in New Preston, Conn.

CHILDREN OF JESSE PECK, (395) ALL BORN IN FARMINGTON, CONN.

[976.]   1. JOEL, (2098) b. Feb. 5, 1808; m. Charlotte M. Scoville, and d., in Farmington, Conn., April 15, 1872.

[977.]   2. MARY, b. May 10, 1809; m. William Frisbie, Sept. 10, 1829, and d., in Westport, N. Y., Dec. 15, 1855.

[978.]   3. SUSAN, b. Feb. 15, 1811, and d., in Farmington, Conn., in Dec. 1812.

CHILDREN OF RICHARD PECK, (396.)

[979]   1. SARAH, b. in Shelburne, Mass., Nov. 13, 1776; m. Jesse Whitcomb, and d., in Indiana, about 1859.

[980.]   2. SAMUEL, (2103) b. in Shelburne, Mass., Jan. 4, 1778; m. Amelia Briggs and d., in Lexington, N. Y., Dec. 21, 1853.

[981.]   3. RICHARD, (2115) b. in Shelburne, Mass., July 23, 1780; m. Permelia Rowley and d., in Windham, N. Y., Dec. 5, 1813.

[982.]   4. TENNANT, (2121) b. in Shelburne, Mass., Jan. 4, 1782; m. Polly Moore and d., in Freeport, Ill., March 21, 1866.

[983.]   5. ELIFF, b. in Shelburne, Mass., in Dec. 1783 ; m. Noah Dimmick and d., in Middletown, N. Y., in June 1817.

[984.]   6. JEMIMA, b. in Spencertown, N. Y., in 1785 ; m. Philemon Chamberlin and d., in Lexington, N. Y., in 1832.

[985.]   7. HANNAH, b. in Spencertown, N. Y., in Oct. 1787 ; m. John E. Burhans, and, in 1870, was living in Venetia, Ulster Co., N. Y.

[986.]   8. JOHN, b. in Woodstock, N. Y.. in 1789, and d., in Windham, N. Y., Jan. 24, 1802.

[987.]   9. POLLY, b. in Woodstock, N. Y., in 1793 ; m. John Beach and d., in Bridgeport, Conn., in 1856.

[988.]   10. PELEG C., b. in Windham; N. Y., April 4, 1796, and d. there unm., Oct. 25, 1815.

[989.]   11. ELIZABETH. b. in Windham, N. Y., April 1, 1798 ; m. Luman Hull, and, in 1875, was living in Durham, N. Y.

[990.]   12. JOHN C., (2131) b. in Windham, N. Y., Aug. 8, 1802 ; m. Nancy Hull, Nov. 18, 1824, and, in 1877, was living in Durham, N. Y.

CHILDREN OF SAMUEL PECK (397) AND LUCRETIA, HIS WIFE, ALL BORN IN LYME, CONN.

[991.]   1. LUCRETIA, b. Aug. 11, 1782, and d. unm., in Albany, N. Y., Oct. 28, 1871.

[992.]   2. FANNY, b. in 1784, and d. unm., in Lyme, Conn., in 1801.

[993.]   3. HANNAH, b. in March 1790, and d. unm., in Albany, N. Y., Aug. 21, 1838.

[994.]   4. FRANCIS, b. Sept. 14, 1792 ; m. Cynthia Newbury, Sept. 19, 1819, and d., in South Wildsor, Conn., Jan. 9, 1857. He had no children.

[995.]   5. SAMUEL, b. in 1794, and d. unm., in Lyme, Conn., in July 1824.

[996.]   6. PETER, (2136) b. July 13, 1796 ; m. Amelia Day, Dec. 29, 1828, and d., in Albany, N. Y., May 24, 1854. His wife d. April 3, 1871, aged 77 years.

CHILDREN OF ABNER PECK (400) AND HANNAH, HIS WIFE, ALL
BORN IN SHELBURNE, MASS.

[997.] 1. HANNAH, b. May 25, 1791, and d. unm., in Shelburne, Mass., Nov. 5, 1815.

[998.] 2. ABNER, (2138) b. May 15, 1793; m. Rebecca
Broad, Nov. 21, 1812; migrated from Lyme, Conn., to Leverett,
Mass., about 1816, and d., in Shelburne, Mass., Feb. 3, 1839.

[999.] 3. PETER, (2145) b. June 16, 1795; m. Ardelia To-
bey, Oct. 21, 1824, and, in 1868, was living in Shelburne, Mass.

[1000.] 4. MARY, b. July 23, 1797, and d. unm., in Shelburne, Mass., Sept. 9, 1856.

[1001.] 5. FANNY, b. June 6, 1800; m. Samuel Nims, in
Sept. 1824, and, in 1868, was living in Grattan, O.

CHILDREN OF JASON PECK (402) AND RHODA, HIS WIFE.

[1002.] 1. PHEBE, b. in Windham, N. Y., Feb. 16, 1796;
m. Nathaniel Sutton. Feb. 5, 1822, and d., in Reading, N. Y.,
Oct. 9, 1832.

[1003.] 2. JASON W., (2151) b. in Windham, N. Y., Aug.
2, 1797; m. Susan Sutten, Oct. 28, 1822, and d., at N. Reading,
N. Y., Nov. 23, 1863.

1004.] 3. ERASTUS, (2160) b. in Windham, N. Y., Dec. 1,
1799; m. Lydia Bailey, Nov. 2, 1831, and d., in Reading, N.
Y., April 22, 1840.

[1005.] 4. TENNANT, (2166) b. in Windham, N. Y., Dec.
19, 1801; m. Dorinda Sutten, and, in 1869, was living in Reading, N. Y.

[1006.] 5. RHODA, b. in Windham, N. Y., Oct. 25, 1803 ·
m. Jacob Gaultry and d., in Tyrone, N. Y., March 21, 1839.

[1007.] 6. BENONI, (2175) b. in Lexington, N. Y., April 4,
1806; m. Clarissa Thompson, June 6, 1831, and, in 1869, was
living at Beaver Dam, N. Y.

[1008.] 7. SOPHRONA, b. in Lexington, N. Y., Feb. 6,
1809; m. Ziba Bailey, and d., at La Porte, Ind., March 13,
1846.

[1009.] 8. ANNIS, b. in Reading, N. Y., May 1, 1812, and was living there unm. in 1869.

CHILDREN OF MARTIN PECK, (495) ALL SAID TO HAVE BEEN BORN IN LYME, CONN., EXCEPT AMANDA AND FANNY, WHO WERE BORN IN HECTOR, N. Y.

[1010.] 1. NANCY, m. David Burman, and d., in Cincinnati, O.

[1011.] 2. LUCY, b. Dec. 7, 1785 ; m. Caleb Smith, March 30, 1806, and d., in Hector, N. Y., Sept. 10, 1838.

[1012.] 3. CLARISSA, b. May 6, 1787 ; m. Charles Everts, and d., in Hector, N. Y., May 6, 1818.

[1013.] 4. JOEL, (2181) b. March 21, 1793 ; m. Nancy Bailey, Feb. 13, 1814, who d. Aug. 10, 1832, and m. 2. Esther Benedict, June 2, 1833, and d., in New York city, Sept. 4, 1837.

[1014.] 5. POLLY, b. Dec. 1, 1794; m. Adam Case, in Dec. 1820, and d., in Hector, N. Y., Sept. 30, 1830.

[1015.] 6. SALLY, b. in 1796 ; m. Isaac Hager, in 1815, and, in 1871, was living in Wellsborough, Penn.

[1016.] 7. PHALLY, m. 1. Daniel Case, and again m. and, in 1871, was living in Kankakee, Ill.

[1017.] 8. AMANDA, b. May 2, 1800 ; m. Lyman Reynolds, Sept. 5, 1818, and d., in Reynoldsville, N. Y., July 5, 1828.

[1018.] 9. FANNY, b. April 23, 1808 ; m. James Reeve, June 24, 1828, and, in 1871, was living in Elmira, N. Y.

CHILDREN OF DARIUS PECK (407) AND LYDIA, HIS WIFE.

[1019.] 1. BETSEY, b. in Lyme, Conn., Oct. 29, 1787 ; m. Isaac Bigelow and d., in Phelps, N. Y.. in 1850.

[1020.] 2. ELISHA, (2192) b. in Conway, Mass., April 11, 1789 ; m. 1. Lucinda Warner, who d. in 1813 ; m. 2. Percy Scott, who d. in 1836, and m. 3. Sarah L. Crouch, and d., in Phelps, N. Y., May 6, 1868.

[1021.] 3. HORACE, (2199) b. in Conway, Mass., Jan. 10, 1790 ; m. Sebe Chapman and d., in Phelps, N. Y., Aug. 3, 1867.

[1022.]   4. LYDIA, b. in Conway, Mass., Oct. 15, 1792 ; m. William Ottley, and, in 1869, was living in Phelps, N. Y.

[1023.]   5. DARIUS, (2207) b. in Conway, Mass., Nov. 20, 1794 ; m. 1. Betsey Raymond, and m. 2. Phebe Williams, and, in 1869, was living in Throopsville, N. Y.

[1024.]   6. ELIJAH, b. in Conway, Mass., Oct. 21, 1796, and d., in Conway, Mass., Nov. 26, 1798.

[1025.]   7. FANNY, b. in Conway, Mass., Aug. 20, 1798 ; m. William Crittenden, and d., in Phelps, N. Y., in 1850.

[1026.]   8. ENOCH, (2212) b. in Conway, Mass., Aug. 22, 1800 ; m. 1. Julitta Ann Jones, who d. April 17, 1835 ; m. 2. Cornelia Ann Swan, who d. Aug. 20, 1848, and m. 3. Almira Dixon, and, in 1869, was living in Phelps, N. Y., where he was a practising physician.

[1027.]   9. IRA, (2216) b. in Conway, Mass., July 20, 1802 · m. Polly Porter, and, in 1869, was living in Phelps, N. Y.

[1028.]   10. ANN, b. in Conway, Mass. ; m. Daniel Stuart and, in 1869, was living in Phelps, N. Y.

[1029.]   11. CHARLES, b. in Phelps, N. Y., and was living there unm. in 1869.

CHILDREN OF JOHN MOORE PECK (410) AND ABIGAIL, HIS WIFE, ALL BORN IN LYME, CONN.

[1030.]   1. DARIUS, b. Dec. 8, 1798, and d. unm., in Leicester, Mass., in 1820.

[1031.]   2. SETH MARVIN, (2220) b. Jan. 4, 1800 ; m. Sarah Pierson, of Lyme, Conn., Sept. 9, 1824, and d., in Bethany, N. Y., March 11, 1868.

[1032.]   3. JOHN MOORE, (2226) b. Aug. 27, 1802 ; m. Lucinda Odiorne, and, in 1869, was living in Jackson, Mich.

[1033.]   4. BETSEY, b. Oct. 21, 1803 ; m. Isaac Perkins, and, in 1869, was living in Wyoming, N. Y.

[1034.]   5. WILLIAM, (2239) b. April 20, 1805 ; m. Pamelia Filkins, and, in 1869, was living in Wyoming, N. Y.

[1035.]   6. JOSHUA, (2258) b. March 22, 1806 ; m. 1. Almena Manwaring ; m. 2. Althea Calhoun, and m. 3. Nancy Turner, and, in 1872, d. at Grass Lake, Mich.

[1036.]   7. DANIEL B., (2247) b. May 23, 1807 ; m. 1. Elizabeth Odiorne and m. 2. Emeline E. Marvin, and, in 1876, was living in Warsaw, N. Y.

[1037.]   8. JEMIMA, b. in 1809 ; m. David Filkins, and, in 1869, was living in Bethany, N. Y.

[1038.]   9. ABIGAIL, b. July 31, 1812 ; m. Samuel Odiorne, and d., in Grand Haven, Mich., in 1868.

[1039.]   10. JOSEPH, (2267) b. Sept. 16, 1814 ; m. Juliet Tubbs, and d., in Bethany, N. Y., Jan. 19, 1867.

[1040.]   11. BENJAMIN, (2271) b. Sept. 16, 1814 ; m. Emily Wells, Sept. 8, 1841, and, in 1869, was living in Staceyville, Iowa.

[1041.]   12. MARGARET, b. in 1816, and d. unm., in Bethany, N. Y., Aug. 6, 1850.

[1042.]   13. SARAH, b. in 1818; m. 1. William Wilson, and m. 2. Jacob Ross, and, in 1869, was living in Conesus, N. Y.

[1043.]   14. PHEBE, b. in Nov. 1820 ; m. Chester W. Durfee, and, in 1869, was living in Bethany, N. Y.

CHILDREN OF TIMOTHY PECK, (414) ALL BORN IN LYME, CONN.

[1044.]   1. CHARLES L., b. Aug. 1806, and d. unm., at Lahina, Sandwich Islands, May 3, 1845.

[1045.]   2. ELISHA S., (2279) b. June 3, 1809 ; m. Caroline Slate March 30, 1855 ; was a physician and d., in Lyme, Jan. 7, 1860.

[1046.]   3. TIMOTHY HOLLIS, (2280) b. Sept. 15, 1812 ; m. Irene E. Gillette, Sept. 30, 1845, and, in 1869, was living in Lyme, Conn.

[1047.]   4. WILLIAM L., b. in 1814, and d. unm., in Lyme, Conn., April 12, 1836.

[1048.]   5. ELIZABETH C., b. in 1816, and d. unm., in Lyme, Conn., May 12, 1836.

[1049.] 6. CAROLINE M., b. April 18, 1818 ; m. Jared Watrous, Dec. 26, 1842, and, in 1869, was living in Lyme, Conn.

[1050.] 7. THOMAS B., b. Sept. 2, 1819 ; m. Hepsibah S. Tooker, Sept. 17, 1850, and, in 1869, was living in Lyme, Conn.

[1051.] 8. LOUISA M., b. Jan. 9, 1822 ; m. Benajah P. Bill, in Sept. 1850, and d., in Lyme, Conn., Jan. 28, 1867.

[1052.] 9. MARION A., b. March 21, 1824 ; m. Frederick Brockway, in April, 1848, and, in 1869, was living in Saybrook, Conn.

[1053.] 10. EMMA E., b. July 12, 1835 , m. John N. Peck, (2230) April 22, 1862, and, in 1869, was living in Jackson, Mich.

CHILDREN OF DANIEL PECK (417) AND PERSIS, HIS WIFE, ALL BORN IN STAFFORD, CONN.

[1054.] 1. ELISHA, (2282) b. in 1798; m. 1. Mary Jane Averill, and m. 2. Sarah O. McLean, Sept. 5, 1839, and d., in New York city, Jan. 18, 1863.

[1055.] 2. ELIZA, b. April 18, 1800; m. Aholiab B. Johnson and, in 1867, was living in Enfield, Conn.

[1056.] 3. CLARISSA, b. March 11, 1802; m. 1. Dr. Horatio Hamilton, and m. 2. Col. Oliver Collins, and, in 1867, was living in Somers, Conn.

[1057.] 4. PERSIS L., b. April 22, 1804 ; m. Rev. Martin Tupper, April 13, 1828, and, in 1867, was living in Hardwick, Mass.

[1058.] 5. DANIEL A., (2286) b. Aug. 4, 1806 ; m. Joanna H. Strickland, May 28, 1835, and, in 1867, was living in Ellington, Conn.

[1059.] 6. ERASMUS D., (2291) b. Sept. 15, 1808. Having early adopted the medical profession, for which he was well educated, he removed from Stafford, Conn., to the State of Ohio, in 1828, and finally settled in Perrysburgh, in that State, where he resided until his decease, Dec. 25, 1876. He m. 1. Mary T. Lincoln, who d., at Washington, D. C., Jan. 20, 1873, and m. 2. Mrs. C. T. Robertson, Sept. 24, 1874. He was very highly respected and esteemed, not only as an able, kind and skillful physician, but as an enterprising business man and a most valuable citizen. He was a representative in the Ohio Legislature from 1855 to 1859, inclusive, and in the 41st and 42d Congresses, from the 10th Congressional District of the State of Ohio, in 1870 to 1873.

[1060.]   7. EMILY A., b. Jan. 6, 1811; m. Henry Gay, and d., in Stafford, Conn., March 2, 1835.

[1061.]   8. AUGUSTA L., b. Jan. 1, 1813 ; m. George Powers, Oct. 10, 1833, and d., in Perrysburgh, Ohio, in Sept. 1872.

[1062.]   9. ELEAZER A., (2292) b. Dec. 15, 1815 ; m. Lucy E. Wildman, of Hartford, Conn., June 4, 1839, and, in 1877, was living in Troy, N. Y.

[1063.]   10. ASENATH, b. Nov. 25, 1818; m. Henry Averill, April 24, 1838, and, in 1877, was living in Perrysburgh, Ohio.

CHILDREN OF EZEKIEL PECK (419) AND LUCINA, HIS WIFE, ALL BORN IN EAST HADDAM, CONN.

[1064.]   1. DANIEL, (2295) b. Oct. 4, 1801 ; m. Maria Olmsted, Nov. 5, 1832, and, in 1867, was living in Millington, Conn.

[1065.]   2. CLARISSA M., b. Oct. 23, 1803 ; m. Dr. Datus Williams, Aug. 25, 1824, and, in 1867, was living in East Haddam, Conn.

[1066.]   3. LUCINA P., b. Oct. 4, 1806 ; m. Halsey Brown, Nov. 22, 1843, and, in 1867, was living in East Haddam, Conn.

[1067.]   4. EZEKIEL Y., (2301) b. Dec. 23, 1808 ; m. Esther J. Eaton, in Nov., 1842, and, in 1867, was living in Akron, Ohio.

[1068.]   5. ERASTUS F., (2307) b. Feb. 6, 1811; m. Sophia Swan, March 13, 1832, and, in 1867, was living in East Haddam, Conn.

[1069.]   6. JERUSHA H., b. May 23, 1813, and d. in infancy, in East Haddam, Conn.

[1070.]   7. ROSWELL C., (2310) b. June 30, 1815 ; m. Elizabeth S. Parker, Nov. 27, 1850, and, in 1867, was living in East Haddam, Conn.

[1071.]   8. THEODORE D., b. Nov. 19, 1817, and d. unm., in New York city, May 26, 1845.

[1072.]   9. ELIZA A., b. June 18, 1820, and, in 1867, was living unm. in East Haddam, Conn.

[1073.]   10. HORATIO H., b. July 28, 1822, and d. unm., in East Haddam, Conn., June 15, 1857.

[1074.]   11. JOSEPH V., (2317) b. July 22, 1825 ; m. Abecca Shull, Sept. 13, 1854, and, in 1867, was living in Penn's Manor, Penn.

CHILDREN OF ELIJAH PECK (425) AND CLARISSA, HIS WIFE.

[1075.]   1. RICHARD E., (2323) b. in Burlington, N. Y., Feb. 8, 1808 ; m. 1. Mary Taft, Feb. 14, 1833 ; m. 2. Almira Taft, Sept. 10, 1840, and m. 3. Olive A. Griggs, Dec. 10, 1857, and, in 1867, was living in Monroe, Ohio.

[1076.]   2. ERASTUS, (2330) b. in Burlington, N. Y., Aug. 20, 1809 ; m. Candace Fox, July 1, 1832, and, in 1867, was living in Kingsville, O.

[1077.]   3. JEDEDIAH, b. in Burlington, N. Y., Dec. 15, 1811, and d unm., in Sheffield, Ohio, Feb. 29, 1832.

[1078.]   4. ELISHA, (2334) b. in Monroe, O., Sept. 7, 1816 ; m. Amanda Richmond. Nov. 26, 1843, and, in 1867, was living in Elkhart, Ind.

[1079.]   5. ELIJAH, (2339) b. in Monroe, O., Dec. 9, 1818 ; m. Adaline Colby, June 7, 1844, and, in 1867, was living in Sheffield, Ohio.

[1080.]   6. CLARISSA, b. in Monroe, O., Oct. 14, 1820, and d. unm., in Sheffield, Ohio, Sept. 7, 1839.

[1081.]   7. DAVID W., (2342) b. in Monroe, O., July 22, 1823 ; m. Julia A. Smith, Feb. 22, 1856, and, in 1867, was living in Denmark, Ohio.

[1082.] 8. EMELINE, b. in Monroe, Ohio, Sept. 22, 1826 ; m. William O. Lillie, Sept. 23, 1853, and, in 1867, was living in Sheffield, Ohio.

CHILDREN OF PETER PECK (426) AND SARAH, HIS WIFE, THE FIRST THREE BORN IN BURLINGTON, N. Y., AND THE LAST THREE BORN IN MONROE, OHIO.

[1083.] 1. ELIJAH, b. Jan. 2, 1810, and d., in Burlington, N. Y., Aug. 21, 1811.

[1084.] 2. POLLY, b. April 21, 1811 ; m. Daniel Campbell, March 25, 1838, and, in 1868, was living in Columbus Grove, Ohio.

[1085.] 3. ESTHER, Sept. 9, 1813 ; m. John Kitchell, March 29, 1833, and, in 1868, was living in Palmyra, Iowa.

[1086.] 4. PETER, (2345) b. Jan. 25, 1818 ; m. 1. Mary Maxwell, Sept. 26, 1836, and m. 2. Sarah Tyler, June 20, 1848, and, in 1868, was living in Millburgh, Mich.

[1087.] 5. SARAH, b. June 18, 1819, and d., in Monroe, O., April 19, 1821.

[1088.] 6. SARAH ANN, b. June 15, 1823 ; m. 1. Joseph Jenkins, July 4, 1844, and m. 2. Lewis Wells, Jan. 25, 1846, and, in 1868, was living in Indianola, Iowa.

ONLY CHILD OF JEDEDIAH PECK, (428.)

[1089.] TABITHA E., b. in Fredericktown, O., June 13, 1829 ; m. Avery D. Martin, Jan. 26, 1859, and, in 1868, was living in Fredericktown, Ohio.

CHILDREN OF WILLIAM E. PECK (429) AND RUAMA, HIS WIFE, ALL BORN IN BURLINGTON, N. Y.

[1090.] 1. RUAMA H., b. Jan. 6, 1811 ; m. 1. Clark Burdick, and m. 2. Nelson Bromley, and, in 1866, was living in York Center, Wis.

[1091.] 2. BETSEY ANN, b. Aug. 31, 1813 ; m. Austin Holdridge, and, in 1866, was living in Holley, Mich.

[1092.] 3. CALVIN H., b. April 15, 1814 ; m. Lydia Briggs, and, in 1866, was living in Ives Grove, Wis.

[1093.] 4. LUCRETIA, b. April 29, 1816 ; m. Alexander Dewey, and, in 1866, was living in Winfield, N. Y.

[1094.] 5. DEBORAH T., b. June 20, 1819 ; m. Welcome Manchester, and, in 1866, was living in Prarie, Wis.

[1095.] 6. JEDEDIAH W., b. July 25, 1821 ; m. Adaline Randall, and, in 1866, was living in Elkhorn, Wis.

[1096.] 7. CAROLINE H., b. July 26, 1823 ; m. ———— Hicks, and, in 1866, was living in Spring Prarie, Wis.

[1097.] 8. CHARALDINE, b. May 11, 1826 ; m. William McLellan and d., in El Paso, Ill., June 24, 1865.

[1098.] 9. ALBERT E., b. July 10, 1834 ; m. Alvira Huntington, and, in 1866, was living in Pleasant Valley, Minn.

CHILDREN OF JOSEPH H. PECK (431) AND SOPHARA, HIS WIFE, ALL BORN IN BURLINGTON, N. Y.

[1099.] 1. ELISHA ERWIN, b. Nov. 11, 1831, and d., in Ypsilanti, Mich., Jan. 23, 1839.

[1100.] 2. ELIZABETH L., was living unm. in Rockford, Ill., in 1865,

CHILDREN OF ELISHA PECK (435) AND OLIVE, HIS WIFE, ALL BORN IN VICTOR, N. Y.

[1101.] 1. MYRON H., (2352) b. May 28, 1828 ; m. Delia M. Bickford, Aug. 22, 1849 ; is a lawyer, and, in 1877, was living in Batavia, N. Y.

[1102.] 2. GEORGE W., b. Dec. 17, 1830, and d., in Victor. N. Y., Aug. 21, 1832.

[1103.] 3. ANNIE E., b. Feb. 6, 1832; m. John A. Guile, Oct. 20, 1859, and, in 1869, was living in Rochester, N. Y.

CHILDREN OF BENJAMIN PECK (436) AND MARY, HIS WIFE.

[1104.] 1. MARY ANN, b. in Cleveland, O., Oct. 1, 1836 ; m. Louis Adleblute, since deeeased, and, in 1865, was living in Delaware, O.

[1105.]   2. SARAH ELLEN, b. in Knox Co., O., March 17, 1838 ; m. Stephen M. Prouty, and, in 1865, was living in Delaware, O.

[1106.]   3. LOUISA JANE, b. in Delaware, O., May 14, 1840 ; m. Richard Heath, and, in 1865, was living in Delaware, Ohio.

[1107.]   4. EDWIN A., b. in Delaware, O., July 1, 1842, and d., March 2, 1850, in Delaware, O.

[1108.]   5. ERVIN B., b. in Delaware, O., Jan. 9, 1844, and, in 1865, was living unm. in Delaware, O.

[1109.]   6. HARRIET A., b. in Delaware, O., Nov. 1, 1846, and, in 1865, was living unm. in Delaware, O.

[1110.]   7. DAVID H., b. in Delaware, O., July 1, 1849, and was living there in 1865.

[1111.]   8. WILLIAM H., b. in Delaware, O., June 1, 1855, and was living there in 1865.

CHILDREN OF SILAS PECK (439) AND MARY, HIS WIFE, THE FIRST
BORN IN RACINE, WIS., THE OTHERS IN BURLINGTON, WIS.

[1112.]   1. NEWTON, b. Sept. 14, 1836, and, in 1865, was unm. and in the U. S. Army.

[1113.]   2. WILLIAM H., b. Jan. 17, 1841, and, in 1865, was living unm. in Burlington, Wis.

[1114.]   3. JULIA, b. Sept. 5, 1844, and, in 1865, was living unm. in Burlington, Wis.

[1115.]   4. ANN ELIZA, b. April 7, 1850, and, in 1865, was living in Burlington, Wis.

[1116.]   5. MENSO W., b. March 23, 1855, and, in 1865, was living in Burlington, Wis.

CHILDREN OF SILAS PECK (441) AND ABBY, HIS WIFE, ALL BORN
IN PITTSFIELD, N. Y., EXCEPT THE LAST THREE, WHO
WERE BORN IN NEW BERLIN, N. Y.

[1117.]   1. NELSON C., (2358) b. July 4, 1811 ; m. 1. Adra Fish, Dec. 8, 1837, who d. May 24, 1842 ; m. 2. Elizabeth Johnson, April 10, 1843, and, in 1870, was living in New Berlin, N. Y.

[1118.]   2. POLLY L., b. Oct. 13, 1813, and d., May 1, 1816, in Pittsfield, N. Y.

[1119.]   3. LYMAN Z., (2364) b. Nov. 6, 1815 ; m. Maria A. Johnson, March 5, 1840, and, in 1870, was living in Pittsfield, N. Y.

[1120.]   4. ANN ELIZA, b. Sept. 23, 1818; m. Isaac Wetmore, Feb. 14. 1841, and, in 1870, was living in New Berlin, N. Y.

[1121.]   5. POLLY M., b. Nov. 1, 1820; m. Milo Goodspeed, June 18, 1867, and, in 1870, was living in Pittsfield, N. Y.

[1122.]   6. ABBY, b. July 26, 1824 ; m. Charles Hitchcock, and, in 1870, was living in Morris, N. Y.

[1123.]   7. DIANA, b. Dec. 30, 1826, and d., Feb. 3, 1829, in New Berlin, N. Y.

[1124.]   8. SILAS H., b. June 21, 1829 ; m. Jane Dixon, July 4, 1853, and, in 1870, was living in New Berlin, N. Y.   He had no children.

[1125.]   9. DELIA, b. Feb. 22, 1832 ; m. George Strator, June 26, 1855, and, in 1870, was living in New Berlin, N. Y.

CHILDREN OF EDWARD C. PECK (442) AND LOUISA, HIS WIFE, ALL
BORN IN NEW LYME, O.

[1126.]   1. SALLY, b. Nov. 5, 1819 ; m. Jonathan Foreman, and, in 1870, was living in Austinburgh, O.

[1127.]   2. HIRAM, (2370) b. March 11, 1821 ; m. Harriet Simmons, May 20, 1851, and, in 1870, was living in Rome, O.

[1128.]   3. EDWARD C., (2374) b. Oct. 18, 1823 ; m. 1. Mary Way ; m. 2. Alice Allen, and d., in New Lvme, O., April 18, 1870.

[1129.]   4. MATTHEW G., (2375) b. May 30, 1826 ; m. Wealthy Knowles, and, in 1870, was living in New Lyme, O.

[1130.]   5. ANSEL, b. March 26, 1828, and d., in New Lyme, O., Dec. 29, 1846.

[1131.] 6. MARIETTE, b. March 30, 1834; m. John Anderson and d., in Trumbull, O., May 3, 1866.

[1132.] 7. LOUISA, b. Feb. 21, 1836; m. Samuel N. Woodruff, and, in 1870, was living in New Lyme, O.

CHILDREN OF LYMAN PECK (445) AND LAURA E., HIS WIFE, ALL BORN IN NEW LYME, OHIO.

[1133.] 1. FENNIMORE E., (2380) b. Feb. 29, 1832; m. Marion Rogers, Dec. 26, 1866, and, in 1870, was living in New Lyme, O.

[1134.] 2. PLUMMER W., b. July 31, 1833, and d., in New Lyme, O., Oct. 14, 1834.

CHILDREN OF WILLIAM D. PECK AND ZIPPORAH, HIS WIFE.

[1135.] 1. WILLIAM S., (2381) b. in New Lyme, O., Dec. 10, 1817; m. Elizabeth Amick, Feb. 7, 1839, and, in 1870, was living in Fairfield, Iowa.

[1136.] 2. MAHALA M., b. in New Lyme, O., July 20, 1819; m. Alanson Cooley in Nov., 1843, and d., in Batavia, Ill., Feb. 2, 1864.

[1137.] 3. BETSEY, b. in New Lyme, O., March 20, 1821; m. David Cipperly, in Nov., 1842, and, in 1870, was living in Beaver, Iowa.

[1138.] 4. LOVISA, b. in New Lyme, O., July 25, 1823; m. John Thompson in Sept., 1850, and, in 1870, was living in St. Louis, Mo.

[1139.] 5. JOSIAH J., (2387) b. in New Lyme, O., Oct. 11. 1828; m. Catharine Scott, Oct. 7, 1850, who d., Dec. 17, 1861 and, in 1870, he was living in Beaver, Iowa.

[1140.] 6. SILAS, (2392) b. in New Lyme, O., May 16, 1830; m. Maria J. Freeland, Oct. 13, 1860, and, in 1870, was living in Beaver, Iowa.

[1141.] 7. NELSON H., (2394) b. in Colebrook, O., April 3, 1833; m. Jane Archer, Nov. 19, 1863, and, in 1870, was living in Beaver, Iowa.

[1142.]   8. LESTER S., (2395) b. in Colebrook, O., Aug. 11 1835;. m. Clara E. Fuller, Feb. 12, 1857, who d. Sept. 19, 1869, and, in 1870, was living in Beaver, Iowa.

[1143.]   9. CHARLES D., b. in New Plato, Ill., Aug. 12, 1837, and d. there in Jan., 1845.

CHILDREN OF JOSIAH J. PECK (447) AND BETSEY, HIS WIFE.

[1144.]   1. BETSEY, b. in New Lyme, O., July 4, 1832; m. Clark Walling, and, in 1870, was living in New Lyme, O.

[1145.]   2. JOSIAH, (2398) b. in Colebrook, O., July 26, 1834 ; m. Minerva Philips, April 20, 1856, and, in 1870, was living in Colebrook, O.

[1146.]   3. JOHN B., (2403) b. in Colebrook, O., Sept. 8, 1837; m. Betsey Hubbard, and d., in New Lyme, O., Feb. 26, 1870.

[1147.]   4. SAMUEL, (2406) b. in Colebrook, O., Oct. 12, 1840 ; m. Jane Beckwith, Dec. 5, 1861, and, in 1870, was living in Colebrook, O.

CHILDREN OF ELIJAH PECK (451) AND PARNY, HIS WIFE, ALL BORN IN NEW LYME, OHIO.

[1148.]   1. THANKFUL M., b. Dec. 29, 1822 ; m. George Smedly, July 29, 1861, and, in 1870, was living in Grundy County, Ill.

[1149.]   2. ANSEL E., b. March 10, 1826, and, in 1870, was living, unm., in New Lyme, O.

[1150.]   3. JOHN S., (2408) b. Dec. 11, 1827 ; m. Antoinette Reeve, Sept. 5, 1852, and, in 1870, was living in New Lyme, O.

[1151.]   4. ZIPPORAH, b. Aug. 11, 1829 ; m. Almeron Howe, Jan. 1, 1849, and, in 1870, was living in Grundy County, Ill.

[1152.]   5. LAMIRA, b. Aug. 30, 1831 ; m. Hezekiah A. Reeve, Jan 1, 1849, and, in 1870, was living in New Lyme, O.

[1153.] 6. MARY ANN, b. April 3, 1833 ; m. Elihu Meigs Feb. 4, 1854, and, in 1870, was living in New Lyme, O.

[1154.] 7. EVELINE A., b. Jan. 29, 1835, and, in 1870, was living unm. in New Lyme, O.

[1155.] 8. MARIA L., b. Jan. 15, 1837 ; m. 1. George Gibbs, Aug. 7, 1860, and m. 2. Chauncey Coon, April 22, 1866, and, in 1870, was living in New Lyme, O.

[1156.] 9. PARNY J., b. Nov. 26, 1838 ; m. Henry Baldwin, in June 1860, and, in 1870, was living in Williamsfield, O.

[1157.] 10. NANCY L., b. Feb. 27, 1842 ; m. Daniel Randall, Sept. 19, 1868, and, in 1870, was living in New Lyme, O.

CHILDREN OF SAMUEL G. PECK (452) AND NANCY E., HIS WIFE.

[1158.] 1. HARRIET E., b. in New Lyme, O., Nov. 13, 1827 ; m. Leander C. Reeve, Jan. 22, 1851, and, in 1870, was living in Rome, O.

[1159.] 2. ZIPPORAH E., b. in New Lyme, O., June 13, 1829 ; m. Sidney Stults, Dec. 24, 1849, and, in 1870, was living in Rome, O.

[1160.] 3. EDWIN A., (2412) b. in New Lyme, O., Oct. 20, 1831 ; m. Urana Palmer, in March 1847, and, in 1870, was living in Orwell, O.

[1161.] 4. AMOS A., (2416) b. in Colebrook, O., Sept. 7, 1834 ; m. Elizabeth Joy, Oct. 1, 1856, and, in 1870, was living in Rome, O.

[1162.] 5. LEWIS G., b. in Colebrook, O., May 31, 1837, and d., in New Plato, Ill., Oct. 5, 1838.

CHILDREN OF SILAS PECK, (453) ALL BORN IN NEW LYME, O.

[1163.] 1. DELINA, b. May 1, 1835 ; m. Albert L. Rathbone, and, in 1870, was living in Morgan, O.

[1164.] 2. HELEN E., b. in Oct. 1839 ; m. John L. Fillmore, Feb. 19, 1865, and, in 1870, was living in New Lyme, O.

[1165.] 3. NINETTE, b. Jan. 5, 1854, and, in 1870, was living unm., in New Lyme, O.

CHILDREN OF LOT PECK (457) AND POLLY, HIS WIFE, ALL BORN
IN LYME, CONN.

[1166.] 1. STEPHEN L., (2421) b. June 5, 1789 ; m. Prudence Lewis, of Lima, N. Y., Feb. 3, 1819, who was living in
Worthington, O., in 1871, where he had d. Oct. 31, 1868.

[1167.] 2. NATHANIEL, b. May 15, 1791, and d., in Lyme,
Conn., Jan. 31, 1794.

[1168.] 3. BETSEY, b. March 9, 1793, and d., in Lyme,
Conn., Feb. 9, 1794.

[1169.] 4. NATHANIEL, again, (2427) b. Oct. 19, 1795 ; m.
Lydia Hatch, of Hebron, N. Y., in March 1821, and d., in
Groveland, Mich., Nov. 2, 1854.

[1170.] 5. CHARLES L., (2436) b. Feb. 15, 1797 ; m. 1.
Louisa Latham, of Granger Co., Tenn., Sept. 27, 1826 ; m. 2.
Mrs. Elizabeth Krider, Feb. 17, 1868, and, in 1871, was living
in Green Co., Mo.

[1171.] 6. ELIZABETH, b. May 26, 1799 ; m. 1. Thomas
Conkey ; m. 2. Abner Clapp, and m. 3. Henry Stiles, and d., in
March 1869, in Worthington, O.

[1172.] 7. MARY, b. in 1802 ; m. —— Peck, and d., in
1821, in the State of Ohio.

CHILDREN OF HARRIS PECK, (462.)

[1173.] 1. HARRIS, (2448) b. in West Bloomfield, N. Y.,
Jan. 17, 1806 ; m. Martha K. Stimson, Aug. 20, 1826, and, in
1871, was living at Albert Lea, Freeborn Co., Minn.

[1174.] 2. FRANCES ELIZA, b. in West Bloomfield, N.
Y., Aug. 21, 1808 ; m. 1. John Matchett, March 20, 1833, who
d. July 17, 1851, and m. 2. Henry King, in July 1853, and, in
1871, was living in Portage, Wood Co., O.

[1175.] 3. HANNAH, b. in West Bloomfield, N. Y., Aug.
21, 1808, and d. there Nov. 20, 1808.

[1176.] 4. MARY E., b. in Mendon, N. Y., Dec. 19, 1812 ;
m. Horace M. Shattuck, April 28, 1834, and, in 1871, was living in Wellington, O.

[1177.]   5. JOHN G., b. in Mendon, N. Y., April 26, 1814, and d. there May 23, 1814.

[1178.]   6. COLEMAN C., (2452) b. in Mendon, N. Y., April 22, 1815 ; m. Betsey Inman, March 4, 1843, and, in 1871, was living in Marcellus, Cass Co., Mich.

[1179.]   7. ABIGAIL J., b. in West Bloomfield, N. Y., April 18, 1817 ; m. Lysander Morse, and d., in Sterling, Ill., April 3, 1865.

[1180.]   8. RICHARD L., (2455) b. May 17, 1821, in West Bloomfield, N. Y.; m. Roxana Fulton, in March 1839, and, in 1871, was living in Wellington, O.

[1181.]   9. SAMUEL I., (2460) b. in West Bloomfield, N. Y., July 18, 1823 ; m. Caroline A. Matcham, May 2, 1848, and, in 1871, was living in Pittsfield, O.

[1182]   10. OSCAR J., (2464) b. in West Bloomfield, N. Y., Aug. 15, 1832 ; m. Charlotte Warren, July 7, 1855, and, in 1871, was living in Wellington, O.

[1183.]   11. JOHN CLARK, (2469) b. in Wellington, O., Dec. 15, 1835 ; m. Huldah Gibbs, in May 1863, and, in 1871, was living in Pittsfield, O.

CHILDREN OF CLARK PECK (465) AND CAROLINE, HIS WIFE, ALL
BORN IN WEST BLOOMFIELD, N. Y.

[1184.]   1. TWINS, b. Dec. 15, 1797, and d., in infancy, in West Bloomfield, N. Y.

[1185.]   2. MIRANDA P., b. April 23, 1799 ; m. 1. William G. Page, in Nov. 1844, and m. 2. David T. Hamilton, Jan. 26, 1869, and d., Jan. 15, 1876, in West Bloomfield, N. Y.

[1186.]   3. PHEBE D., b. Jan. 16, 1801, and d., Sept. 26, 1805, in West Bloomfield, N. Y.

[1187.]   4. CAROLINE, b. Jan. 31, 1805, and d., Nov. 4, 1815, in West Bloomfield, N. Y.

[1188.]   5. JASPER C., (2471) b. May 24, 1807 ; m. Mary C. Snow, March 12, 1844, and, in 1871, was living in West Bloomfield, N. Y.   His wife d. there Oct. 15, 1871.

[1189.]   6. ABEL H., (2475) b. Dec. 5, 1808 ; m. Sarah Darrow, March 24, 1834, and, in 1869, was living in Leavenworth, Kansas.

[1190.]   7. JOSEPH A., (2478) b. Julv 28, 1817 : m. Susan H. Richardson, March 18, 1844, and, in 1869, was living in Kalamazoo, Mich.

CHILDREN OF PALMER PECK (466) AND CLARISSA, HIS WIFE, ALL BORN IN WEST BLOOMFIELD, N. Y.

[1191.]   1. RICHARD D., b. March 28, 1804, and d. unm., in Dubuque, Iowa, July 28, 1834.

[1192.]   2. LORENZO D., b. April 15, 1806, and d., in West Bloomfield, N. Y., March 18, 1819.

[1193.]   3. DUDLEY, b. March 26, 1808, and d. unm., at Little Turkey River, Iowa, Sept. 28, 1839

[1194.]   4. NANCY D., b. May 4, 1810 ; m. Origen Dunnell, and, in 1867, was living in Wethersfield, N. Y.

[1195.]   5. FANNY M., b. March 28, 1812, and d. unm., in Wethersfield, N. Y., July 26, 1857.

[1196.]   6. MATTHEW D., b. Aug. 12, 1814, and, in 1867, was living unm. in Clayton, Iowa.

[1197.]   7. SAMUEL D., (2482) b. June 29, 1817 ; m. Nancy W. Moreland, and, in 1867, was living in Colony, Iowa.

[1198.]   8. DOUGLASS, (2490) b. Jan. 6, 1821 ; m. 1. Catharine Gillett, Sept. 20, 1848, who d. June 9, 1856, and m. 2. Mary Haught, Julv 13, 1858, and, in 1867, was living in Clayton, Iowa.

CHILD OF OLIVER PECK (469) AND AMY, HIS WIFE, BORN IN LYME, CONN.

[1199.]   OLIVER, (2495) b. Nov. 12, 1798 ; m. Huldah Maria Ensign, March 20, 1823 ; is a physician, and, in 1875, was living in Sheffield, Mass.

CHILDREN OF MATTHEW PECK (472) AND LOIS, HIS WIFE, ALL
BORN IN LYME, CONN.

[1200.]   l. PHEBE DORR, b. Oct. 1, 1809, and, in 1869,
was living unm. in West Bloomfield, N. Y.

[1201.]   2. MARY HAINES, b. June 26, 1811; m. Joel
Miner, in Nov. 1840, and, in 1869, was living in Lyme, Conn.

[1202.]   3. LUCY BURNHAM, b. Jan. 11, 1814; m. Randall Drake, July 26, 1843, and, in 1869, was living in Kalamazoo, Mich.

[1203.]   4. LOIS CATHARINE, b. Nov. 17, 1816; m. Loren
Whittemore, May 4, 1837, and, in 1869, was living in Mundy,
Mich.

[1204.]   5. HANNAH HALL, b. March 13, 1820; m. George
Ingersoll, Nov. 2, 1840, and d., in Marengo, Mich., April 14,
1844.

[1205.]   6. MATTHEW J., (2496) b. July 14, 1822; m Marianna Hendee, Dec. 17, 1856, and, in 1869, was living in West
Bloomfield, N. Y.

CHILDREN OF RICHARD SEARS PECK (473) AND PHEBE, HIS
WIFE, ALL BORN IN CHATHAM, N. Y.

[1206.]   1. RICHARD H., (2498) b. March 9, 1815 ; m. Mary
Ten Eyck, June 23, 1841, and, in 1869, was living in Austin,
Texas.

[1207.]   2. OLIVER J., (2503) b. March 28, 1817 ; m. Angeline R. Dorr, May 4, 1848; is a physician, and, in 1877, was
living in Chatham, N. Y.

[1208.]   3. EDWARD R., (2506) b. Feb. 29, 1819 ; m. Mary
Champlin in 1858 ; is a lawyer, and, in 1875, was living in
Kinderhook, N. Y.

CHILDREN OF JOHN SEARS PECK (477) AND BETSEY, HIS WIFE,
ALL BORN IN WEST BLOOMFIELD, N. Y.

[1209.]   1. JUDITH, d. in infancy in West Bloomfield,
N. Y.

[1210.]   2. PALMER, (2508) b. Oct. 10, 1797 ; m. Sela Lawrence, April 24, 1825, and d., in Adrian, Mich, March 26, 1864.

[1211.]   3. ELISHA, b. in 1802, and d. unm., in West Bloomfield, N. Y., in Feb. 1834.

[1212.]   4. JEREMIAH, (2509) b. May 5, 1809 ; m. Julia A. Lawrence, Jan. 29, 1831, and d., in West Bloomfield, N. Y., Nov. 3, 1838.

[1213.]   5. NATHAN, (2513) b. May 9, 1812; m. Mary Latty, Nov. 15. 1835, and d., in Lima, N. Y., in Aug. 1870.

CHILDREN OF THOMAS PECK (479) AND SARAH, HIS WIFE, ALL BORN IN LIMA, N. Y.

[1214.]   1. HENRY, (2524) b. July 8, 1800 ; m. 1. Lucretia Tinker, Oct. 16, 1823, and m. 2. Hannah Comstock, July 18, 1856, and, in 1869, was living in Victor, N. Y.

[1215.]   2. MYRTA, b. Dec. 17, 1802; m. Isaac N. Stage, Jan. 20, 1824, and, in 1869, was living in Cleveland, O.

[1216.]   3. WILLIAM, b. March 14, 1804, and d., in Lima, N. Y., Jan. 13, 1813.

[1217.]   4. MARIA, b. March 3, 1807 ; m. Amos Dann, Jan. 30, 1830, and, in 1869, was living in Avon, N. Y.

[1218.]   5. JUDITH, b. July 8, 1809 ; m. Samuel March, Jan. 21, 1829, and, in 1869, was living in Oconomowoc, Wis.

[1219.]   6. RICHARD, (2528) b. Nov. 30, 1811 ; m. 1. Elizabeth Case, Sept. 15, 1833 ; m. 2. Rebecca Jefferds, Oct. 15, 1845, and, in 1869, was living in Lima, N. Y.

[1220.]   7. ELSA, b. Feb. 3, 1814; m. Philip Riley, Nov. 19, 1835, and, in 1869, was living in Holland, N. Y.

[1221.]   8. CHRISTINA, b. Nov. 7, 1818; m. John Case, April 2, 1841, and, in 1869, was living in Aurora, N. Y.

[1222.]   9. SYLVANUS, (2531) b. Dec. 15, 1821 ; m. Jemima Van Houter, Dec. 19, 1840, and d., in Lima, N. Y., Sept. 22, 1851.

CHILDREN OF WATROUS PECK, (480) ALL BORN IN WEST BLOOM-
FIELD, N. Y.

[1223.] 1. EMILY E., b. Dec. 6, 1805; m. William Arnold,
Sept. 1, 1831, and d., in Lima, N. Y., Feb. 13, 1845.

[1224.] 2. EDWARD W., (2534) b. March 19, 1807; m. 1.
Lucy B. Frost, June 26, 1833, who d. July 5, 1840; m. 2. Mary
A. James, June 26, 1842, who d. Jan. 13, 1866, and m. 3. Eliza-
beth G. Greeley, Dec. 25, 1867, and, in 1873, was living in
Pontiac, Mich.

[1225.] 3. JOSEPH FRANKLIN, (2537) b. May 20, 1810;
m. Clarissa Miner, Nov. 14, 1833, and, in 1870, was living in
Springfield, Mass.

[1226.] 4. LOUISA L., b. Aug. 25, 1813, and d., in West
Bloomfield, N. Y., Oct. 30, 1814.

[1227.] 5. WILLIAM B., b. Jan. 22, 1816; m. Ann Middle-
ton, June 24, 1841, and d., in Keokuk, Iowa, April 8, 1850.

[1228.] 6. JOHN SEARS, (2541) b. Sept. 2, 1818; m. Mary
Fisher, March 8, 1848, and, in 1869, was living in Oberlin, O.

[1229.] 7. CHARLES W., b. June 27, 1820, and d., in West
Bloomfield, N. Y., Feb. 14, 1821.

[1230.] 8. SARAH E., b. Aug. 6, 1828; m. Clark Allen,
Sept. 3, 1850, and, in 1869, was living in West Bloomfield,
N .Y.

CHILDREN OF GEORGE PECK (481) AND MARTHA, HIS WIFE, ALL
BORN IN WEST BLOOMFIELD, N. Y.

[1231.] 1. DESMOND G., (2547) b. Oct. 14, 1807; m. Harriet Wilson, Oct. 17, 1833, and d., in East Troy, Wis., Oct. 30,
1844.

[1232.] 2. LODEMA A. B., b. April 10, 1810; m. Gardner
Gould, Dec. 29, 1834, and d., in Knowlesville, N. Y., Jan. 26,
1868.

[1233.] 3. DEBORAH B., b. Dec. 12, 1812; m. Ward
Mann, June 20, 1833, and d., in West Bloomfield, N. Y., Oct.
14, 1834.

[1234.]   4. ALMIRA A., b. Jan. 14, 1815 ; m. Nathaniel R. Wilson, Feb. 14, 1837, and, in 1869, was living in West Bloomfield, N. Y.

[1235.]   5. GEORGE N., b. Sept. 14, 1819, and d. unm., in West Bloomfield, N. Y., Aug. 13, 1845.

[1236.]   6. SOPHIA F., b. Jan. 7, 1822 ; m. Nathan H. Wheeler, Jan. 1, 1852, and d., in West Bloomfield, N. Y., Feb. 13, 1860.

CHILDREN OF ABNER PECK (482) AND MARIA, HIS WIFE, ALL BORN IN WEST BLOOMFIELD, N. Y.

[1237.]   1. LOUISA M., b. May 6, 1820 ; m. Frederick W. Patterson, and, in 1869, was living in Buffalo. N. Y.

[1238.]   2. MARY JANE, b. July 21, 1823 ; m. Samuel Beckwith, and, in 1869, was living in Greenport, L. I., N. Y.

[1239.]   3. CARRIE N., b. Dec. 21, 1831, and, in 1869, was living unm. in Buffalo, N. Y.

CHILDREN OF REYNOLD PECK (484) AND NANCY, HIS WIFE, ALL BORN IN WEST BLOOMFIELD, N. Y.

1240.]   1. VINTON, (2551) b. Nov. 21, 1816 ; m. 1. Roxey E. Humphrey, June 23 1841, who d. July 13, 1866, and m. 2. Libbie Sterling, Jan. 8, 1868, and, in 1869, was living in West Bloomfield, N. Y.

[1241.]   2. MINERVA L., b. Feb. 8, 1818 ; m. Elisha F. Leach, Dec. 30, 1839, and, in 1869, was living in West Bloomfield, N. Y.

[1242.]   3. AMANDA A., b. May 29, 1821 ; m. Robert T. Leach, March 4, 1841, and, in 1869, was living in West Bloomfield, N. Y.

[1243.]   4. SARAH A., b. May 14, 1824 ; m. Seth L. Lee, July 12, 1845, and, in 1869, was living in West Bloomfield, N. Y.

[1244.]   5. THOMAS R., (2554) b. June 21, 1826 ; m. Julia F. Hopkins, May 26, 1857, and, in 1870, was living in Waterloo, N. Y.

[1245.]   6. LYDIA E., b. Sept. 8, 1829; m. Roswell C. Munson, June 8, 1853, and d , in Oshawa, C. W., Jan. 23, 1861.

[1246.]   7. EMILY M., b. Jan. 4, 1832; m. Charles C. Latimer, July 21, 1858, and, in 1869, was living in Princeton, Ill.

[1247.]   8. REYNOLD MARVIN, b. Feb. 16, 1834; m. Isabella L. Ainsworth, Sept. 21, 1860, and, in 1869, was living in West Bloomfield, N. Y., having no children.

[1248.]   9. N. JENNETTE, b. April 5, 1836; m. William N. Page, Sept. 20, 1862, and, in 1869, was living in Jacksonville, Florida.

CHILDREN OF STEPHEN L. PECK (487) AND DIANA, HIS WIFE, ALL
BORN IN LYME, CONN.

[1249.]   1. STEPHEN L., b. Jan. 2, 1833, and d. unm., in Lyme, Conn., Dec. 14, 1860.

[1250.]   2. KATE LAY, b. Jan. 31, 1836; m. Ezra C. Smith, Aug. 16, 1871, and, in 1875, was living in Lyme, Conn.

[1251.]   3. FANNIE JANE, b. June 1838; m. John C. Way of New Lyme, O., in Sept. 1869, and was living there in 1875.

[1252.]   4. LOUISA MATILDA, b. Sept. 28, 1841; m. Thomas J. Warren, Oct. 7, 1863, and, in 1875, was living in Saybrook, Ill.

CHILDREN OF JOHN PECK (493) AND MARY, HIS WIFE.

[1253.]   1. MARGARET DeVAN, b. in Whitestown, N. Y., April 30, 1823; m. N. Emmet Lyman, and d., in Staunton, Va., May 23, 1871.

[1254.]   2. THOMAS R. GOLD, (2559) b. in Whitestown, N. Y., Feb. 28, 1827; graduated at Yale College in 1848; m. Susan Jane Egbert, Sept. 8, 1859, and, in 1875, was settled as a minister at Hastings upon Hudson, N. Y.

[1255.]   3. SARAH WALTON, b. in New York city, Aug. 23, 1828, and d., in Brooklyn, N. Y., May 11, 1830.

[1256.]   4. JOHN SEDGWICK, b. in New York city, March 27, 1830, and d., in Savannah, Ga., March 12, 1850.

[1257.] 5. HENRY DWIGHT, (2561) b. in New York city Jan. 22, 1836 ; m. Jennie M. Tucker, adopted dau. of H. L. Sill, of Lyme, Conn., June 8, 1868, and, in 1875, was living in Staunton, Va.

CHILDREN OF SETH S. PECK (494) AND SARAH, HIS WIFE, ALL
BORN IN WHITESTOWN, N. Y., EXCEPT THE OLDEST,
WHO WAS BORN IN LYME, CONN.

[1258.] 1. MARY LAY, b. July 17, 1816, and, in 1875, was living unm. in St. Augustine, Florida.

[1259.] 2. REBECCA, b. July 27, 1818, and, in 1875, was living in St. Augustine, Florida.

[1260.] 3. JOHN ELISHA, b. Dec. 12, 1820 ; is a physician, and, in 1875, was living unm. in St. Augustine, Florida.

[1261.] 4. LUCY ROCKWELL, b. July 7, 1827 ; m. George Burt, of Vermont, and d., in St. Augustine, Florida, March 22, 1856.

[1262.] 5. SARAH, b. April 7, 1830, and d., in St. Augustine, Florida, June 19, 1836.

CHILDREN OF CHARLES L. PECK (495) AND HANNAH AUGUSTA,
HIS WIFE, ALL BORN IN LYME, CONN.

[1263.] 1. JAMES MITCHELL, b. Dec. 6, 1823, and, in 1875, was living unm. in Lyme, Conn.

[1264.] 2. ELISHA, b. Nov. 4, 1825, and d., in Lyme, Conn., June 11, 1827.

[1265.] 3. ALDEN STEPHEN, b. Aug. 16, 1828 ; was a physician and d. unm., in Lyme, Conn., Nov. 16, 1860.

[1266.] 4. CHARLES WILLIAM, b. Sept. 17, 1830, and, in 1875, was living unm. in New York city.

[1267.] 5. JOHN HENRY, (2562) b. Oct. 22, 1832 ; m. Julia E. Mann, June 11, 1859, and, in 1875, was living in Chicago, Ill.

[1268.] 6. AUGUSTA MITCHELL, b. March 16, 1836 ; m. Joseph S. Lyman, of Toledo, Ohio, Sept. 12, 1853 ; again m.

Elizur Clark, of Syracuse, N. Y., Nov. 4, 1869, and, in 1875, was living in Syracuse, N. Y.

CHILDREN OF JOHN M. PECK (505) AND ADELINE, HIS WIFE.

[1269.]   1. DAVID C., b. in Nassau, N. Y., Nov. 21, 1830, and d. there Dec. 13, 1830.

[1270.]   2. WILLIAM L., b. in Nassau, N. Y., Jan. 8, 1832, and d. unm. in Acton, Ill., Sept. 4, 1855.

[1271.]   3. MINDWELL A.. b. at Sandy Creek, N. Y. Feb. 8, 1835, and d. unm., in Albany, Dec. 25, 1865.

[1272.]   4. EUNICE E., b. at Sandy Creek, N. Y., Feb. 21, 1839, and, in 1877, was living in Albany, N. Y.

[1273.]   5. MARTHA T., b. in Troy, N. Y., Aug. 3, 1843, and d. unm., in Albany, N. Y., July 31, 1862.

[1274.]   6. SAMUEL, b. in Troy, N. Y., July 2, 1845, and d., in Troy, N. Y., July 17, 1845.

[1275.]   7. MARION A., b. in Troy, N. Y., Nov. 6, 1848, and, in 1877, was living unm. in Albany, N. Y.

CHILDREN OF EZRA M. PECK (511) AND EUNICE, HIS WIFE, ALL BORN IN LYME, CONN.

[1276.]   1. WILLIAM K., (2566) b. March 13, 1809 ; m. Eliza Fulton in 1835, and d., in Rising Sun, Ind., June 17, 1846.

[1277.]   2. CHARLES C., (2567) b. Nov. 20, 1811 ; m. 1. Elizabeth Wardell, Oct. 20, 1836 ; m. 2. Angeline Stagg, Nov. 2, 1854, and, in 1875, was living in New York city.

[1278.]   3. HORACE E., (2569) b. May 3, 1813 ; m. Emma Newell, in March 1843, and, in 1861, was living in Vincennes, Ind.

[1279.]   4. ELEAZER C., (2570) b. March 11, 1816 ; m. Eunice H. Warren, Jan. 11, 1842, and, in 1875, was living in Lyme, Conn.

[1280.]   5. MARIA E., b. Sept. 13, 1818 ; m. William W. J. Warren, Nov. 2, 1841, and, in 1875, was living in Lyme, Conn.

[1281.] 6. ORRIN M., b. May 8, 1821, and d. unm., in Charleston, S. C., March 21, 1848.

CHILD OF JOSEPH PECK (512) AND ANN, HIS WIFE.

[1282.] SARAH ANN, b. in Lyme, Conn., in 1825, and, in 1875, was living unm. in Haddam, Conn.

CHILD OF DANIEL PECK, (515.)

[1283.] K—— K., was living in 1864 at LeSueur City, Minn. Nothing further can be ascertained about him, or whether Daniel Peck (515) had any other children.

CHILDREN OF JOSEPH PECK (520) AND ANNA, HIS WIFE, ALL BORN IN LYME, CONN.

[1284.] 1. ESTHER, b. Dec. 10, 1799; m. Joseph H. Mather, Oct. 10, 1826, and d., in Saybrook, Conn., Dec. 3, 1828.

[1285.] 2. GEORGE R., (2578) b. Oct. 1, 1801 ; m. Elizabeth S. Lee, Jan. 12, 1825, and d., in 1872, in Lyme, Conn.

CHILDREN OF MATHER PECK (526) AND JULIA ANN, HIS WIFE, ALL BORN IN BETHANY, N. Y.

[1286.] 1. GILBERT M., (2588) b. April 19, 1814; m. Sarah B. Thompson, June 15, 1837, and, in 1869, was living in East Bethany, N. Y.

[1287.] 2. JULIA, b. April 23, 1817, and d. unm., in East Bethany, N. Y., Dec. 20, 1835.

[1288.] 3. ESTHER, b. Jan. 20, 1820, and, in 1869, was living unm. in East Bethany, N. Y.

[1289.] 4. LAVINIA, b. April 18, 1822 ; m. Utley Lathrop, Feb. 10, 1842, who d. March 19, 1848, and, in 1869, was living in East Bethany, N. Y.

[1290.] 5. MARY, b. Nov. 28, 1826, and, in 1869, was living unm. in East Bethany, N. Y.

[1291.] 6. HENRY, b. March 30, 1828, and d., in East Bethany, N. Y., March 26, 1837.

[1292.]   7. MARTHA, b. Sept. 13, 1830 ; m. John C. Clark, June 2, 1852, and, in 1869, was living in Kingston, C. W.

[1293.]   8. JULIA AMANDA, b. Jan. 20, 1836 ; m. Dan V. Brooks, Sept. 3, 1863, and, in 1869, was living in Alton, Ill.

CHILDREN OF DAVID H. PECK (525) AND HANNAH, HIS WIFE.

[1294.]   1. NEWTON L. F., (2592) b. in Richmond, N. Y., Dec. 22, 1814 ; m. Samantha White, Sept. 16, 1846, and, in 1870, was living in Springville, Iowa.

[1295.]   2. OVANDO S. X., (2599) b. in Richmond, N. Y., Aug. 9, 1816 ; m. 1. Susan Tyler, and m. 2. Maria E. Stout, and, in 1873, was living in New York city.

[1296.]   3. HOMER P. K., (2600) b. in Richmond, N. Y., Oct. 11, 1818 ; m. 1. Jane Jones and m. 2. Rebecca Lefferson and, in 1871, was living in Rochester, N. Y.

[1297.]   4. JOHN P. P., (2607) b. in Richmond, N. Y., Aug. 15, 1820 ; m. 1. Dorothy Rick ; m. 2. Eliza Marshall, and m. 3. Frances Fulton, and, in 1870, was living in Hamilton, O.

[1298.]   5. ELIZA A., b. in Stafford, N. Y., Sept. 8, 1822 ; m. Ralph Hueston, and, in 1875, was living in Peakesville, Clarke Co., Mo.

[1299.]   6. MARY M., b. in Stafford, N. Y., Oct. 25, 1824, and d. unm., in Middletown, O., Nov. 25, 1848.

[1300.]   7. LIBERTY B., b. in Stafford, N. Y., Oct. 15, 1826, and d., in Mayville, N. Y., April 1, 1837.

[1301.]   8. HARRIET J., b. in Stafford, N. Y., Sept. 20, 1828 ; m. Lewis B. Wynne, and, in 1871, was living in Washington city.

[1302.]   9. DELIA A., b. in Mayville, N. Y., Dec. 14, 1830 ; m. John W. Fuller, and d., in Auburn, N. Y., March 12, 1865.

[1303.]   10. CHARLOTTE N., b. in Mayville, N. Y., Sept. 10, 1832, and d. there March 20, 1834.

[1304.]   11. FRANCES A., b. in Mayville, N. Y., Sept. 25, 1834, and, in 1875, was living, unm., at Peakesville, Clarke County, Mo.

[1305.] 12. RHUAMA, b. in Mayville, N. Y., Sept. 6, 1836, and d. the same day.

CHILDREN OF JESSE PECK (527) AND ASENATH, HIS WIFE, ALL BORN IN LYME, CONN.

[1306.] 1. JESSE MARVIN, b. in 1820, and d. unm., in Lyme, Conn., April 5, 1855.

[1307.] 2. PETER LORD, b. in Feb., 1823, and, in 1867, was living unm., in Lyme, Conn.

[1308.] 3. DAVID M., b. May 25, 1825, and d. unm., at Fair Haven, Conn., Sept. 26, 1848.

[1309.] 4. CAROLINE, b. March 23, 1834 ; m. Joseph Thompson, and, in 1867, was living in the State of Minnesota.

[1310.] 5. LYDIA A., b. July 4, 1836, 'and d. unm., in Lyme, Conn., Nov. 28, 1857.

[1311.] 6. JOHN SMITH, b. in June, 1837, and, in 1867, was living unm., in New York City.

[1312.] 7. JOSEPH, b. in July, 1838, and d., in Lyme, Conn., in Sept., 1838.

CHILDREN OF BENJAMIN K. PECK, (538.)

[1313.] 1. LUCY, b. in Lima, N. Y., Aug. 24, 1811, and d. unm., in Utica, N. Y., in 1849.

[1314.] 2. MARY, b. in Lima, N. Y., Nov. 26, 1814, and d. unm., in Mendon, N. Y., in Dec. 1838.

[1315.] 3. MATTHEW G., (2613) b. in Lima, N. Y., Sept. 22, 1818; m. 1. Aristine Bingham, in Nov. 1851, and m. 2. Catharine Gibson, March 26, 1862, and, in 1869, was living in Pontiac, Mich.

[1316.] 4. HELEN C., b. in Lima, N. Y., Nov. 2, 1820, and, in 1869, was living unm. in Rochester, N, Y.

[1317.] 5. PASCAL P., (2615) b. in Lima, N. Y., May 15, 1822; m. Alexine McCall, Nov. 5, 1850, and, in 1869, was living in Nashville, Tenn.

[1318.] 6. HENRY K., b. in Lima, N. Y., Jan. 20, 1826, and d. unm., in Shelbyville, Tenn., June 5, 1863.

[1319.] 7. MYRON G., b. in Lima, N. Y., July 30, 1829, and, in 1869, was living unm. in Heidleberg, Germany.

[1320.] 8. EMILY, b. in East Bethany, N. Y., in Dec. 1835, and, in 1869, was living in New Bedford, Mass.

[1321,] 9. MARY E., b. in Pittsford, N. Y., in April 1838 and d. unm. in Colerain, Mass., July 9, 1851.

CHILDREN OF WILLIAM PECK (540) AND MARIETTA, HIS WIFE, ALL BORN IN WEST BLOOMFIELD, N. Y.

[1322.] 1. MEHITABLE C., b. June 20, 1828 ; m. D. H. Hastings, May 6, 1851, and d., in Mendon, N. Y., Dec. 25, 1858.

[1323.] 2. WILLIAM H., b. Jan. 10, 1831, and d., in West Bloomfield, N. Y., Sept. 3, 1832.

[1324.] 3. GEORGE, b. Jan. 31, 1833, and d., in West Bloomfield, N. Y., Dec. 9, 1849.

[1325.] 4. CHARLES L., b. March 9, 1835, and, in 1869, was living unm. in Muir, Mich.

[1326.] 5. FRANCIS H., b. March 20, 1837, and d., in West Bloomfield, N. Y., Sept. 14, 1850.

[1327.] 6. CARRIE W., b. Sept. 6, 1839 ; m. Wells Baker, Feb. 27, 1861, and, in 1869, was living in West Bloomfield, N. Y.

[1328.] 7. WATSON C., b. Dec. 6, 1841, and d. unm., in Livonia, N. Y., May 31, 1862.

[1329.] 8. FREDERICKA E., b. Aug. 8, 1844 ; m. Daniel J. Hamilton, Feb. 20, 1867, and, in 1869, was living in Muir, Ionia, Co., Mich.

CHILDREN OF RICHARD PECK (543) AND CATHARINE H., HIS WIFE, ALL BORN IN BETHANY, N. Y.

[1330.] 1. ELIZABETH M., b. Feb. 8, 1817 ; m. 1. Abner Goodell, and m. 2. Hezekiah Manwaring, and d., Jan. 12, 1873, at St. George, Gore Dist., C. W.

[1331.]   2. MARIA LOUISA, b. April 5, 1818 ; m. Alvan Peck, and, in 1870, was living in Albion, Mich.

[1332.]   3. NATHANIEL, (2617) b. Nov. 17, 1819 ; m. Althea M. Churchill, and d., at Crawfordsville, Ind., Aug. 14, 1850.

[1333.]   4. RICHARD, (2618) b. July 18, 1821 ; m. Sylvia A. Gillett, and d., in Palmyra, Ill., Jan. 12, 1877.

[1334.]   5. ISRAEL M., (2621) b. April 8, 1823 ; m. Frances C. Fargo, and, in 1877, was living in Stafford, N. Y.

[1335.]   6. CATHARINE H., b. Sept. 25, 1825 ; m. Ransom E. Aldrich, and, in 1870, was living in the State of Mississippi.

[1336.]   7. MARY ANN, b. Aug. 11, 1827 ; m. William H. Van Epps, and, in 1870, was living in Dixon, Ill.

[1337.]   8. BENJAMIN F., (2624) b. July 16, 1829 ; m. Phebe R. Peck, (2221) and, in 1870, was living in East Bethany, N. Y.

[1338.]   9. LUCY JANE, b. May 21, 1831 ; m. Seth M. Peck, Jr., (2223) and d., in Bethany, N. Y., in Oct. 1873.

[1339.]   10. CHARLES A., b. Oct. 23, 1832, and d. unm., at Dixon's plantation, Miss., July 19, 1863.   He was a soldier in the war of the rebellion.

[1340.]   11. ROBERT C., b. July 11, 1837, and d., in Bethany, N. Y., April 9, 1841.

EIGHTH GENERATION.

CHILDREN OF JOEL PECK, (545) ALL BORN IN NORWICH, N. Y.

[1343.]   1. PHEBE, b. Aug. 17, 1796 ; m. Abijah Dann, and, in 1861, was living in Canton, Penn.

[1344.]   2. SALLY, b. May 14, 1798 ; m. Alva June, and d., at Annin Creek, Penn., in May 1872.

[1345.]   3. JOEL M., b. Dec. 12, 1799 ; m. Amanda Purdy, Feb. 22, 1821, and, in 1675, was living in Palmyra, Wis.   He had sons living in 1875, viz.: *Oscar D.*, in Oshkosh, Wis.; *Charles B.*, in Detroit, Mich., and *George R.*, in Topeka, Kansas, the latter being a lawyer and U. S. Attorney there, and having been a soldier and officer in the Atlanta campaign and in Gen. Sherman's army in its march to the sea.   In 1868 he was clerk of the Circuit Court, Rock Co., Wis.

[1346.]   4. MEHITABLE, b. Feb. 5, 1801; m. Jesse Porter, and, in 1861, was living at Centreville, town of Portland, Chatauqua Co., N. Y.   Her husband d. about 1851.

[1347.]   5. DELILAH, b. Oct. 18, 1802; d. in North Norwich, N. Y, in May 1806.

[1348.]   6. JOHN, b. March 1, 1806; m. Sarah Franklin, and, about 1866, was living in Castalia, O.

[1349.]   7. LEWIS, b. March 15, 1809; m. Lucy Akley, Sept. 4, 1834; was a Justice of the Peace; resided in North Norwich, N. Y., and d. there April 2, 1871.   His sons, *Winfield S.*, b. Aug. 7, 1844, and *Walter W.*, b. Feb. 27, 1850, were living in North Norwich in 1875.

[1350.]   8. HULDAH, b. Nov. 18, 1811; m. George W. Record, Jan. 21, 1839, and d., in Cortlandville, N. Y., Oct. 5, 1855.

[1351.]   9. WEALTHY, b. Nov. 29, 1814; m. Artemas B. Cleveland, Jan. 13, 1844, and, in 1875, was living in Fabius, N. Y.

[1352.]   10. LUCINDA, b. July 15, 1817; m. Smith Titus, and d., in North Norwich, N. Y., March 16, 1869.

CHILDREN OF STEPHEN NORTHRUP PECK (550) AND LYDIA, HIS WIFE, ALL BORN IN SOLON, N. Y.

[1353.]   1. POLLY, b. Sept. 22, 1801; m. Samuel Chapman, and d., in Crete, Will Co., Ill., Nov. 13, 1854.

[1354.]   2. LYMAN, b. Dec. 24, 1803; m. Almira Thompson, Sept. 25, 1828, and, in 1875, was living in Cortland village, N. Y.   He had sons living in 1875, viz.: *Northrup J.*, surgeon dentist at Independence, Iowa; *Lyman, Jr.*, farmer and Justice of the Peace in Solon, N. Y.; *Rufus T.*, Post Master and School Commissioner of Cortland county; *Charles T.*, merchant at Solon, N. Y., and *Melvin D.*, physician and surgeon in the Pension Department at Washington, D. C.

[1355.] 3. HIRAM, b. May 25, 1806 ; m. Nancy Cameron, and d., in Solon, N. Y., Jan. 4, 1865.

[1356.] 4. NATHAN, b. Jan. 31, 1809 ; m. Polly Thompson and d., in Solon, N. Y., March 21, 1856.

[1357.] 5. EMILY, b. Oct. 15, 1811 ; m. Charles Burlingham, and, in 1875, was living at McGrawville, N. Y.

[1358.] 6. STEPHEN N., b. May 13, 1814 ; m. Belinda J., Thompson, and d., in New Market, C. W., May 4, 1865.

[1359.] 7. PLATT, b. June 11, 1817 ; m. Mary Ann Kinney, and, in 1875, was living in Solon. N. Y.

[1360.] 8. SMITH W., b. March 25, 1820, and d., unm., in Watertown, Wis., June 25, 1845.

[1361.] 9. JOHN, b. June 10, 1823, and, in 1875, was living in Solon, Cortland Co., N. Y.

[1362.] 10. SALLY, b. Oct. 8, 1825 ; m. Jairus Davis, and d., in Solon, Cortland Co., N. Y., Dec. 22, 1870.

CHILDREN OF JOHN PECK (551) AND SARAH, HIS WIFE.

[1363.] 1. DARIUS, (2628) b. in Norwich, Chenango county, N. Y., June 5, 1802 ; prepared for college under Rev. Daniel Hascall and Mr. Zenas Morse, Principal of Hamilton Academy, N. Y.; in Oct. 1822 entered the Sophomore class of Hamilton College, N. Y., at which he graduated in August 1825 ; studied law with Hon. Ambrose L. Jordan and William Slosson, in the cities of Hudson and New York; was admitted to the bar of the Supreme Court of the State of New York in August 1828, and in 1829 settled as a lawyer at the city of Hudson, N. Y., where, until the present date, he has continued his professional career.   In February, 1833, he was appointed by the Governor and Senate of the State of New York, Recorder of the city of Hudson, then a judicial officer, as well as a member of the

Common Council of that city, which office he held until April 1843. He was married to Harriet M. Hudson, of the city of Troy, N. Y., Sept. 12, 1836 ; was for several years Superintendent of Schools and Master in Chancery ; was appointed, in April 1843, by the said Governor and Senate, a Judge of the Court of Common Pleas of the County of Columbia, N. Y., and in November 1855 was elected, and in November 1863 and 1867 re-elected, County Judge of Columbia County aforesaid. His wife d. April 18, 1863, aged 49 years.

[1364.] 2. MARY P., b. in Norwich, N. Y., Jan. 25, 1804 ; m. John Fiske, of Cazenovia, N. Y., Sept. 20, 1821, and d., in Cazenovia, N. Y., Dec. 10, 1855. Her husband d., in Detroit, Mich., Aug. 27, 1866, aged 75 years. She had children : 1. *Mary A.*, b. Dec. 2, 1823 ; 2. *Sarah E.*, b. April 24, 1826 ; m. Solon Prentiss, Nov. 24, 1853—has an only child, Mary E., b. July 30, 1856 ; 3. *Julia M.*, b. April 22, 1828 ; m. Artemas C. Bacon, Aug. 29, 1848, and d., Sept. 8, 1867 ; 4. *John P.*, b. Sept. 2, 1830 ; m. Lucy A. Fuller, June 16, 1858, and, in 1877, was a wholesale merchant in Detroit, Mich. ; 5. *Edwin D.*, b. Nov. 8, 1835 ; was a graduate of Michigan University ; m. Myra A. Trall, July 26, 1860, and d. June 7, 1873, leaving an only child, Julia Frances, b. Oct. 7, 1867. The above named *Julia M.* and *Edwin D.* died in Detroit, Mich., and *Sarah E.* was living there in 1877.

[1365.] 3. JOHN, b. in Cazenovia, N. Y., April 11, 1808 and d. there Feb. 16, 1810.

[1366.] 4. PHILETUS B., (2629) b. in Cazenovia, Madison county, N. Y., November 29, 1809. Early evincing great mental activity and an ardent thirst for knowledge, opportunity of preparation for a liberal education was afforded him at Hamilton Academy, N. Y., which, however, failing health ventually obliged him to forego, and he then engaged for a considerable period in agricultural pursuits. He was married to Nancy Morse, of Cazenovia, N. Y., May 30, 1831, and soon after resolved to resume his studies and devote himself to the work of the ministry. In the Spring of 1834 he entered the Hamilton Literary and Theological Institution, now Madison University, from which, having gone through the regular course, he graduated in August 1838. He was ordained in March 1839, and in June following settled as pastor of the Baptist church in Owego, Tioga county, N. Y. After an uncommonly successful ministry at Owego, he died suddenly of malignant dysentery while on a visit to his father and mother at Cazenovia, October 6, 1847. He was an instructive and earnest preacher and an untiring and devoted pastor, and distinguished for his benevolence, frankness, sound judgment, executive abilities and decision of character. His widow was living at Owego, N. Y., in 1877.

[1367.] 5. JULIA M., b. in Cazenovia, N. Y., March 13, 1816 ; m. Rev. William M. Pratt, Aug. 22, 1839, and d., in Crawfordsville, Ind., Oct. 14, 1839.

[1368.] 6. LINUS M., b. in Cazenovia, Madison county, N. Y., February 3, 1818. He entered the Sophomore class of Hamilton College in September, 1838 ; sustained, during his whole course, a superior position as a scholar, and graduated in July, 1841, receiving one of the highest honors of his class. After leaving college he taught a year in the Hamilton Academy, N. Y., and subsequently pursued the study of law until the Autumn of 1843, when he concluded to discontinue his legal studies and prosecute a theological course, preparatory to his entrance on the Christian ministry. Having devoted a year to the pre-requisite study of Hebrew and been duly licensed to preach, in August, 1844, he entered the Theological Institution at Hamilton, N. Y., in the following October, where he took the regular course of two years and graduated in Oct. 1846. In the Summer of 1845 he had been appointed a tutor in Hamilton College, and though the acceptance of the appointment was urgently requested by the Faculty he respectfully declined it as precluding his immediate entrance on the duties of the ministry. He was married to Cordelia C.

Kendrick. of Hamilton, N. Y., Sept. 17, 1846. He preached in Lebanon, N. Y., for several months prior to July, 1847, when he commenced preaching to the church in Hamilton, N. Y., and continued his labors there, with great acceptance, until his death, at Cazenovia, October 4, 1847, of the same malignant disease which a few hours afterward proved fatal to his brother, Philetus B. Peck, both having the same funeral obsequies, and both being borne together to their last resting place. He naturally possessed a vigorous and logical mind, and superior powers of analysis. His intellectual training was thorough and complete. He was kind-hearted, zealous and laborious, an excellent public speaker, and distinguished for his chaste and manly eloquence.

CHILDREN OF NATHAN PECK (552) AND SALLY, HIS WIFE.

[1369.] 1. TAMMA, b. in Plymouth, N. Y., Dec. 5, 1804, and d., in Norwich, N. Y., Oct. 15, 1806.

[1370.] 2. CELISTA, b. in Plymouth, N. Y., Oct. 28, 1806 · m. Benjamin Salisbury, April 6, 1831, and, in 1875, was living in Cortlandville, N. Y.

[1371.] 3. STEPHEN N., b. in Plymouth, N. Y., Sept. 14, 1808 ; m. Almira Ferris, who d., in Aug. 1850, at Whitewater, Wis.

[1372.] 4. URINA, b. in Solon, N. Y., Oct. 15, 1810 ; m. Thomas Derby, April 13, 1833, and d., in Cortlandville, N. Y., Oct. 8, 1866.

[1373.] 5. TAMMA A., b. in Solon, N. Y., Nov. 6, 1812 ; m. Chauncey Mahan, July 11, 1837, and d., in Cortlandville, N. Y., Nov. 5, 1845.

[1374.] 6. HANNAH, b. in Solon, N. Y., Aug. 11, 1814 ; m. Joseph D. Chaffee, March 19, 1837, and, in 1872, was living in Cortlandville, N. Y.

[1375.] 7. DeWITT C., b. in Nelson, N. Y., Aug. 6, 1816 ; m. 1. Caroline Clark, Oct. 21, 1841, and m. 2. Eliza R. Kinne, Sept. 17, 1850, and, in 1872, was living in Hillsdale, Mich.

[1376.]   8. NATHAN, b. in Nelson, N. Y., Dec. 17, 1818, and d., in Nelson, N. Y., Jan. 29, 1821.

[1377.]   9. SALLY MARIA, b. in Nelson, N. Y., Oct. 4, 1821; m. Reuben Bennett, Nov. 17, 1843, and, in 1875, was living in Cortlandville, N. Y.

[1378.]   10. NATHAN B., b. in Nelson, N. Y., Nov. 28, 1823; m. Laura Hopkins, March 31, 1849, and, in 1875, was living in Cortlandville, N. Y.

[1379.]   11. JOHN D., b. in Nelson, N. Y., June 6, 1827; m. Sarah J. Osborn, May 24, 1854, and, in 1875, was living in Conneaut, Ashtabula Co., O.

CHILDREN OF JAMES PECK (555) AND HANNAH, HIS WIFE, ALL BORN IN GREENWICH, CONN.

[1380.]   1, DEBORAH, b. Feb. 23, 1804; m. Warren W. Sellick, June 15, 1826, and d., in Bridgeport, Conn., June 8, 1834.

[1381.]   2. BENJAMIN, (2630) b. Nov. 5, 1805; m. Asenath Florence, Nov. 25, 1829, and d., in Port Chester, N. Y., April 10, 1864, where his widow resided in 1877.

[1382.]   3. ALICE E., b. July 27, 1808; m. James Green, in 1827, and, in 1874, was living in Bridgeport, Conn.

[1383.]   4. SARAH A., b. Aug. 7, 1814; m. Thomas Benedict, in 1836, and, in 1874, was living in New Haven, Conn.

CHILDREN OF HEATH PECK (556) AND SALLY, HIS WIFE, BOTH BORN IN GREENWICH, CONN.

[1384.]   1. RUTH, b. March 7, 1802; m. Gideon Reeves, who has died, and she was living in Lodi, N. Y., in 1872.

[1385.]   2· ELSEY, b. Oct. 22, 1804; m. Isaiah Allen, and, in 1870, was living at Gratiot Center, Mich.

CHILDREN OF NATHAN PECK (559) AND NANCY, HIS WIFE, ALL BORN IN WATERVLIET, N. Y.

[1386.]   1. ROBERT K., b. June 22, 1827, and d., in Watervliet, N. Y., Aug. 29, 1827.

[1387.]   2. NATHAN G., (2631) b. April 12, 1829 ; m. 1. Catharine H. Williams, and m. 2. Content Brockway, and, in 1875, was living in Junction City, Kansas.

[1388.]   1. CAMPBELL· K., (2632) b. April 8, 1831 ; m. Helen A. Higbie, and, in 1875, was living in Keokuk, Iowa.

CHILDREN OF SOLOMON C. PECK, (560) ALL BORN IN CLIFTON PARK, N. Y.

[1389.]   1. DAVID A., (2633) b. Aug. 23, 1820 ; m. Susan Foot ; was ordained a Baptist minister, Sept. 6, 1848, and, in 1875, was living in Rockwood, N. Y.

[1390.]   2. LYDIA, b. Sept. 5, 1823 ; m. Martin Woodward, and, in 1870, was living in Clifton Park, N. Y.

[1391.]   3. MARGARET. b. Aug. 26, 1825, and d., in Clifton Park, N. Y., Dec. 6, 1825.

[1392.]   4. CATHARINE, b. Dec. 13, 1826 ; m. Samuel Smith, and, in 1870, was living in Clifton Park, N. Y.

[1393.]   5. SOLOMON T., (2634) b. Feb. 7, 1831; m. Mary Hosmer, and, in 1875, was living in Belle Prairie, Ill.

[1394.]   6. SARAH, b. Aug. 14, 1833 ; m. John D. Darling, and d., in Watervliet, N. Y., Aug. 15, 1869.

[1395.]   7. NATHAN E., b. May 13, 1837 ; m. Sarah Fellows, April 26, 1863, and, in 1875, was living in Clifton Park, N. Y.   He had no children.

[1396.]   8. MARY A., b. July 1, 1840 ; m. John A. Vedder, Nov. 22, 1865, and, in 1870, was living in Schenectady, N. Y.

CHILDREN OF ABIJAH PECK, (562) ALL BORN IN CLIFTON PARK, N. Y.

[1397.]   1. ELIZABETH, b. April 5, 1823, and d. unm., in Clifton Park, N. Y., April 16, 1844.

[1398.]   2. STEPHEN V., b. Feb. 21, 1826, and d., in Clifton Park, N. Y., Aug. 2, 1826.

[1399.]   3. JOHN, (2635) b. Aug. 19, 1827; m. Penina M. Clark, June 14, 1854, and, in 1877, was living in Clifton Park, N. Y.

[1400.] 4. REED, b. Dec. 7, 1832, and d., in Clifton Park, N. Y., Aug. 21, 1849.

[1401.] 5. CAROLINE V., b. May 20, 1838, and d., in Clifton Park, N. Y., Aug. 19, 1851.

CHILDREN OF JOHN PECK (564) AND MARIA, HIS WIFE, ALL BORN IN CLIFTON PARK, N. Y.

[1402.] 1. CAROLINE, b. Aug. 18, 1830; m. Dudley E. Jones, Sept. 12, 1855, and, in 1869, was living at Little Rock, Arkansas.

[1403.] 2. MONTGOMERY, b. July 29, 1833, and d., in Clifton Park, N. Y., May 5, 1838.

[1404.] 3. SOPHIA, b. June 28, 1835; m. Luman S. Clark, in Oct. 1859, and, in 1869, was living in Little Rock, Ark.

[1405.] 4. ELIZA, b. April 17, 1837, and d., in Clifton Park, N. Y., May 18, 1855.

[1406.] 5. MARIA, b. April 22, 1839; m. John M. Clark, in Nov. 1858, and, in 1870, was living in Clifton Park, N. Y.

[1407.] 6. JENNIE, b. Aug. 24, 1841; m. Cyrus P. Rogers, Dec. 31, 1862, and, in 1869, was living in Frederica, Del.

[1408.] 7. HATTIE, b. Feb. 4, 1844; m. Charles D. Thurber, Dec. 2, 1868, and, in 1875, was living at Saratoga Springs, N. Y.

[1409.] 8. JOHN A., b. Feb. 8, 1847, and d., in Clifton Park, N. Y., Feb. 10, 1850.

CHILDREN OF SAMUEL PECK (565) AND ABIGAIL, HIS WIFE, ALL BORN IN GREENWICH, CONN.

[1410.] 1. TAMMA R., b. Oct. 22, 1799, and d., in Stamford, Conn., Ang. 14, 1815.

[1411.] 2. GEORGE, b. Sept. 6, 1801, and d., in Greenwich, Conn., Nov. 17, 1814.

[1412.] 3. SYLVANUS, b. Aug. 14, 1803, and d. unm., in Stamford, Conn., Aug. 13, 1823.

[1413.] 4. HANNAH, b. Aug. 14, 1803 ; m. Rev. Elijah Hibbard, March 18, 1834, and d., in Geneva, N. Y., Feb. 27, 1858.

[1414.] 5. ELIZA, b. Aug. 10, 1805, and d. unm., in Waterloo, N. Y., June 8, 1845.

[1415.] 6. SAMUEL, b. Dec. 20, 1806, and m. Widow Mary P. Jackson, dau. of Deborah P. Ferris, (567) Jan. 20, 1833, and, in 1861, was living in Greenwich, Conn.

[1416.] 7. EMELINE, b. Nov. 16, 1808, and d. unm., in Greenwich, Conn., Feb. 13, 1831.

[1417.] 8. DARIUS, b. July 27, 1811, and d. unm.. in Greenwich, Conn., March 10, 1851.

CHILDREN OF SAMUEL PECK (570) AND SARAH, HIS WIFE, ALL BORN IN GREENWICH, CONN.

[1418.] 1. ELIZABETH, b. July 23, 1815 ; m. Edward Derby, and, in 1861, was living in Greenwich, Conn.

[1419.] 2. DAVID B., b. April 17, 1817 ; m. Harriet Frashay, and, in 1861, was living in Greenwich, Conn.

[1420.] 3. HARRIET, b. April 12, 1819 ; m. Floyd Palmer, and d., in North Castle, N. Y., April 8, 1840.

[1421.] 4. HENRY, b. April 20, 1822, and d. unm., in Greenwich, Conn., Oct. 8, 1849.

[1422.] 5. HANNAH, b. May 22, 1824; m. Edgar L. Brundage, and d., in Greenwich, Conn., Dec. 14, 1861.

[1423.] 6. MARY, b. April 22, 1826 ; m. Richard Smith, and, in 1861, was living in Greenwich, Conn.

CHILDREN OF ENOCH P. PECK (573) AND MARY, HIS WIFE, ALL BORN IN SHARON, CONN.

[1424.] 1. AUGUSTUS L., b. Sept. 8, 1816 ; m. Mary L. Parsons, Jan. 4, 1841, and, in 1877, was living in Sharon Conn.

[1425.] 2. ELIAS R., b. Oct. 10, 1824 ; m. Euphemia E. Nodine, Oct. 28, 1854, and d., in Sharon, Oct. 21, 1864.

[1426.]   3. CHARLES W., b. Dec. 18, 1831; m. Julia M. Cartwright, Nov. 3, 1858, and, in 1873, was living in Sharon, Conn.

CHILDREN OF GEORGE W. PECK (574) AND HANNAH, HIS WIFE, ALL BORN IN SHARON, CONN

[1427.]   1. CHARLES M., b. July 29, 1820, and d., in Sharon, Conn., April 13, 1822.

[1428.]   2. BETSEY L., b. Oct. 31, 1823; m. James Allen, May 22, 1850, and, in 1870, was living in Bethlem, Conn.

[1429.]   3. EMILY, b. July 29, 1826; m. 1. Sanford Peck, (866) Nov. 28, 1850, and m. 2. John Trowbridge, Sept. 21, 1869, and, in 1870, was living in Bethlem, Conn.

[1430.]   4. JOHN C., b. Oct. 6, 1828; m. Josephine Hoyt, May 4, 1853, and, in 1870, was living in Atlanta, Ga.

[1431.]   5. AMARILLIS, b. Aug. 25, 1830; m. Watson Cartwright, April 7, 1856, and, in 1870, was living in Hamden, Conn.

[1432.]   6. CAROLINE M., b. June 22. 1833, and d., in Sharon, Conn., June 13, 1844.

[1433.]   7. SARAH A., b. April 16, 1838; m. Roderick B. Judson, Oct. 2, 1858, and, in 1870, was living in Woodbury, Conn.

CHILDREN OF JOHN C. PECK (579) AND SARAH, HIS WIFE, BORN IN CATSKILL, N. Y.

[1435.]   1. LAURA, b. July 20, 1834; m. William H. Russ, June 6, 1852, and d., in Catskill, N. Y., Feb. 21, 1870.

[1436.]   2. REBECCA, b. Aug. 14, 1835; m. Orrin R. Bouton, Aug. 18, 1857, and, in 1870, was living in Roxbury, N. Y.

ONLY CHILD OF SAMUEL F. PECK (580) AND LAURA ANN, HIS WIFE, BORN IN SHARON, CONN.

[1437.]   CHARLOTTE A., b. July 12, 1832; m. Edmond Peck, (864) Dec. 25, 1855, and d., in Sharon, Conn., Feb. 4, 1856.

CHILDREN OF SAMUEL PECK (581) AND ELIZA, HIS WIFE, ALL
BORN IN NEW YORK CITY.

[1438.]　1. GEORGE, b. May 8, 1829, and d., in New York
city, Sept. 10, 1829.

[1439.]　2. ALONZO R., b. July 19, 1831; m. Lydia A.
Stuart, and, in 1877, was living in New York city.

[1440.]　3. WILLIAM H., b. Nov. 2, 1833 ; m. Mary Van
Dusen, and, in 1875, was living in New York city

[1441.]　4. ADELAIDE, b. Dec. 22, 1837, and, in 1875, was
living in New York city.

[1442.]　5. CATHARINE R., b. March 25, 1839, and, in
1875, was living in New York city.

[1443.]　6. ALBERT, b. April 18, 1840, and, in 1875, was
living in New York city.

[1444.]　7. SUSAN, b. Aug. 11, 1845, and, in 1875, was living in New York city.

[1445.]　8. ELIZA, b. June 12, 1851, and, in 1875, was living
in New York city.

CHILDREN OF WILLIAM PECK (583) AND LYDIA A., HIS WIFE, ALL
BORN IN GREENWICH, CONN.

[1446.]　1. EDWIN, b. March 27, 1834, ; was m. and d., in
Brooklyn, N. Y., June 12, 1872.

[1447.]　2. ADALINE, b. Feb. 11, 1836 ; m. and, in 1875,
was living in Brooklyn, N. Y.

[1448.]　3. SARAH, b. Dec. 20, 1837, and, in 1875, was living in Brooklyn, N. Y.

[1449.]　4. AUGUSTUS, b. Feb. 10, 1840 ; m. and, in 1875,
was living in New York city.

[1450.]　5. MARY, b. March 24, 1842 ; m. and, in 1875, was
living in Philadelphia, Penn.

[1451.]　6. BENJAMIN, b. May 11, 1844, and, in 1875, was
living unm. in New York city.

[1452.]　7. CORNELIA, b. Sept. 11, 1846 ; m. and, in 1875,
was living in Philadelphia, Penn.

[1453.] 8. WILLIAM T., b. Aug. 22, 1849, and, in '1875' was living unm. in Norwalk, Conn.

[1454.] 9. ISAAC, b. May 28, 1851, and d. unm. in Greenwich, Conn.

[1455.] 10. JOHN B., b. July 6, 1852 and, in 1875, was living unm. in New York city.

[1456.] 11. CHARLES, b. Feb. 16, 1856, and, in 1875, his residence was unknown.

CHILDREN OF EDWIN PECK (584) AND MARTHA, HIS WIFE, ALL
BORN IN NEW YORK CITY.

[1457.] 1. MARY A., b. May 17, 1842 ; m. Seymour N. Gimbrede April 15, 1862, and, in 1876, was living in New York city.   Her husband d. there Sept. 9, 1868.

[1458.] 2. ISABEL, b. Aug. 24, 1846 ; m. Jerome Badgley, and, in 1876, was living in New York city.

[1459.] 3. ELOISE, b. Aug. 24, 1846, and d., in New York city, July 23, 1848.

[1460.] 4. FLORENCE LOISE, b. March 1856 ; m. and, in 1876, was living in New York city.

CHILDREN OF ENOS K. PECK (590) AND MARY, HIS WIFE, ALL
BORN IN MADISON, GEORGIA.

[1461.] 1. CHARLES E., b. Aug. 12. 1830, and, in 1854, was living unm. in Arkansas.

[1462.] 2. FRANCES ANN, b. April 12, 1833 ; m. Richard A. Jones, and, in 1861, was living in Madison, Ga.

[1463.] 3. DAVID W., b. May 7, 1834, and, in 1860, was living unm. in Wood Co., Texas.

CHILDREN OF GEORGE A. PECK (600) AND ANN ELIZA, HIS WIFE,
ALL BORN IN NEW YORK CITY, EXCEPT THE LAST,
WHO WAS BORN IN GREENWICH, CONN.

[1464.] 1. HENRY V., b. July 5, 1842, and, in 1870, was living unm. in Greenwich, Conn.

[1465.]   2. FRANCES C., b. Dec. 14, 1843, and d., in Greenwich, Conn., April 7, 1858.

[1466.]   3. MARY E., b. Aug. 14, 1847, and, in 1870, was living unm. in Greenwich, Conn.

[1467.]   4. GEORGE A., b. July 19, 1849, and, in 1870, was living unm. in Greenwich, Conn.

[1468.]   5. JANE A., b. Dec. 12, 1851, and d., in New York city, July 22, 1853.

[1469.]   6. JANE A., again, b. July 9, 1854, and, in 1870, was living in Greenwich, Conn.

[1470.]   7. JOSEPH E., b. Feb. 29, 1856, and, in 1870, was living in Greenwich, Conn.

[1471.]   8. EMMA F., b. Feb. 12, 1859, and, in 1870, was living in Greenwich, Conn.

CHILDREN OF SOLOMON PECK (601) AND MARY, HIS WIFE, ALL BORN IN GREENWICH, CONN.

[1472.]   1. FERRIS, b. Oct. 14, 1830, and d., in July, 1863, in Greenwich, Conn.

[1473.]   2. JOSEPH, b. May 24, 1832; m. Catharine M. Whiting, Oct. 18, 1852, and, in 1870, was living in New York city.

[1474.]   3. SOLOMON, b. April 9, 1834, and, in 1870, was living in Stamford, Conn.

[1475.]   4. EMELINE W., b. July 17, 1836, and, in 1870, was living in Greenwich, Conn.

[1476.]   5. CAROLINE E., b. April 12, 1845, and, in 1870, was living in Greenwich, Conn.

CHILDREN OF JEDUTHAN PECK (603) AND MARY, HIS WIFE, ALL BORN IN GREENWICH, CONN.

[1477.]   1. SAMUEL J., b. Feb. 14, 1846, and, in 1861, was living in Greenwich, Conn.

[1478.]   2. ISAAC A., b. Aug. 20, 1848, and, in 1861, was living in Greenwich, Conn.

[1479.]   3. JOHN F., b. Nov. 26, 1858, and, in 1861, was living in Greenwich, Conn.

[1480.]   4. WILLIAM F., b. Feb. 26, 1860, and, in 1861, was living in Greenwich, Conn.

ONLY CHILD OF JESSE PECK (607) AND ROSENA, HIS WIFE, BORN IN BEDFORD N. Y.

[1481.]   JOHN, b. Feb. 4, 1844, and, in 1861, was living in Bedford, N. Y.

CHILDREN OF WILLIAM H. PECK (609) AND JANE, HIS WIFE, ALL BORN IN NEW YORK CITY, EXCEPT THE LAST, WHO WAS BORN IN SING SING, N. Y.

[1482.]   1. MARY C., b. June 29, 1823 ; m. Enoch R. Ware, and, in 1873, was living near Yonkers, N. Y,

[1483.]   2. SARAH E., b. July 21, 1825, and d. unm., in Sing Sing, June 12, 1866.

[1484.]   3. WILLIAM H., b. July 24, 1827, and d., in New York city, March 24, 1832.

[1485.]   4. GILBERT C., b. Aug. 5, 1831, and d., in New York city, March 17, 1837

[1486.]   5. WILLIAM H., again, b. July 9, 1835 ; m. Isabella Bard, of Sing Sing, N. Y., June 27, 1866, and was living there in 1873.

[1487.]   6. JANE S., b. July 9, 1835, and, in 1873, was living unm. in Sing Sing, N. Y.

[1488.]   7. EMMA, b. March 13, 1838, and, in 1873, was living in Sing Sing, N. Y.

[1489.]   8. ISAAC C., b. April 22, 1841, and d., March 10, 1843, in Sing Sing, N. Y.

CHILDREN OF EDMUND PECK (616) AND MARY, HIS WIFE.

[1490.]   1. CHARLES E., b. in New York city, May 1, 1844 and, in 1873, was living in Jersey City, N. J.

[1491.]   2. WALLACE F., b. in New York city, Nov. 7, 1846, and, in 1873, was living in Jersey City, N. J.

[1492.] 3. LEVAN S., b. in Sing Sing, N. Y., Nov. 13, 1850, and, and, in 1873, was living in Jersey City, N. J.

[1493.] 4. T. SMULL, b. Feb. 12, 1854, in Sing Sing, N. Y., and d., in Carbon Co., near White Haven, Luzerne Co., Penn., July 4, 1858.

CHILDREN OF CHARLES H. PECK (628) AND REBECCA, HIS WIFE, ALL BORN IN ST. LOUIS, MO., AND ALL LIVING THERE IN 1861.

[1494.] 1. AUSTIN, b. Jan. 29, 1841.
[1495.] 2. CHARLES H., b. Jan. 15, 1843.
[1496.] 3. RUDOLPH A., b. Oct. 28, 1845.
[1497.] 4. STEPHEN, b. Aug. 14, 1847.
[1498.] 5. RODERICK A., b. Aug. 16, 1849.
[1499.] 6. REBECCA, b. March 12, 1852.
[1500.] 7. WILLIAM W., b. Jan. 10, 1855.
[1501.] 8. BELLE, b. Jan. 16, 1857.
[1502.] 9. JOHN A., b. Feb. 13, 1859.

CHILDREN OF JOHN WALTER PECK, (624) ALL BORN IN ST. LOUIS, MO., AND ALL LIVING THERE IN 1861.

[1503.] 1. CHARLES W., b. Sept. 8, 1847.
[1504.] 2. WILLIAM H., b. June 14, 1850.
[1505.] 2. EDWARD B., b. Dec. 28, 1851.
[1506.] 4. GEORGE W., b. Jan. 19, 1854.

CHILDREN OF WILLIAM H. PECK (629) AND MARY, HIS WIFE.

[1507.] 1. ELIZABETH A., b. in Stamford, Conn., Sept. 30, 1848, and, in 1870, was living in Greenwich, Conn.

[1508.] 2. GEORGE F., b. in Greenwich, Conn., July 18, 1851, and, in 1870, was living in Greenwich, Conn.

[1509.] 3. CHARLES T., b. in Greenwich, Conn., Dec. 31, 1856, and, in 1870, was living in Greenwich, Conn.

CHILDREN OF STEPHEN PECK (632) AND SUSAN A., HIS WIFE, BOTH
BORN IN STAMFORD, CONN.

[1510.] 1. CHARLES HENRY, b. Oct. 4, 1848, and, in 1861, was living in Stamford, Conn.

[1511.] 2. LEWIS F., b. April 12, 1850, and, in 1861, was living in Stamford, Conn.

CHILDREN OF JOHN ALBERT PECK (633) AND JANE A., HIS WIFE,
BOTH BORN IN STAMFORD, CONN.

[1512.] 1. WILLIAM H., b. March 29, 1849, and, in 1861, was living in Stamford, Conn.

[1513.] 2. EVA JANE, b. June 26, 1854, and, in 1861, was living in Stamford, Conn.

CHILDREN OF WALTER PECK (634) AND CATHARINE, HIS WIFE,
ALL BORN IN NEW YORK CITY.

[1514.] 1. EMELINE A., b. June 22, 1806, and d., unm., in Sept., 1875, in Greenwich, Conn.

[1515.] 2. EBENEZER W., b. Nov. 12, 1807 ; m. Elizabeth Williams, and, in 1870, was living in East New York, Kings Co., N. Y.

[1516.] 3. ABRAHAM D., b. Feb. 19, 1809 ; m. Sarah J. Campbell, and had d., in Brighton, near Ann Arbor, Mich., prior to 1877.

[1517.] 4. CORDELIA, b. Nov. 29, 1810, and d., in Greenwich, Conn., Oct. 18, 1817.

[1518.] 5. WALTER C., b. Sept. 12, 1812, and d., in New York city, Feb. 4, 1819.

[1519.] 6. LOUISA, b. April 16, 1814 ; m. Pardon D. Davis and, in 1869, was living in Yonkers, N. Y.

[1520.] 7. GEORGE W., b. May 18, 1816 ; m. Sophia Lee ; has been a member of Congress from Michigan, and, in 1869, was said to be living in East Saginaw, Mich.

[1521.] 8. OPHELIA, b. July 2, 1818 ; m. Leonard Hess, and, in 1870, was living in Brooklyn, N. Y.

[1522.]   9. CATHARINE A., b. April 8, 1819, and d., in New York city, July 27, 1820.

[1523.]   10. WALTER, b. July 21, 1821, and d. unm., in Chicago, Ill., June 17, 1855.

[1524.]   11. CATHARINE M., b. April 4, 1823, and d., in New York city, Oct. 22, 1824.

[1525.]   12. LaFAYETTE, b. Feb. 6, 1825, and d., in New York city, June 12, 1826.

[1526.]   13. CORNELIA, b. Jan. 4, 1827, and d., in New York city, May 6, 1827.

[1527.]   14. WILLIAM TAPPAN, b. March 18, 1828, and d., in New York city, Dec. 21, 1829.

[1528.]   15. EDWARD H., b. May 6, 1830 ; m. Susan Miller, and, in 1870, was supposed to be living in Canada.

CHILDREN OF RALPH PECK (640) AND ELIZABETH, HIS WIFE, ALL BORN IN NEW YORK CITY.

[1529.]   1. FRANCES E., b. June 10, 1827, and d., in New York city, June 19, 1827.

[1530.]   2. CATHARINE E., b. Oct. 31, 1828 ; m. William H. Reading, June 1, 1848, and d., in Indianapolis, Ind., July 17, 1854.

[1531.]   3. JULIA W., b. June 20, 1830 ; m. William M. Clark, Jan. 29, 1855, and, in 1870, was living at Mianus, Conn.

[1532.]   4. DEBORAH S., b. Oct. 30, 1831, and, in 1870, was living at Mianus, Conn.

CHILDREN OF WILLIAM PECK, (644) ALL BORN IN NEW YORK CITY.

[1533.]   1. WILLIAM H., b. Nov. 24, 1808 ; m. Ellen Ann Hitt, was several years Post Master of Brooklyn, N. Y., and d. there May 15, 1868.

[1534.]   2. ALFRED, b. July 28, 1810, and d., in Newark, N. J., in 1818.

[1535.]   3. WALTER b. March 30, 1812 ; m. 1. Maria Hitt, and m. 2. Anna Gotsberger, and, in 1860, was living in New Orleans, La.

[1536.]   4. JANE, b. Feb. 2, 1814 ; m. Luke Roscoe, and, in 1860, was living in Lapeer, Mich.

CHILDREN OF ABRAHAM PECK (651) AND MARGARET ANN, HIS WIFE.

[1537.]   1. TUNIS, b. in Rotterdam, N. Y., Sept. 11, 1835 ; m. 1. Anna Lasher, Sept. 11, 1862, who d. June 11, 1866 ; m. 2. Susan M. Miller, Feb. 13, 1868, and, in 1877, was living in Amsterdam, N. Y.

[1538.]   2. BENJAMIN, b. in Glenville, N. Y., Jan. 3, 1838, and d. there March 12, 1838.

CHILDREN OF EDWARD PECK, (653) ALL BORN IN WESTFIELD, N. Y., AND ALL, EXCEPT MARY ANN AND ISABELLA, LIVING THERE IN 1861.

[1539.]   1. MARY ANN, b. May 18, 1831, and d., in West-field, N. Y., about 1839.

[1540.]   2. ISABELLA, b. Nov. 15, 1837, and d., in West-field, N. Y., Jan. 26, 1841.

[1541.]   3. EDWARD, b. Oct. 14, 1839 ; m. Joanna Dewey.

[1542.]   4. HIRAM R., b. Aug. 12, 1841.

[1543.]   5. DELOS, b. May 3, 1843.

[1544.]   6. ROLLIN, b. July 8, 1845.

[1545.]   7. FRANK, b. Aug. 3, 1849.

[1546.]   8. MARYETTE, b. Oct. 14, 1851.

CHILDREN OF HARVEY PECK (657) AND MINERVA, HIS WIFE, ALL BORN IN WESTFIELD, N. Y., AND ALL, EXCEPT ELLEN M., LIVING THERE IN 1861.

[1547.]   1. HOLLISTER H., b. Nov. 16, 1835.

[1548.]   2. ELLIOTT S., b. Feb. 5, 1842.

[1549.]   3. MARY L., b. March 13, 1845.

[1550.]   4. ELLEN M., b. Sept. 29, 1847, and d., in West-field, N. Y., May 26, 1850.

[1551.]   5. HENRY S., b. May 25, 1849.

CHILDREN OF JONATHAN PECK (660) AND CAROLINE, HIS WIFE, ALL BORN IN FLUSHING, N. Y.

[1552.] 1. CORNELL, b. March 14, 1809 ; m. Mary Nelson, of Flushing, N. Y., April 16, 1839, and, in 1860, was living in Flushing, N. Y.

[1553.] 2. ANN ELIZA, b. June 9, 1811 ; m. William H. Fairweather, of Flushing, N. Y., Nov. 10, 1831, and, in 1860, was living in Flushing, N. Y.

[1554.] 3. JAMES, b. April 25, 1813 ; m. Sarah Bush, of Brooklyn, N. Y., Jan, 5, 1847, and d., in Flushing, N. Y., Oct. 15, 1855.

[1555.] 4. RICHARD, b. Dec. 28, 1815 ; m. Ann Eliza Haviland, of New York city, Feb. 21, 1839, and m. 2. Mary Ann Smith, of New Haven, Conn., and, in 1873, was living in New Haven, Conn.

[1556.] 5. THOMAS LAVENDER, b. Nov. 21, 1817 ; m. 1. Clarissa Fairweather, Oct. 18, 1838, who d. Aug. 31, 1858, and m. 2. Sarah E. Bootman, of New York city, June 21, 1860, and, in 1860, was living in Norwalk, Conn.

[1557.] 6. CAROLINE, b. March 14, 1819 ; m. William Henry Roe, of Flushing, N. Y., Oct. 3, 1839, and d., in Flushing, N. Y., April 16, 1854.

[1558.] 7. JANNETT, b. May 2, 1821 ; m. Theodore D. Dumont, Nov. 5, 1851, and, in Oct. 1860, was living in Williamsburgh, N. Y.

[1559.] 8. SUSAN ANN, b. Dec. 18, 1823 ; m. William Augustus Mitchell, of Flushing, N. Y., Sept. 10, 1846, and, in 1860, was living in Manhasset, N. Y.

[1560.] 9. JONATHAN, b. Aug. 27, 1825 ; m. Mary Antolnette Poole, of Flushing, N, Y., Aug. 4, 1847, and, in 1874, was living in Long Island city, N. Y.

[1561.] 10. HENRY AUGUSTUS, b. Sept. 18, 1829 ; m. Mary Duryea, of Flushing, in Feb. 1857, and, in 1870, was living in Brooklyn, N. Y.

[1562.] 11. WILLIAM LEWIS, b. Sept. 2, 1831 ; m. Phebe Ann Wright, of Flushing, in Oct. 1855, and, in 1870, was living in New York city.

CHILDREN OF CURTIS PECK, (661) ALL BORN IN FLUSHING, N. Y.

[1563.] 1. MARY, b. Feb. 10, 1808 ; m. Stephen Mills, of Flushing, N. Y., in 1827, and, in 1860, was living in Brooklyn, N. Y.

[1564.] 2. SARAH P., b. Jan. 16, 1810 ; m. Alfonso Delgado, of Mexico, in 1826, and d., in the city of Mexico, in Feb. 1834.

[1565.] 3. WILLIAM HENRY, b. Nov. 30, 1812 ; m. Eliza B. Robinson, of Bridgeport, Conn., Jan. 19, 1835, and, in 1872, was living in Flushing, N. Y.

[1566.] 4. AGNES, b. Sept. 19, 1814 ; m. James B. Thompson, of New York city, in 1830, and, in 1860, was living in New York city.

[1567.] 5. ANN REBECCA, b. Aug. 25, 1816 ; m. Darius A. Nash, of New York city, in 1837, and d., in Maspeth, N. Y., July 15, 1844.

[1568.] 6. ELIZABETH ANN, b. Aug. 17, 1818 ; m. Henry Brooks, of New York city, in 1834, and d., in New York city, Dec. 26, 1834.

[1569.] 7. CURTIS, b. Aug. 27, 1820 ; m. 1. Hannah Maria Allen, and m. 2. Catalina Meserole, in 1840, and, in 1860, was living in New Rochelle, N. Y.

[1570.] 8. JOHN FORBES, b. Dec. 27, 1821 ; m. Loretta Reynolds, of Port Chester, N. Y., in 1838, and, in 1860, was living in Hartford, Conn.

[1571.] 9. P. GALATIAN, b. Sept. 10, 1823 ; m. Ann Reynaud, of New York city, in 1839, and, in 1860, was living in New York city.

[1572.] 10. ALFONSO DELGADO, b. Sept. 4, 1825 ; m. Elizabeth Gould, of Fairfield, Conn., in 1847, and, in 1860, was living in California.

[1573.]   11. HANNAH MARIA, b. July 15, 1828, and d. unm., in Brooklyn, N. Y., June 20, 1846.

[1574.]   12. LOUISA, b. Sept. 11, 1832 ; m. Robert J. Davies, of Brooklyn, N. Y., in 1848, and was living there in 1860.

[1575.]   13. SARAH E., b. Sept. 9, 1836 ; m. Joseph Hart, of Brooklyn, N. Y., in 1857, and was living there in 1860.

CHILDREN OF CHARLES PECK, (662) THE FIRST FOUR BORN IN NEW YORK CITY, AND THE LAST THREE IN FLUSHING, N. Y.

[1576.]   1. HANNAH, b. April 25, 1810 ; m. James W. Harper, of New York city, March 13, 1827, and, in 1860, was living in Brooklyn, N. Y.

[1577.]   2. ELIZABETH ANN, b. Nov. 2, 1816 ; m. Amasa Newman, of Brooklyn, N. Y., April 5, 1836, and, in 1860, was living in Brooklyn, N. Y.

[1578.]   3. CHARLES BENSON, b. Dec. 19, 1818 ; m. Sarah Wright, Sept. 10, 1839, and d., in Brooklyn, N. Y., July 5, 1841.

[1579.]   4. ESTHER ELIZA, b. March 31, 1821 ; m. John Habberton, of Brooklyn, N. Y., March 19, 1841, and, in 1860, was living in Brooklyn, N. Y.

[1580.]   5. MARY MARTHA, b. June 2, 1823 ; m. Rev. Solomon Parsons, Oct. 10, 1859, and, in 1860, was living in Perth Amboy, N. J.

[1581.]   6. HARRIET NEWELL, b. Sept. 28, 1826 ; m. Daniel Baker, M. D., Aug. 1, 1858. and, in 1860, was living in Chatham, N. J.

[1582.]   7. RICHARD SEAMAN, b. Aug. 23, 1828 ; m. Catharine Emmons, of Brooklyn, N. Y. Nov. 3, 1856.

CHILDREN OF ISAAC PECK (663) AND AGNES, HIS WIFE, ALL BORN IN FLUSHING, N. Y.

[1583.]   1. HAMILTON, b. May 4, 1815 ; m 1. Jane Morgan, July 15, 1845, and m. 2. Anna M. Johnson, Aug. 13, 1857, and, in 1860, was living in Watertown, N. Y.

[1584.] 2. ADALINE, b. Sept. 29, 1816 ; m. Rev. Samuel M. Haskins, July 27, 1842, and d., in Williamsburgh, N. Y., Jan. 19, 1858

[1585.] 3. ISAAC, b. Feb. 23, 1820 ; m. Abby P. Beers, dau. of Dr. Timothy P. Beers, of New Haven, Conn., March 17, 1841, and, in 1860, was living in Flushing, N. Y.

[1586.] 4. GEORGE WARNER, b. Jan. 5, 1822 ; m. Adaline A. Vassar, of Poughkeepsie, N. Y., Sept. 7, 1843. and, in 1877, was living in Flushing, N. Y.,

[1587.] 5. JAMES MILNER, b. Nov. 14, 1824 ; m. Anna Leverich, of Flushing, N. Y., Sept. 11, 1860, and, in 1860, was living in Flushing, N. Y.

[1588.] 6. MARIA GREEN, b. Oct. 31, 1826 ; m. Rev. William Parot, of New York city, who was an Episcopal clergyman, and, in 1860, was living at Pierrepont, N. Y.

CHILDREN OF ELIJAH PECK, (664) ALL BORN IN FLUSHING, N. Y.

[1589.] 1. MARGARET ANN, b. March 27, 1817; m. James Udall, Feb. 11, 1834, and, in 1860, was living at Great Neck, N. Y.

[1590.] 2. JONATHAN RICHARD, b. July 6, 1822 ; m. Elizabeth Bennett, Sept. 4, 1853, and, in 1860, was living in Brooklyn, N. Y.

[1591.] 3. ELIJAH, b. Dec. 23, 1824 ; m. Susan C Jones, April 28, 1847, and d., in Great Neck, N. Y., Feb. 2, 1856.

[1592.] 4. CHARLOTTE LOUISA, b. Nov. 8, 1828 ; m. Robert M. Ward, of New York city, Feb. 10, 1847, and was living there in 1870.

ONLY CHILD OF ALEXANDER PECK (665) AND REBECCA, HIS WIFE, BORN IN FLUSHING, N. Y.

[1593.] ALEXANDER, b. Aug. 2, 1818 ; entered the U. S. Navy and is supposed to have d. there unm. many years since.

CHILDREN OF WILLIAM PECK (666) AND LYDIA ANN, HIS WIFE,
THE OLDEST BORN IN SAVANNAH, GA., AND THE
OTHERS IN FLUSHING, N. Y.

[1594.] 1. WILLIAM HOWARD, b. May 18, 1821; m. Laura C. Kinne, of Port Jefferson, N. Y., Dec. 1, 1841, and d., in Brooklyn, N. Y., Jan. 27, 1852.

[1595.] 2. THEODOSIA, b. April 19, 1823; m. William Habberton, of Brooklyn, N. Y., March 31, 1842, and, in 1860, was living at Mt. Carmel, Ill.

[1596.] 3. MARGARET ELIZABETH, b. Dec. 16, 1825; m. Charles Barnum, of Flushing, N. Y.. Sept. 11, 1843, and, in 1860, was living in Flushing, N. Y.

[1597.] 4. HARRIET KEITH, b. Nov. 29, 1827, and d. unm., in Flushing, N. Y., April 10, 1846.

[1598.] 5. EDWARD L., b. Sept. 1, 1834, and, in 1860, was living unm. at Glen Cove, N. Y.

[1599.] 6. ELIJAH W., b. March 17, 1836, and, in 1860 was living unm. in Terre Haute, Ind.

CHILDREN OF RICHARD PECK (667) AND HARRIET, HIS WIFE,
ALL BORN IN SHELDON, VT.

[1600.] 1. RICHARD, b. March 3, 1832, and d. unm., in Sheldon, Vt., March 19, 1855.

[1601.] 2. JANNETT, b. Feb. 17, 1836, and, in 1860, was living unm. in Sheldon, Vt.

[1602.] 3. THEODOSIA, b. April 23, 1838, and, in 1860, was living unm. in Sheldon, Vt.

[1603.] 4. HANNAH, b. Nov. 11, 1841, and, in 1860, was living unm. in Sheldon, Vt.

CHILDREN OF CHARLES E. PECK (673) AND MARY, HIS WIFE, THE
FIRST FOUR BORN IN NEWBURGH, N. Y., AND THE OTHERS
IN NEW YORK CITY, AND ALL, EXCEPT CHARLES E.,
AND MARIA T., LIVING THERE IN 1861.

[1604.] 1. ELIZABETH T., b. Aug. 6, 1836.

[1605.]   2. CHARLES E., b. March 25, 1838, and d., in New-burgh, N. Y., May 25, 1842.

[1606.]   3. CATHARINE A., b. March 4, 1840.

[1607.]   4. GEORGIANNA, b. Jan. 20, 1844.

[1608.]   5. WILLIAM P., b. Oct. 9, 1846.

[1609.]   6. ALPHONSO, b. April 16, 1849.

[1610.]   7. MARIA T., b. Oct. 19, 1851, and d., in New York city, Aug 19, 1852.

[1611.]   8. CHARLES E., again, b. Aug. 15, 1855.

CHILDREN OF FREDERICK PECK (677) AND SARAH, HIS WIFE.

[1612.]   1. CHARLES F., b. in Greenwich, Conn., Dec. 6, 1832 ; m. Sarah Moore, of New Hampshire, and, in 1860, was living in Boston, Mass.

[1613.]   2. THEODORE H., b. in Stamford, Conn., June 27 1839, and was living there in 1860.

[1614.]   3. EMELINE H., b. in Stamford, Conn. Feb. 25 1842, and was living there in 1860.

CHILDREN OF WILLIAM H. PECK (678) AND MARY, HIS WIFE.

[1615.]   1. MARY E., b. in New York city, Dec. 17, 1832 ; m. James Donnelly, of New York city, and was living there in 1860.

[1616.]   2. SARAH S., b. in New York city, Sept. 30. 1834, and was living there unm. in 1860.

[1617.]   3. HANNAH M., b. in New York city, Oct. 17, 1840 ; m. Henry Herbert, of New Haven, Conn., and, in 1860, was living in New York city.

[1618.]   4. JOHN W., b. in Greenwich, Conn., Oct. 29, 1842, and, in 1860, was living unm. in New York city.

[1619.]   5. MOSES, b. in Greenwich, Conn., Dec. 24, 1844 and, in 1860, was living unm. in New York city.

[1620.]   6. GEORGE, b. in New York city, Sept. 16, 1847, and, in 1860, was living unm. in New York city.

CHILDREN OF ISAAC PECK (685) AND MARGARET, HIS WIFE, ALL
BORN IN NEW YORK CITY.

[1621.] 1. GEORGE C., b. Oct. 17, 1841, and, in 1860, was
living in Greenwich, Conn.

[1622.] 2. ADDISON, b. Jan. 24, 1844, and, in 1860, was
living in Greenwich, Conn.

[1623.] 3. JAMES L, b. April 26, 1847, and, in 1860, was
living in Greenwich, Conn.

[1624.] 4. ANNIE, b. in 1850, and, in 1860, was living in
Greenwich, Conn.

CHILDREN OF DAVID PECK (686) AND SARAH, HIS WIFE, BOTH
BORN IN NEWBERN, N. C.

[1625.] 1. EDWIN, b. in May 1801, and d., in Newbern, N.
C., May 19, 1802.

[1626.] 2. ANN AUGUSTA, b. June 29, 1802; m. James
Rikeman, and, in 1868, was living at Rye Neck, near Mamaroneck, N. Y. Her children were *David P.*, b. Aug. 9, and d.
Aug. 16, 1832, and *Ann Augusta*, b. Nov. 30, 1833, and, in
1868, was living at Rye Neck, N. Y.

CHILDREN OF BENONI PECK (694) AND HULDAH, HIS WIFE, ALL
BORN IN GREENWICH, CONN.

[1627.] 1. HANNAH, b. Sept. 13, 1813, and, in 1861, was
living unm. in Genoa, N. Y.

[1628.] 2. ISAAC, b. May 4, 1815; m. 1. Margaret Smith,
who d. Dec. 28, 1849, and m. 2. Phebe Jane Stoddard, Jan. 28,
1858, and, in 1861, was living in Genoa, N. Y.

[1629.] 3. RHODA, b. April 11, 1818; m. Sereno E. Todd,
June 19, 1844, and, in 1861, was living in Lansing, N. Y.

[1630.] 4. AMY ELIZA, b. Sept. 11, 1821; m. Josiah
Todd, Jr., Jan. 29, 1852, and, in 1861, was living in Lansing,
N. Y.

[1631.] 5. CORNELIUS, b. June 27, 1823, and d., in Greenwich, Conn., Oct. 18, 1826.

[1632.]   6. DAVID, b. Feb. 16, 1825 ; graduated at Yale College in 1849 ; m. Frances Maria Jocelyn, of New Haven, Conn., Sept. 8, 1852 ; was a Congregational minister, and d., at Sunderland, Mass., Jan. 31, 1874, where he was settled as such minister.

[1633.]   7. SARAH, b. Jan. 31, 1827 ; m. Lucius A. Brown, March 27, 1854, and, in 1861, was living in Deposit, N. Y.

[1634.]   8. CORNELIUS, again, b. Sept. 30, 1829 ; m. Mary Wood, Feb. 12, 1862, and was then living in Genoa, N. Y.

CHILDREN OF ELIPHALET PECK (701) AND DEBORAH, HIS WIFE, ALL BORN IN GREENWICH, CONN.

[1635.]   1. CELISTA, b. Oct. 3, 1824 ; m. Joseph Bounty, Jan. 15, 1851, and, in 1861, was living in N. Stamford, Conn.

[1636.]   2. MARY, b. April 15, 1830 ; m. Harvey Slater, in Jan. 1853, and, in 1861, was living in Greenwich, Conn.

[1637.]   3. SAMUEL, b. Aug. 20, 1833, and d., in Greenwich, Conn., Aug. 23, 1833.

[1638.]   4. JARED, b. Sept. 14, 1834 ; m. Julia Ann Peck, (1740) Jan. 17, 1866, and was then living in Greenwich, Conn.

[1639.]   5. WILLIAM E., b. May 5, 1838 ; m. Emily Peck, (788) April 16, 1860.

CHILDREN OF DAVID PECK (703) AND MARY B., HIS WIFE, ALL BORN IN GREENWICH, CONN.

[1640.]   1. CEPHAS, b. Jan. 3, 1830 ; m. Josephine Ferris, Dec. 31. 1857, and, in 1861, was living in Port Chester, N. Y.

[1641.]   2. ANDREW, b. May 7, 1831, and d., in Greenwich, Conn., Sept. 15, 1831.

[1642.]   3. ANNA AUGUSTA, b. Sept. 9, 1833 ; m. Samuel Peck, (747) Dec. 17, 1855, and, in 1861, was living in Bridgeport, Conn.

[1643.]   4. MARY AMANDA, b. Jan. 27, 1835 ; m. Samuel Wilcox, May 17, 1852, and, in 1861, was living in Greenwich, Conn.

[1644.] 5. STEPHEN C., b. April 2, 1836 ; m. Eliza B. Sherwood, Nov. 20, 1865, and, in 1867, was living in Greenwich, Conn.

[1645.] 6. CLARISSA R., b. Oct. 9, 1838, and d., in Greenwich, Conn , Oct. 19, 1839.

[1646.] 7. CATHARINE M.. b. Dec. 30, 1839, and d., in Greenwich, Conn., March 4, 1863.

[1647.] 8. SARAH M., b. June 29, 1841, and d., in Greenwich, Conn., Aug. 15, 1843.

[1648.] 9. ALVORD, b. June 26, 1843.

[1649.] 10. ELIZABETH C., b. June 23, 1847.

CHILDREN OF GIDEON PECK (709) AND PHEBE W., HIS WIFE, ALL
BORN IN NEW YORK CITY, EXCEPT THE OLDEST,
WHO WAS BORN IN GREENWICH, CONN.

[1650.] 1. EBENEZER, b. July 19, 1814 ; m. Catharine M. Franklin, and, in 1861, was living in New York city.

[1651.] 2. CHARLES HENRY, b. Nov. 25, 1815, and d., in New York city, March 20, 1820.

[1652.] 3. EUNICE ELIZABETH, b. April 13, 1818, and d., in New York city, March 21, 1820.

[1653.] 4. GIDEON M., b. April 15, 1820 ; m. Mary Eugenia Wicks, and, in 1861, was living in New York city.

[1654.] 5. MARY ELIZABETH, b. May 6, 1822, and d., in New York city, Jan. 16, 1827.

[1655.] 6. HENRY WILLIS, b. July 19, 1824, and d., in New York city, Dec. 21, 1825.

[1656.] 7. JOHN WESLEY, b. Dec. 26, 1826 ; m. Betsey B. Lyon, Nov. 11, 1847, and, in 1861, was living in New York city.

[1657.] 8. CAROLINE FRANCES,. b. Oct. 13, 1828, and d., in New York city, May 4, 1830.

[1658.] 9. ANN ELIZA MERRITT, b. Oct. 8, 1832, and d., in New York city, Oct. 28, 1834.

[1659.] 10. JULIA MERRITT, b. April 7, 1835, and, in 1861, was living unm. in New York city.

[1660.] 11. PHŒBE WILLIS, b. June 27, 1837 ; m. George H. French, and, in 1861, was living in New York city.

CHILDREN OF THEOPHILUS PECK (712) AND SARAH, HIS WIFE, ALL BORN IN NEW YORK CITY.

[1661.] 1. WILLIAM LEWIS, b. Sept. 22, 1823 ; m. Hannah M. Purdy, and, in 1851, was living in New Castle, N. Y.

[1662.] 2. ELIZABETH MARY, b. July 22, 1825 ; m. George O. Close. May 1, 1848, and, in 1861, was living in Brooklyn, N. Y.

[1663.] 3. JULIA FRANCES, b. Feb. 21, 1827 ; m. Van Kleeck Deyo, Dec. 3, 1850, and, in 1861, was living in Monroe, Mich.

[1664.] 4. EDWARD MILLS, b. Nov. 27, 1828 ; m. Susan M. Drake, Oct. 17, 1854 ; is an Episcopal clergyman, and, in 1877, was settled as such at Richfield Springs, N. Y.

CHILDREN OF THOMAS PECK (715) AND JANE, HIS WIFE, ALL BORN IN POUNDRIDGE, N. Y.

[1665.] 1. SARAH ANN, b. April 25, 1846 ; m. James Bates, in 1868, and, in 1870, was living in Brooklyn, N. Y.

[1666.] 2. BENJAMIN, b. July 13, 1847, and, in 1870, was living unm. in Lewisboro', N. Y.

[1667.] 3. ANDREW, b. Sept. 26, 1850, and, in 1870, was living in Lewisboro', N. Y.

[1668.] 4. JAMES, b. July 22, 1855, and, in 1870, was living unm. in Lewisboro', N. Y.

CHILDREN OF EZRA R. PECK (717) AND CATHARINE, HIS WIFE, ALL BORN IN POUNDRIDGE, N. Y.

[1669.] 1. ELIPHALET N., b. Nov. 15, 1835 ; m. Mary E. Buckley, and, in 1870, was living in Stamford, Conn.

[1670.] 2. DAVID H., b. May 18, 1840 ; m. Elizabeth Van Wart, and, in 1870, was living in New York city.

[1671.]   3. HULBERT, b. July 23, 1842; m. Mary Fenton, and, in 1870, was living in New York city.

[1672.]   4. CLARA ELIZA, b. July 7, 1846; m. Andrew Jones, and, in 1870, was living in Stamford, Conn.

[1673.]   5. JOHN P., b. June 26, 1849, and d., in Bedford, N. Y., Aug. 18, 1854.

ONLY CHILD OF ARAD PECK (719) AND ELIZA, HIS WIFE.

[1674.]   EDWARD A., b. in Greenwich, Conn., Oct. 22, 1834 ; was m. and, in 1875, was living in Greenwich, Conn.

CHILDREN OF OBADIAH PECK (723) AND LIZETTA, HIS WIFE.

[1675.]   1. MYRTILLA M., b. in New York city, Oct. 11, 1819; m. Rev. J. W. Alvord, and, in 1861, was living in Boston, Mass.

[1676.]   2. ANNA MARIA, b. in New York city, Aug. 18, 1823, and, in 1861, was living unm. in Brooklyn, N. Y.

[1677.]   3. LIZETTA, b. in New York city, June 11, 1829, and, in 1861, was living unm. in Brooklyn, N. Y.

[1678.]   4. LEWIS M., b. in Greenwich, Conn., Sept. 10, 1832 ; was Colonel and Brevet Brigadier-General in the War of the Rebellion, and, in 1875, was living in Brooklyn, N. Y.

[1679.]   5. SAMUEL C., b. in Greenwich, Conn., Aug. 23 1834, and d. unm., in Greenwich, Conn., Sept. 23, 1857.

CHILDREN OF ISAAC PECK (729) AND JULIA, HIS WIFE, BOTH BORN IN GREENWICH, CONN.

[1680.]   1. SOPHIA, b. May 6, 1842, and d., in Greenwich, Conn., Oct. 7, 1861.

[1681.]   2. ZENAS M., b. Aug. 9, 1844, and, in 1870, was living in Greenwich, Conn.

CHILDREN OF WHITMAN PECK (730) AND RUTH MARIA, HIS WIFE.

[1682.]   1. GERTRUDE M., b. in Genoa, N. Y., Nov. 27, 1846, and, in 1868, was living in Ridgefield, Conn.

[1683.]   2. MARY M., b. in Genoa, N. Y., Jan. 7, 1849, and, in 1868, was living in Ridgefield, Conn.

[1684.]   3. ANNA K., b. in North Branford, Conn., Feb. 5, 1853, and, in 1868, was living in Ridgefield, Conn.

[1685.]   4. EDWARD S., b. in North Branford, Conn., June 23, 1855, and, in 1868, was living in Ridgefield, Conn.

CHILDREN OF WILLIAM PECK (736) AND NANCY, HIS WIFE, ALL BORN IN RYE, N. Y.

[1685.]   1. CAROLINE, b. in Dec. 1820, and d. unm., in New York city, in the Winter of 1839.

[1686.]   2. WILLIAM C., b. Dec. 25, 1821 ; m. Lydia Hampton, May 23, 1842, and. in 1872, was living in New York city.

[1687.]   3. ANN MARIA, b. in 1824 ; m. Charles Burt, in 1853, and, in 1861, was living in New York city.

CHILDREN OF JAMES HERVEY PECK (736) AND PHEBE C., HIS WIFE, ALL BORN IN PORT CHESTER, N. Y.

[1688.]   1. JEANNETTE E., b. Oct. 29, 1840 ; m. D. A. B. Davis, Feb. 3, 1864, and, in 1873, was living in Port Chester, N. Y.

[1689.]   2. GEORGE A., b. March 25, 1843, and d., in Port Chester, N. Y., Aug. 5, 1851.

[1690.]   3. JAMES H., b. July 9, 1845 ; m. Isabella ———, July 8, 1863, and, in 1873, was living in Port Chester, N. Y.

[1691.]   4. MARY H., b. June 14, 1847, and d., in Port Chester, N. Y., March 19, 1853.

[1692.]   5. SARAH E., b. Jan. 27, 1849 ; m. Walter B. Toucey, April 14, 1869, and, in 1873, was living in Rye, N. Y.

[1693.]   6. GEORGIANNA, b. Aug. 3, 1851, and, in 1873, was living in Port Chester, N. Y.

[1694.]   7. WILLIAM E., b. Feb. 19, 1854, and, in 1873, was living in Port Chester, N. Y.

[1695.]   8. CARRIE W., b. Dec. 31, 1856, and, in 1873, was living in Port Chester, N. Y.

CHILDREN OF CHARLES A. PECK (738) AnD MARY H., HIS WIFE,
ALL BORN IN NEW YORK CITY.

[1696.] 1. ANNA LOUISA, b. Aug. 3, 1828, and, in 1861,
was living unm. in New York city.

[1697.] 2. JOHN B., b. Aug. 16, 1830 ; m. Anna Van Nor-
den, July 13, 1853, and, in 1874, was living in Yonkers, N. Y.

[1698.] 3. THOMAS B., b. Dec. 28, 1832, and, in 1874, was
living in Rye, N. Y.

[1699.] 4. CHARLES A., b. March 10, 1835, and d. unm.,
in New York city, July 25, 1861.

[1700.] 5. JAMES W., b. Nov. 3, 1837, and, in 1864, was
living unm. in New York city.

[1701.] 6. SARAH ELIZABETH, b. May 8, 1840, and, in
1861, was living unm. in New York city.

[1702.] 7. JARED V., b. May 23, 1843, and, in 1861, was
living in New York city.

CHILDREN OF JARED V. PECK (742) AND PHEBE, HIS WIFE.

[1703.] 1. WILLIAM, b. in New York city, Jan. 27, 1857,
and d. there March 25, 1857.

[1704.] 2. LOTTIE M., b. in New York city, Aug. 15, 1861,
and, in 1873, was living in Rye, N. Y.

CHILDREN OF ISAAC PECK (744) AND CATHARINE CORNELIA,
HIS WIFE.

[1709.] 1. CATHARINE SARAH SCHUYLER, b. in New
York city Oct. 1, 1842, and, in 1869, was living in Greenwich,
Conn.

[1710.] 2. SAMUEL JONES, b. in New York city, Jan. 1,
1845, and, in 1869, was living in Greenwich, Conn.

[1711.] 3. ROBERT SCHUYLER, b. in New York city,
Nov. 16, 1846, and d., at Peekskill, N. Y., Sept. 7, 1866.

[1712.] 4. FRANCES REGINA CORNELIA, b. in Greenwich, Conn., June 14, 1857, and was living there in 1869.

ONLY CHILD OF SAMUEL PECK (747) AND ANNA AUGUSTA, HIS WIFE.

[1713.]   ELOISE, b. in Bridgeport, Conn., Sept. 21, 1859, and was living there in 1861.

CHILDREN OF BENJAMIN PECK (752) AND ELIZABETH, HIS WIFE.

[1714.]   1. LAVINA, b. in New York city, April 27, 1835, and d., in Greenwich, Conn., April 23, 1837.

[1715.]   2. ARTHUR, b. in New York city, Dec. 22, 1838, and d., in Greenwich, Conn., Dec. 19, 1842.

[1716.]   3. NATHAN E., b. in Greenwich, Conn., July 26, 1841 ; m. Mary Sarles, of Bedford, N. Y., and, in 1870, was living in Greenwich, Conn.

[1717.]   4. ARTHUR, again, b. in Greenwich, Conn., Nov. 6, 1843, and d., in Greenwich, Conn., March 31, 1845.

CHILDREN OF EBENEZER PECK (754) AND ELIZA R., HIS WIFE, ALL
BORN IN NEW YORK CITY, EXCEPT THE LAST, WHO WAS BORN
IN PERTH AMBOY, N. J., AND ALL, EXCEPT THE FIRST
THREE, LIVING IN PERTH AMBOY, N. J., IN 1861.

[1718.]   1. JAMES R., b. Feb. 26, 1838 ; m. Emma Cooper, in 1860, and was living in New York city, in 1875.

[1719.]   2. CHARLOTTE E , b. Feb. 27, 1840, and d., in New York city, Sept. 9, 1841.

[1720.]   3. EBENEZER, b. Feb. 18, 1842, and d., in New York city, April 2, 1842.

[1721.]   4. CHARLOTTE, again, b. March 6, 1843.

[1722.]   5. SILAS R., b. April 26, 1845.

[1723.]   6. ELIZA A., b. June 14, 1847.

[1724.]   7. SARAH K., b. Dec. 2, 1849.

[1725.]   8. EBENEZER H., b. March 4, 1852.

[1726.]   9. ADELAIDE B., b. Feb. 19, 1855.

[1727.]   10. ALFRED B., b. Oct. 14, 1856.

[1728.]   11. ESTELLE B., b. June 18, 1859.

CHILDREN OF ELIAS PECK (759) AND ELLEN E., HIS WIFE, ALL
BORN IN NEW LONDON, CONN., EXCEPT THE OLDEST,
WHO WAS BORN IN NEW YORK CITY.

[1729.]   l. CHARLES H., b. April 9, 1851, and, in 1861, was living in New York city.

[1730.]   2. WILLIAMINA, b. July 13, 1852 ; m. Selah Young, Jr., of Brooklyn, N. Y., Dec. 28, 1825, she then living in New London, Conn.

[1731.]   3. ELIAS J., b. Dec. 2, 1854, and d., in New London, Conn., March 5, 1855.

[1732.]   4. ELLEN R., b. April 27, 1858, and, in 1861, was living in New London, Conn.

CHILDREN OF ABNER N. PECK, (760) ALL BORN IN NEW YORK CITY.

[1736.]   1. ALBERT M., b. Dec. 29, 1834, and d., in Greenwich, Conn., Dec. 21, 1839.

[1737.]   2. SARAH ANN, b. Nov. 18, 1850, and d., in New York city, Nov. 19, 1850.

[1738.]   3. ANNIE C., b. April 17, 1852, and d., in New York city, June 20, 1753.

[1739.]   4. ALBERT C., b. June 30, 1855, and, in 1861, was living in New York city.

CHILDREN OF WILLIAM PECK (762) AND CAROLINE, HIS WIFE,
ALL BORN IN GREENWICH, CONN.

[1740.]   1. JULIA A., b. Oct. 15, 1839 ; m. Jared Peck, (1638) Jan. 17, 1866, and, in 1867, was living in Greenwich, Conn.

[1741.]   2. ELIAS S., b. Feb. 6, 1842, and, in 1861, was living in Port Chester, N. Y.

[1742.]   3. HARRIET E., b. July 20, 1844, and, in 1861, was living unm. in Greenwich, Conn.

[1743.]   4. OSCAR, b. March 1, 1847, and, in 1861, was living unm. in Greenwich, Conn.

[1744.] 5. JOHN W., b. Oct. 28, 1849, and d., in Greenwich, Conn., July 27, 1850.

[1745.] 6. MARY E., b. Sept. 12, 1851, and, in 1861, was living in Greenwich, Conn.

[1746.] 7. ALBERT M., b. Sept. 19, 1853, and, in 1861, was living in Greenwich, Conn.

CHILDREN OF JOHN PECK (764) AND SARAH N., HIS WIFE.

[1747.] 1. WILLIAM LEWIS, b. in Greenville, Ia., Aug. 17, 1850, and, in 1861, was living at Travers des Sioux, Nicolet Co., Minn.

[1748.] 2. WALTER HYER, b. in Rockville, Ill., Aug. 28, 1853, and, in 1861, was living at Travers des Sioux, Nicolet Co., Minn.

[1749.] 3. HELEN BREMNER, b. in Hoboken, N. J., Dec. 26, 1855, and, in 1861, was living at Travers des Sioux, Nicolet Co., Minn.

CHILDREN OF ABRAHAM H. PECK (765) AND SUSAN, HIS WIFE, ALL BORN IN GREENWICH, CONN.

[1750.] 1. ELIAS R., b. Nov. 12, 1848, and, in 1861, was living in New York city.

[1751.] 2. ADDISON, b. Dec. 22, 1850, and, in 1861, was living in New York city.

[1752.] 3. ELIZABETH R., b. Feb. 9, 1853, and, in 1861, was living in New York city.

CHILDREN OF WILLIAM J. PECK, (771) ALL BORN IN NEW YORK CITY.

[1753.] 1. MARY B., b. March 7, 1845, and, in 1869, was living in New York city.

[1754.] 2. WILLIAM J., b. Dec. 10, 1848, and d., in New York city, June 19, 1852.

[1755.] 3. SYLVANUS G., b. Dec. 30, 1850, and d., in Mamaroneck, N. Y., Dec. 9, 1851.

[1756.]   4. EDWIN H., b. Nov. 8, 1855, and, in 1869, was living in New York city.

[1757.]   5. WALTER L., b. June 6, 1857, and, in 1869, was living in New York city.

[1758.]   6. KATE L., b. Feb. 19, 1859, and, in 1869, was living in New York city.

CHILDREN OF JOSHUA S. PECK (772) AND SARAH, HIS WIFE, ALL BORN IN NEW YORK CITY.

[1759.]   1. NATHAN, b. April 16, 1848 ; m. Ella M. Thacher, May 11, 1870, and was then living in New York city.

[1760.]   2. GEORGE K., b. Dec. 17, 1850, and d., in New York city, June 10, 1855.

[1761.]   3. WILLIAM J., b. Aug. 6, 1853, and, in 1861, was living in New York city.

[1762.]   4. ELLA K., b. Aug. 2, 1857, and, in 1861, was living in New York city.

[1763.]   5. CHARLES B., b. Jan. 9, 1860, and, in 1861, was living in New York city.

CHILDREN OF ELIAS PECK (776) AND CATHARINE ISABELLA, HIS WIFE, ALL BORN IN NEWBURGH, N. Y.

[1764.]   1. THOMAS M., b. Feb. 16, 1835 ; m. Mrs. Mary L. Harris, of Brooklyn, N. Y., Jan. 8, 1873, and was then living in Newburgh, N. Y.

[1765.]   2. ANNIE M., b. July 20, 1836, and, in 1873, was living unm. in New York city.

[1766.]   3. MARTHA E., b. June 12, 1840, and d., in Newburgh, N. Y., Feb. 2, 1843.

[1767.]   4. JOHN E., b. March 4 1844, and, in 1877, was living at Grand Rapids, Mich.

[1768.]   5. CATHARINE A., b. June 4, 1845, and, in 1873, was living unm. in New York city.

CHILDREN OF ISRAEL PECK (782) AND NANCY, HIS WIFE, ALL
BORN IN NEW YORK CITY, EXCEPT ISABELLA G.,
WHO WAS BORN IN SOUTHOLD, N. Y.

[1769.] 1. EMMA LOUISA, b. Aug. 17, 1841; m. J. G.
Hunting, June 23, 1864, and was then living in Southold, N. Y.

[1770.] 2. SARAH ELIZA, b. Nov. 29, 1843, and, in 1861.
was living in Southold, N. Y.

[1771.] 3. ANNA MARIA, b. Jan. 7, 1846, and, in 1861,
was living in Southold, N. Y.

[1772.] 4. CAROLINE MATILDA, b. May 21, 1848, and,
in 1861, was living in Southold, N. Y.

[1773.] 5. ISABELLA G., b. July 17, 1851, and, in 1861,
was living in Southold, N. Y.

[1774.] 6. LUCY ADELAIDE, b. Oct. 31, 1853. and, in
1861, was living in Southold, N. Y.

ONLY CHILD OF NEHEMIAH PECK (785) AND MARY, HIS WIFE.

[1775.] CHARLES A., b. in New York city, Nov. 21, 1847,
and, in 1861, was living in New York, and is said to have
since died there.

CHILDREN OF ALPHEUS PECK (786) AND LOUISA A., HIS WIFE,
BOTH BORN IN NEW YORK CITY.

[1777.] 1. NATHANIEL L., b. July 8, 1852, and d., in
New York city, Jan. 7, 1855.

[1778.] 2. ALPHEUS, b. April 28, 1856, and, in 1861, was
living in New York city.

CHILDREN OF HERMON PECK, (791) ALL BORN AT GLEN'S FALLS, N. Y.

[1779.] 1. DANIEL, b. Feb. 25, 1831; m. Abby Mayo, and,
in 1870, was living at Glen's Falls, N. Y.

[1780.] 2. JANE, b. Dec. 23, 1832; m. Alexander Robinson,
in 1855, and, in 1869, was living at Glen's Falls, N. Y.

[1781.] 3. AMANDA, b. Jan. 14, 1835; m. Meredith B.
Little, and, in 1869, was living at Glen's Falls, N. Y.

[1782.]   4. HARRIET, b. Dec. 25, 1839, and, in 1869, was living unm. at Glen's Falls, N. Y.

[1783.]   5. ASHUR N., b. Aug. 12, 1841, and d. unm., at Glen's Falls, N. Y., March 6, 1869.

[1784.]   6. HENRY, b. April 29, 1848, and, in 1869, was living at Glen's Falls. N. Y.

[1785.]   7. HENRIETTA, b. April 29, 1848, and, in 1869, was living at Glen's Falls, N. Y.

CHILDREN OF WILLIAM PECK (798) AND HANNAH, HIS WIFE, ALL BORN AT GLEN'S FALLS, N. Y.

[1786.]   1. GEORGE N., b. Feb. 26, 1838, and d., at Glen's Falls, N. Y., July 16, 1839.

[1787.]   2. REUBEN N., b. May 3, 1840, and, in 1869, was living at Glen's Falls, N. Y.

[1788.]   3. MARY E., b. Nov. 26, 1842, and, in 1869, was living unm. at Glen's Falls, N. Y.

[1789.]   4. EMMA J., b. Dec. 29, 1847, and, in 1869, was living unm. at Glen's Falls, N. Y.

CHILDREN OF BENJAMIN PECK (801) AND SARAH H., HIS WIFE, ALL BORN AT GLEN'S FALLS, N. Y.

[1790.]   1. JULIA A. b. March 23, 1842, and, in 1869, was living unm. at Queensbury, N. Y.

[1791.]   2. TENTY A., b. Nov. 13, 1848, and, in 1869, was living unm. in Queensbury, N. Y.

[1792.]   3. LYDIA O., b. Aug. 2, 1852, and d., at Glen's Falls, N. Y., Sept. 17, 1852.

CHILDREN OF NATHANIEL S. PECK (802) AND HARRIET, HIS WIFE, BORN IN SPRING TOWNSHIP, PENN.

[1793.]   1. SARAH JANE, b. Dec. 29, 1856, and, in 1870, was living in Spring Township, Penn.

[1794.]   2. HIRAM B., b. Jan. 20, 1859, and, in 1870, was living in Spring Township, Penn.

[1795.] 3. WILLIAM B., b. March 16, 1861, and, in 1870, was living in Spring Township, Penn.

[1796.] 4. LYDIA ANN, b. Jan. 25, 1863, and, in 1870, was living in Spring Township, Penn.

[1797.] 5. JESSE D., b. Feb. 9, 1865, and, in 1870, was living in Spring Township, Penn.

[1798.] 6. FREDERICK C., b. Jan. 17, 1867, and, in 1870, was living in Spring Township, Penn.

[1799.] 7. CHARLES, b. Aug. 10, 1869, and, in 1870, was living in Spring Township, Penn.

CHILDREN OF CHARLES PECK (803) BOTH BORN AT GLEN'S FALLS, N. Y.

[1800.] 1. DANIEL E., b. April 11, 1849, and, in 1869, was living at Glen's Falls, N. Y.

[1801.] 2. CHARLOTTE A., b. July 27, 1857, and, in 1869, was living at Glen's Falls, N. Y.

CHILDREN OF DARIUS PECK (806) AND MARY S., HIS WIFE.

[1802.] 1. SARAH E., b. at Glen's Falls, N. Y., Aug, 2 1830; m. Rev. Horace G. Mason, a Baptist minister, and, in 1869, was living in Meriden, Conn.

[1803.] 2. EDWIN O., b. at Glen's Falls, N. Y., Aug. 22, 1832; m. Sarah Philips, and, in 1869, was living in Morristown, N. J.

[1804.] 3. ELLEN M., b. in Saratoga, N. Y., July 2, 1836, and, in 1869, was liviug unm. in Newark, N. J.

[1805.] 4. NANCY M., b. at Glen's Falls, N. Y., July 3, 1838 ; m. Joseph S. Scofield, and, in 1869, was living in Madison, N. J.

[1806.] 5. GEORGE D., b. at Glen's Falls, N. Y., Aug. 16, 1840, and, in 1869, was living unm. in Newark, N. J.

[1807.] 6. HENRY T., b. at Glen's Falls, N. Y., March 1, 1844, and, in 1869, was living unm. in Newark, N. J.

CHILDREN OF PHILO PECK, (810) ALL BORN IN VAN BUREN, N. Y.

[1808.]   1. ASA B., b. Feb. 8, 1828; m. Mary Waterman, and, in 1875, was living in Van Buren, N. Y.

[1809.]   2. LUCIAN, b. Oct. 25, 1829; m. Ruana Peck, (1811) and, in 1875, was living in Lansing, Mich.

[1810.]   3. HOMER, b. Aug. 12, 1838; m. Helen Fish, and, in 1875, was living in Van Buren, N. Y.

CHILDREN OF ETHAN PECK (815) AND ALMA, HIS WIFE, ALL
BORN IN LANSING, MICH., EXCEPT RUANA, WHO
WAS BORN IN VAN BUREN, N. Y.

[1811.]   1. RUANA, b. May 10, 1842; m. Lucian Peck, (1809) and, in 1870, was living in Lansing, Mich.

[1812.]   2. DeFOREST, b. March 3, 1844, and, in 1870, was living in Lansing, Mich.

[1813.]   3. FLETCHER, b. June 23, 1847, and, in 1870, was living in Lansing, Mich.

[1814.]   4. JANE, b. Feb. 7, 1851, and, in 1870, was living in Lansing, Mich.

[1815.]   5. EMILY, b. April 6, 1853, and, in 1870, was living in Lansing, Mich.

[1816.]   6. LUCIAN, b. March 16, 1855, and, in 1870, was living in Lansing, Mich.

[1817.]   7. RANSEL, b. Oct. 26, 1857, and, in 1870, was living in Lansing, Mich.

[1818.]   8. ELIHU, b. Feb. 10, 1860, and, in 1870, was living in Lansing, Mich.

[1819.]   9. MARY, b Sept. 6, 1862, and, in 1870, was living in Lansing, Mich.

[1820.]   10. ELLEN, b. Jan. 26, 1870, and, in 1870, was living in Lansing, Mich.

CHILDREN OF LYMAN PECK, (817) ALL BORN IN CAMILLUS, N. Y.

[1821.]   1. FRANCES, b April 14, 1848; m. George Green, and, in 1875, was living in Camillus, N. Y.

[1822.] 2. RUANA, b. Oct. 1, 1850; m. Joseph Harvey, and, in 1875, was living in Camillus, N. Y.

[1823.] 3. MARY, b. Aug. 19, 1851; m. Frank Fish, and, in 1870, was living in Syracuse, N. Y.

[1824.] 4. WILLY, b. Aug. 30, 1857, and, in 1875, was living in Camillus, N. Y.

[1825.] 5. NATHAN, b. Oct. 7, 1865, and, in 1875, was living in Camillus, N. Y

CHILDREN OF ELIHU PECK (818) AND AGNES, HIS WIFE.

[1826.] 1. JANE A., b. in Camillus, N. Y., April 25, 1850, and, in 1875, was living unm. in Lansing, Mich.

[1827.] 2. EMMA LOUISE, b. in Camillus, N. Y., Nov. 30, 1853, and, in 1875, was living unm. in Lansing, Mich.

[1828.] 3. FLORA ISADORE, b. in Delta, Mich., Feb. 10, 1857, and, in 1875, was living unm. in Lansing, Mich.

ONLY CHILD OF DANIEL PECK (822) AND BETSEY, HIS WIFE, BORN IN VAN BUREN, N. Y.

[1829.] EUNICE, b. in 1855, and, in 1875, was living in Van Buren, N. Y.

CHILDREN OF WILLIAM PECK (823) AND MATILDA, HIS WIFE, BORN IN VAN BUREN, N. Y.

[1830.] 1. TAMMY E., b. Nov. 29, 1855, and, in 1875, was living in Van Buren, N. Y.

[1831.] 2. WILLIE A., b. March 27, 1859, and, in 1875, was living in Van Buren, N. Y.

[1832.] 3. JAMES L., b. Aug. 24, 1861, and, in 1875, was living in Van Buren, N. Y.

[1833.] 4. WILBUR H., b. June 18, 1863, and, in 1875, was living in Van Buren, N. Y.

[1834.] 5. LeROY J., b. May 16, 1865, and, in 1875, was living in Van Buren, N. Y.

[1835.]   6. JOHN P., b. Dec. 3, 1867, and, in 1875, was living in Van Buren, N. Y.

[1836.]   7. GEORGE H , b. Sept. 27, 1869, and, in 1875, was living in Van Buren, N. Y.

ONLY CHILD OF ISAAC PECK (824) AND TAMMY, HIS WIFE.

[1837.]   ANNIE L., b. in Camillus, N. Y., June 11, 1845; m. Ransen Gardenier, and, in 1876, was living in Valatie, N. Y.

CHILDREN OF AARON PECK (825) AND CAROLINE, HIS WIFE, ALL BORN IN CAMILLUS, N. Y.

[1838.]   1. MARTHA L., b. April 13, 1846; m. James M. Ellis, and, in 1875, was living in Elbridge, N. Y.

[1839.]   2. HELEN I., b. May 13, 1848; m. Ira Hinsdale, and, in 1870, was living in Sedalia, Mo.

[1840.]   3. CHARLES H., b. Sept. 14, 1858, and, in 1875, was living in Camillus, N. Y

CHILDREN OF EDWIN PECK (827) AND SARAH, HIS WIFE, ALL BORN IN CAMILLUS, N. Y.

[1841.]   1. WILLIE M., b. Aug. 22, 1850, and d., in Camillus, N. Y., Aug. 21, 1869.

[1842.]   2. MARY A., b. June 2, 1856, and, in 1875, was living in Camillus, N. Y.

[1843.]   3. JANE H., b. Oct. 18, 1858, and, in 1875, was living in Camillus, N. Y.

CHILDREN OF RICHARD PECK (828) AND MARY, HIS WIFE, ALL BORN IN VAN BUREN, N. Y.

[1844.]   1. ALBERT A., b. Jan. 6, 1843; m. Ursula Brown, Aug. 3, 1869, and, in 1870, was living in Tioga County, N. Y.

[1845.]   2. ISAAC V., b. Aug. 3, 1845, and, in 1870, was living in Van Buren, N. Y.

[1846.]   3. JAMES H., b. Aug. 11, 1847, and, in 1870, was living in Van Buren, N. Y.

[1847.]   4. EMMA JANE, b. Sept. 7, 1849, and, in 1870, was living in Van Buren, N. Y.

[1848.]   5. NATHANIEL, b. Feb. 8, 1852, and, in 1870, was living in Van Buren, N. Y.

[1849.]   6. HATTIE, b. April 7, 1856, and, in 1770, was living in Van Buren, N. Y.

[1850.]   7. LUCY M., b. June 6, 1858, and, in 1870, was living in Van Buren, N. Y.

CHILDREN OF LEONARD PECK (829) AND SUSAN, HIS WIFE.

[1851.]   1. LeROY S., b. in Camillus, N. Y., March 17, 1848, and, in 1875, was living in Groton, N. Y.

[1852.]   2. ADDISON, b. in Groton, N. Y., Sept. 29, 1851, and, in 1875, was living in Groton, N. Y.

[1853.]   3. GEORGE, b. in Groton, N. Y., March 22, 1854, and, in 1875, was living in Groton, N. Y.

CHILDREN OF ENOS PECK (830) AND ESTHER, HIS WIFE, BOTH BORN IN VAN BUREN, N. Y.

[1854.]   1. LEWIS, b. in 1853, and, in 1875, was living in Camillus, N. Y.

[1855.]   IDA M., b. in 1858, and, in 1875, was living in Camillus, N. Y.

CHILDREN OF HORACE PECK, (834) ALL BORN IN THE STATE OF MICHIGNA.

[1856.]   1. MARY F., b. in 1857, and, in 1870, was living in the State of Michigan.

[1857.]   2. ISAAC H., b. in 1859, and, in 1870, was living in the State of Michigan.

[1858.]   3. LAURA J., b. in 1862, and, in 1870, was living in the State of Michigan.

CHILDREN OF ROBERT PECK (845) AND SARAH ELIZABETH, HIS WIFE, ALL BORN IN GREENWICH, CONN.

[1859.]   1. LAVINA, b. Sept. 16, 1818, and d., in Greenwich, Conn., Sept. 15, 1820.

[1860.] 2. WILLIAM ROBERT, b. Dec. 25, 1820, and d., in Greenwich, Conn., Aug. 9, 1835.

[1861.] 3. ZUCKNER M., b. Feb. 9, 1823, and d., in Greenwich, Conn., March 13, 1824.

[1862.] 4. RUTH M., b. Feb. 14, 1825 ; m. Humphrey Denton, of Greenwich, Conn., Nov. 3, 1845, and d., in Greenwich, Jan. 7, 1857.

[1863.] 5. EMILY ANN, b. Feb. 25, 1827, and d., in Greenwich, Conn., Oct. 25, 1831.

[1864.] 6. JOSEPH A., b. June 5, 1830 ; m. Sarah Jane Guernsey, Nov. 28, 1853, and d., in Greenwich, Conn.

CHILDREN OF WILSON PECK (847) AND PHEBE, HIS WIFE.

[1865.] 1. CHARLES W., b. in Canton, Ill., Nov. 12, 1845, and, in 1872, was m. and living in the State of Kansas.

[1866.] 2. BENJAMIN W., b. in Vermont, Ill., May 20, 1850, and, in 1872, was living in the State of Kansas.

[1867.] 3. MARY A., b. in Astoria, Ill., Sept. 5, 1851, and, in 1872, was living in Henry, Ill.

[1868.] 4. ALBERT, b. in Astoria, Ill., Jan. 12, 1854, and d. there Feb. 29, 1856.

[1869.] 5. ELISHA R., b. in Astoria, Ill., April 25, 1857, and, in 1861, was living in Astoria, Ill.

[1870.] 6. WILLIAM, b. in Astoria, Ill., June 4, 1860, and, in 1872, was living in Henry, Ill.

[1871.] 7. WILLETTE, b. in Astoria, Ill., June 4, 1860, and, in 1872, was living in Henry, Ill.

CHILDREN OF ELIAS REED PECK AND EUNICE, HIS WIFE.

[1872.] 1. MARGARET ANN E., b. in Canton, Ill., March 11, 1841 ; m. Samuel H. Wright, Feb. 21, 1861, and d., in Wyoming Territory, May 4, 1873.

[1873.] 2. SAMUEL M., b. in Canton, Ill., Aug. 28, 1842 ; m. Amelia A. Drake, Oct. 14, 1863.

[1874.]   3. EUNICE L., b. in Canton, Ill., Sept. 27, 1844; m. Robert J. Wagoner, Jan. 20, 1872.

[1875.]   4. MARY JANE M., b. in Canton, Ill., March 3, 1847, and d. there March 28, 1847.

[1876.]   5. AMANDA C., b. in Canton, Ill., Jan. 28, 1849, and d. there Feb. 20, 1850.

[1877.]   6. MARY JANE M., again, b. in Canton, Ill., Jan. 28, 1849, and, in 1874, was living in Prairie City, Iowa.

[1878.]   7. THOMAS J. L., b. in Canton, Ill., Jan. 20, 1851, and d. there Nov. 1, 1851.

[1879.]   8. THOMAS J. L., again, b. in Canton, Ill., Sept. 28, 1852, and, in 1874, was living in Prairie City, Iowa.

[1880.]   9. DELIA A., b. in Mound Prairie, Iowa, Jan. 19, 1856, and, in 1874, was living in Prairie City, Iowa.

[1881.]   10. MALVINA A., b. in Mound Prairie, Iowa, Dec. 3, 1859, and, in 1874, was living in Prairie City, Iowa.

[1882.]   11. SALINA CAROLINE, b. in Prairie City, June 23, 1863, and was living there in 1874.

CHILD OF JONATHAN PECK (850) AND FRANCES S., HIS WIFE.

[1882.]   ELLA, b. and said to have d. six months after her birth, in LaSalle, Ill.

CHILDREN OF JOSEPHUS PECK (852) AND AMY JANE, HIS WIFE, THE OLDEST BORN IN BEDFORD, N. Y., AND THE OTHERS IN STAMFORD, CONN.

[1883.]   1. HENRIETTA D., b. May 22, 1849; m. John F. Jackson, Jan. 29, 1868, and d., in Stamford, April 24, 1873.

[1884.]   2. PHEBE ANN, b. Feb. 26, 1852, and, in 1869, was living in Stamford, Conn.

[1885.]   3. JULIA, b. Jan. 15, 1854, and, in 1869, was living in Stamford, Conn.

[1886.]   4. SAMUEL W., b. July 23, 1857, and, in 1869, was living in Stamford, Conn.

[1887.]   5. MARY, b. Aug. 18, 1859, and, in 1869. was living in Stamford, Conn.

CHILDREN OF WILLIAM R. PECK (854) AND LUCRETIA LOUISA, HIS WIFE.

[1888.] 1. SARAH L., b. in Hyde Park, N. Y., March 23, 1833, and d., in Bowling Green, O., May 10, 1848.

[1889.] 2. MARY L., b. in Miltonville, O., July 10, 1836, and, in 1870, was living unm. in Ellsworth, Conn.

[1890.] 3. FRANCES E., b. in Miltonville, O., Feb. 13, 1839, and d., in Bowling Green, O., Aug. 30, 1842.

[1891.] 4. EMMA C., b. in Bowling Green, O., Oct. 14, 1841, and d. there Aug. 9, 1844.

[1892.] 5. LEWIS WILLIAM, b. in Bowling Green, O., Oct. 5, 1843, and d. there June 28, 1844.

[1893.] 6. FREDERICK WILLIAM, b. in Bowling Green, O., April 9, 1845, and d., in Cincinnati, O., Jan. 30, 1864.

CHILDREN OF CALVIN F. PECK (856) AND MARY L., HIS WIFE, BOTH BORN IN SHARON, CONN.

[1894.] 1. GEORGE H., b. Aug. 12, 1846, and, in 1870, was living unm. in Sharon, Conn.

[1895.] 2. ALBERT L., b. Nov. 20, 1849, and d., in Sharon, Conn., Sept. 29, 1861.

CHILDREN OF CHARLES H. PECK (858) AND FANNIE M., HIS WIFE.

[1896.] 1. LEWIS, b. in Camden, S. C., May 8, 1854, and, in 1870, was living in Ellsworth, Conn.

[1897.] 2. WILLIAM, b. in Camden, S. C., Sept. 3, 1856, and, in 1870, was living in Clarksville, N. Y.

[1898.] 3. JAMES B. C., b. in Albany, N. Y, in April, 1859, and d., in Camden, S. C., in Jan. 1860.

CHILDREN OF EDMOND PECK (864) AND CHARLOTTE A., HIS WIFE.

[1899.] 1. CHARLOTTE A., b. in Sharon, Conn., June 14, 1857, and d. there Dec. 31, 1872.

[1900.] 2. MARY E., b. in Sharon, Conn., Nov. 3, 1863, and, in 1870, was living in West Haven, Conn.

[1901.] 3. LAURA B., b. in Sharon, Conn., Aug. 6, 1867 and, in 1870, was living in West Haven, Conn.

CHILD OF SANFORD PECK (866) AND EMILY, HIS WIFE.

[1902.] 1. GEORGE W., b. in Woodbury, Conn., Feb. 8 1854, and was living in Bethlem, Conn.

CHILDREN OF WILLIAM PECK (867) AND MARY ANN, HIS WIFE, ALL BORN IN CHESHIRE, CONN.

[1903.] 1. MATILDA, b. Oct. 14, 1815 ; m. Lambert Sanford, Sept. 12, 1838, and, in 1861, was living in Windsor, N. Y.

[1904.] 2. WILLIAM, b. Nov. 10, 1819 ; m. Maria Louisa Smith, and, in 1861, was living in Southington, Conn.

[1905.] 3. MARY ANN, b. April 11, 1824 ; m. Hiram A. Peck, (1921) March 25, 1850, and, in 1861, was living in Cheshire, Conn.

CHILDREN OF BURTON PECK (872) AND CAROLINE, HIS WIFE.

[1906.] 1. ELLA, b. in Cheshire, Conn., June 29, 1825, and d. unm., in Burton, O., Oct. 4, 1841.

[1907.] 2. CELIA, b. in Canton, N. Y., July 16, 1828 ; m. Merriman Barnes, April 1, 1850, and, in 1861, was living in Troy, O.

[1908.] 3. JOEL, b. in Canton, N. Y., Aug. 26, 1829, and d., in Canton, N. Y., Aug. 28, 1831.

[1909.] 4. JOHN, b. in Canton, N. Y., May 13, 1831; m. Lois Manly, May 8, 1852, and, in 1861, was living in Madison, O.

[1910.] 5. LAURA M., b. in Burton, O., Feb. 9, 1834 ; m. Uzziel Balch, who d. July 7, 1861, and she was then living in Concord, O.

[1911.] 6. WILLIAM H., b. in Burton, O., Aug. 7, 1837 ; m. Aloiza Haines, April 3, 1860 ; was 1st Lieutenant in the war of the Rebellion, and then resided in Illinois.

[1912.] 7. CATHARINE, b. in Burton, O., Dec. 13, 1839, and d. there May 7, 1841.

[1913.] 8. NELSON E. b. in Burton, O., March 29, 1841; was in service in the war of the Rebellion, and then resided in Illinois.

[1914.] 9. ANN, b. in Burton, O., April 29, 1842, and, in 1861, was living unm. in Chardon, O.

[1915.] 10. MARIANNE, b. in Munson, O., July 3, 1849, and, in 1861, was living in Burton, O.

CHILDREN OF CLEMENT PECK (873) AND DAMARIS, HIS WIFE, ALL BORN IN CHESHIRE, CONN.

[1916.] 1. CECILIA NANCY, b. Aug. 8, 1815; m. Alfred S. Baldwin, Oct. 4, 1860, and d., in Cheshire, Conn., Jan. 9, 1847.

[1917.] 2. ELIZABETH ANN, b. June 12, 1817; m. George D. Allen, June 3, 1842, and d., in Cheshire, Conn., Jan. 18, 1852.

[1918.] 3. CLEMENT A., b. May 24, 1821; m. Sarah Norton, and, in 1861, was living in Cheshire, Conn.

[1919.] 4. CHARLOTTE M., b. Nov. 22, 1825, and d., in Cheshire, Conn., Oct. 10, 1834.

[1920.] 5. MARY A., b. Jan. 1, 1831, and, in 1861, was living unm. in Cheshire, Conn.

CHILDREN OF CHAUNCEY PECK, (874) ALL BORN IN CHESHIRE, CONNECTICUT.

[1921.] 1. HIRAM A., b. Sept. 16, 1821; m. Mary Ann Peck, (1905) March 25, 1850, and, in 1861, was living in Cheshire, Conn.

[1922.] 2. SARAH R., b. April 17, 1824; m. Jesse Hall, of Waterbury, Conn., Nov. 26, 1848, and was living there in 1861.

[1923.] 3. JOSEPH C., b. Dec. 20, 1831; m. —— Prichard, of Waterbury, Conn., and was living there in 1861.

[1924.] 4. LAURA M., b. Dec. 20, 1831, and d., in Cheshire, Conn., Nov. 17, 1835.

CHILDREN OF ASA PECK, (875) ALL BORN IN LOUDON COUNTY, VA.

[1925.] 1. CLEMENT A., b. Sept. 14, 1823 ; m. Mary Jane Saunders, Dec. 18, 1849, who d. March 17, 1858, and, in 1861, was living in Georgetown, D. C.

[1926.] 2. JOHN ASA, b. April 10, 1825, and d., in Leesburgh, Va., Sept. 16, 1831.

[1927.] 3. EDWIN, b. March 23, 1826, and d., in Leesburgh, Va., Sept. 16, 1831.

[1928.] 4. MARY E., b. Oct. 29, 1827 ; m. Lewis L. Wilkinson, Jan. 15, 1856, and, in 1861, was living in Georgetown, D. C.

[1929.] 5. JULIUS J., b. May 28, 1829 ; m. Amanda W. Temple, Feb. 1, 1853, and, in 1861, was living in Fairfax Co., Virginia.

[1930.] 6. CHARLES T., b. Oct. 15, 1830, and, in 1861, was living unm. in Loudon Co., Va.

[1931.] 7. ASA JAMES, b. Jan. 1, 1833, and, in 1861, was living in Fairfax Co., Va.

[1932.] 8. AMELIA P., b. Jan. 1, 1833, and d. in Leesburgh, Va., Oct. 3, 1833.

CHILDREN OF JOHN PECK, (877) ALL BORN IN CHESHIRE, CONN.

[1933.] 1. STELLA T., b. Aug. 15, 1823, and d., in Cheshire, Conn., Sept. 6, 1829.

[1934.] 2. ANN ELIZA, b. Feb. 21, 1825 ; m. Titus Ives, Jan. 1, 1857, and, in 1861, was living in Cheshire, Conn.

[1935.] 3. JOHN A., b. March 12, 1836, and, in 1861, was living unm. in Cheshire, Conn.

[1936.] 4. MARY E., b. Nov. 24, 1839, and, in 1861, was living unm. in Cheshire, Conn.

CHILDREN OF JUSTUS PECK, (880.)

[1937.] 1. HARRY F., b. in Cheshire, Conn., Jan. 25, 1840, and d., in Cheshire, Conn., June 4, 1842.

[1938.] 2. MARIETTA J., b. in Cheshire, Conn., May 27, 1841, and, in 1861, was living in Bethany, Conn.

[1939.] 3. HARRY F., again, b. in Bethany, Conn., Aug. 5, 1843, and, in 1861. was living in Bethany, Conn.

[1940.] 4. CHARLOTTE F., b. in Bethany, Conn., Nov. 12, 1845, and, in 1861, was living in Bethany, Conn.

CHILDREN OF GEORGE PECK (882) AND LYDIA, HIS WIFE, ALL BORN IN CHESHIRE, CONN

[1941.] 1. GEORGE, b. July 7, 1824 ; m. Charlotte Blakesley, April 11, 1849, and, in 1861, was living in Cheshire, Conn.

[1942.] 2. BENJAMIN, b. July 11, 1830 ; m. Eliza Ann Hubbel, Feb. 26, 1861, and was then living in Cheshire, Conn.

[1943.] 3. LYDIA, b. Aug. 8, 1834, and, in 1861, was living unm. in Cheshire, Conn.

[1944.] 4. LEVI, b. Sept. 4, 1837 ; m. Celestia Hubbel, Jan. 19, 1860, and, in 1861, was living in Cheshire, Conn.

[1945.] 5. ESTHER, b. Oct. 15, 1840, and, in 1861, was living unm. in Cheshire, Conn.

CHILDREN OF LEVI PECK (883) AND ESTHER LAVINIA, HIS WIFE, ALL BORN IN CHESHIRE, CONN.

[1946.] 1. LEVI N., b. Aug. 28, 1837, and d., in East Haven, Conn., in Dec. 1860.

[1947.] 2. ESTHER L., b. Aug. 16, 1842, and d., in Cheshire, Conn., Oct. 11, 1849.

[1948.] 3. BIRDSEYE D. W., b. June 26, 1845, and d., in Cheshire, Conn., Sept. 7, 1859.

[1949.] 4. EDWARD, b. Aug. 27, 1847, and d., in Cheshire, Conn., Sept. 11, 1849.

[1950.] 5. BIRDSEYE, again, b. May 27, 1849, and, in 1861, was living unm. in East Haven, Conn.

[1951.] 6. EDWARD, again, b. Jan. 17, 1852, and d., in East Haven, Conn., May 31, 1859.

[1952.] 7. CLARENCE, b. in 1854, and d., in East Haven, Conn., Feb. 16, 1858.

CHILDREN OF EDWARD PECK (885) AND PERSIS S., HIS WIFE.

[1953.] 1. S. EUGENE, b. ın Wyoming, N. Y., Dec. 20, 1838.

[1954.] 2. ELLA M., b. in Wyoming, N. Y., Dec. 13, 1840, and d. there Feb. 23, 1842.

[1955.] 3. EDWARD S., b. in Wyoming, N. Y., Nov. 3, 1842.

[1956.] 4. EMILY A., b. in Clinton, Mich., Aug. 19, 1844.

[1957.] 5. PHINEAS C., b. in Clinton, Mich., June 17, 1846, and d., in Napoleon, Mich. Aug. 9, 1848.

[1958.] 6. FLORA J., b. in Napoleon, Mich., Jan. 9, 1849.

[1959.] 7. PHINEAS P., b. in Napoleon, Oct. 7, 1851.

CHILDREN OF SAMUEL B. PECK (886) AND DENCY, HIS WIFE.

[1960.] 1. AMBROSIA J., b. in Covington, N. Y., July 3, 1834; m. Samuel R. Sanford, July 7, 1858.

[1961.] 2. MELLECENT M., b. in Covington, N. Y., Oct. 22, 1835.

[1962.] 3. CORNELIA N., b. in Gorham, N. Y., Aug. 22, 1845, and d. there Dec. 15, 1852.

CHILDREN OF ENOS T. PECK (888) AND HENRIETTA, HIS WIFE, ALL BORN IN DOVER, N. J.

[1963.] 1. JOSEPHINE E., b. May 20, 1836; m. Hiram B. Fargo, Dec. 20, 1861.

[1964.] 2. SOLON L., b. Dec. 5, 1838.

[1965.] 3. HELEN M., b. Oct. 15, 1839.

[1966.] 4. M. IMOGENE, b. Oct. 17, 1844.

[1967.] 5. WHITFIELD H., b. May 16, 1846.

[1968.] 6. EMERSON, b. July 5, 1848.

CHILD OF FREDERICK B. PECK (892) AND SARAH, HIS WIFE.

[1969.] FREDERICK L., b. in Orleans, N. Y., April 2, 1852.

CHILDREN OF FRANK S. PECK (893) AND CAROLINE, HIS WIFE, BORN IN GREENVILLE, MICH.

[1970.]   1. EDWARD W., b. Sept. 4, 1859.

[1971.]   2. EMILY C., b. Oct. 27, 1861.

CHILDREN OF JOHN A. PECK (894) AND IMOGENE L., HIS WIFE.

[1972.]   1. WILLIAM S., b. in Greenville, Mich., July 18, 1858.

[1973.]   2. HARRIET M., b. in Muskegon, Mich., March 29, 1861.

CHILDREN OF CHARLES PECK (898) AND SARAH, HIS WIFE, ALL BORN IN LEXINGTON, NOW JEWETT, N. Y., EXCEPT WILLIAM AND GEORGE, WHO WERE BORN IN HUNTER, N. Y.

[1974.]   1. ALFRED, b. Dec. 22, 1814 ; m. 1. Jane Peck (931) ; m. 2. Lydia B. Peck (932), and, in 1875, was living in Great Barrington, Mass.

[1975.]   2. HENRY G., b. March 16, 1817, and d., in Lexington, now Jewett, N. Y., Nov. 17, 1817.

[1976.]   3. CATHARINE, b. Oct. 13, 1818 ; m. Benjamin Jones, and, in 1876, was living in Jewett, N. Y.

[1977.]   4. MARY, b. Feb. 23, 1821 ; m. Munson Peck (933), and, in 1875, was living in Great Barrington, Mass.

[1978.]   5. HENRY, b. Feb. 26, 1823 ; m. Julia North, and, in 1875, was living at Malad City, Idaho Territory.

[1979.]   6. SARAH, b. April 3, 1825, and d. unm., in Jewett, N. Y., Sept. 13, 1843.

[1980.]   7. ELIAS F., b. June 4, 1827 ; m. Adeline Peck (2035), and, in 1870, was living in Great Barrington, Mass.

[1981.]   8. LUCINDA, b. Sept. 11, 1829, and, in 1870, was living unm. in Great Barrington, Mass.

[1982.]   9. WILLIAM, b. July 16, 1831 ; m. Sarah Johnson, and, in 1870, was living in English Neighborhood, N. J.

[1983.]   10. CHARLES D., b. Nov. 18, 1833 ; m. Sidney Davis, May 15, 1866, and, in 1870, was living in Pueblo. Colorado.

[1984.]   11. GEORGE, b. Feb. 2, 1836 ; m. Rosette E. Rice, March 13, 1866, and, in 1875, was living at Pueblo, Colorado.

[1985.]   12. WALTER B., b. Oct. 23, 1838 ; m. Ellen Rice, and, in 1870, was living at South Egremont, Mass.

CHILDREN OF JOEL PECK, (899) ALL BORN IN LEXINGTON, NOW JEWETT, N. Y.

[1986.]   1. SETH, b. Sept. 20, 1812, and d. unm., in Rome, N. Y., Nov. 1, 1839.

[1987.]   2. ELIZABETH, b. May 1, 1816 ; m. Ira Smalling, and, in 1874, was living at or in the vicinity of Jaynesville Iowa.

[1988.]   3. JULIUS, b. Nov. 1, 1817 ; m. Amanda Whittaker, and, in 1874, was living at or in the vicinity of Jaynesville, Iowa.

[1989.]   4. HARRIET, b. March 10, 1820 ; m. William Smith, and, in 1874, was living at or in the vicinity of Jaynesville, Iowa.

[1990.]   5. MILO, b. Sept. 12, 1824 ; m. Maria Saunders, and d., in Lockport, N. Y., in 1864 or 1865.

[1991.]   6. EUNICE, b. Oct. 11, 1826, and d., in Jewett, N. Y., in 1829.

[1992.]   7. ORINDA, b. Nov. 16, 1828, and d. unm. in Belleville, Wis., Feb. 4, 1858.

[1993.] ˙ 8. HELEN, b. Nov, 13, 1834, and d., in Windham, N. Y., Nov. 7, 1837.

[1994.]   9. HARRISON, b. Dec. 24, 1836 ; m. Jane Carr, and, in 1866, was living in Metropolis City, Ill.

CHILDREN OF CHAUNCEY PECK (902) AND MINERVA, HIS WIFE, ALL BORN IN LEXINGTON, NOW JEWETT, N. Y.

[1995.]   1. EVELINE, b. Oct. 25, 1818 ; m. Edward Holaday, Feb. 23, 1842, and, in 1870, was living in Rockland, N. Y.

[1996.]   2. VOLUTIA, b. July 28, 1820 ; m. Calvin Wood, Feb. 24, 1846, and, in 1870, was living in Margaretville, N. Y.

[1997.] 3. HENRY, b. Jan. 17, 1823, and d., in Lexington, now Jewett, N. Y., Jan. 31, 1823.

[1998.] 4. LUCY L., b. Feb. 9, 1824; m. Robert Sheely, Sept. 20, 1846, and, in 1861, was living in Rockland, N. Y.

[1999.] 5. ORLANDO, b. July 23, 1826, and d., in Lexington, now Jewett, N. Y., Oct. 17, 1827.

[2000.] 6. SAMUEL, b. Dec. 11, 1829 ; m. Nancy Gage, Jan. 17, 1861, and, in 1875, was living in Colchester, N. Y.

[2001.] 7. CHAUNCEY, b. Sept. 26, 1832 ; m. Arametta Kimball, Jan. 14, 1858, and, in 1870, was living in Rockland, N. Y.

CHILDREN OF JOHN PECK (907) AND JANE, HIS WIFE, ALL BORN IN LEXINGTON, NOW JEWETT, N. Y.

[2002.] 1. HENRY H., b. May 13, 1834; m. Julia A. North, and, in 1875, was living in Sheffield, Mass.

[2003.] 2. MYRA, b. Nov. 3, 1836 ; m. Egbert Bogert, Feb. 18, 1863, and, in 1876, was living in Catskill, N. Y.

[2004.] 3. PHILO, b. May 11, 1841 ; m. Frances Crapsey, and, in 1876, was living at Palenville, Greene Co., N. Y.

CHILDREN OF IRA PECK (911) AND PENELOPE, HIS WIFE, ALL BORN IN MARION, GA., EXCEPT HENRY K. AND EMELINE, WHO WERE BORN IN ASHFORD, CONN.

[2005.] 1. HENRY K., b. May 12, 1824; m. Frances B. Johnson, Oct. 31, 1867, and, in 1875, was living in Cornwall, N. Y.

[2006.] 2. JOHN, b. Oct. 17, 1825, and d., in Marion, Ga., Nov. 14, 1825.

[2007.] 3. CORNELIA C., b. Aug. 24, 1827, and, in 1875, was living unm. in Hartford, Conn.

[2008.] 4. EMELINE A., b. Oct. 16, 1829, and d., in Marion, Ga., July 4, 1831.

[2009.] 5. IRA H., b. April 16, 1832, and, in 1875, was living unm. in Hartford, Conn.

[2010.] 6. MARY J., b. March 25, 1834 ; m. in Paris, France, Giovanni Danesi, an Italian, Jan. 14, 1873, and, in 1875, was living at Nice, France.

[2011.] 7. WILLIAM H., b. March 14, 1836, and d., in Marion, Ga., July 6, 1837.

[2012.] 8. WILLIAM H., again, b. April 19, 1838 ; m. Georgia C. Roberts, Dec. 11, 1862, and, in 1875, was living in Hartford, Conn.

[2013.] 9. CAROLINE, b. Oct. 4, 1840 ; m. Henry A. Redfield, May 20, 1862, and, in 1875, was living in Hartford, Conn.

CHILDREN OF GEORGE PECK (912) AND PERMELIA, HIS WIFE, ALL BORN IN FARMINGTON, CONN.

[2014.] 1. JOHN C., b. Jan. 11, 1816 ; m. 1. Mary J. Gray, and m. 2. Irene Bevins, and, in 1875, was living in Hillsdale, Mich.

[2015.] 2. EUNICE H., b. Aug. 3, 1820 ; m. Shubael Thompson, Feb. 12, 1846, and, in 1875, was living in West Avon, Conn.

[2016.] 3. GEORGE C., b. Feb. 4, 1824, and d. unm. in Farmington, Conn., Oct. 16, 1843.

[2017.] 4. JULIUS B., b. April 4, 1830, and d., in Hillsdale, Mich., Oct. 24, 1873.

CHILDREN OF CALEB PECK (913) AND LUCY, HIS WIFE, BOTH BORN IN SOUTHINGTON, CONN.

[2018.] 1. IRA, b. March 23, 1818, and, in 1874, was living in Southington, Conn.

[2019.] 2. SOPHIA, b. April 11, 1821 ; m. Henry Hart, Aug. 25, 1842, and d. in Southington, Conn.

CHILDREN OF CHAUNCEY PECK (916) AND LURA, HIS WIFE.

[2020.] 1. JOHN L., b. in Hunter, N. Y., Aug. 29, 1825, and d. unm. in Malden, N. Y., Aug. 15, 1855.

[2021.]   2. ADELINE, b. in Hunter, N. Y., Dec. 3, 1827, and d., in Hunter, N. Y., Aug. 1, 1829.

[2022.]   3. CHAUNCEY M., b. in Hunter, N. Y., Dec. 13, 1829, and, in 1870, was living unm. in Windham, N. Y.

[2023.]   4. AUGUSTA, b. in Thompson, N. Y., Nov. 1, 1833, and, in 1870, was living unm. in Windham, N. Y.

[2024.]   5. MARK, b. in Lexington, now Jewett, N. Y., May 3, 1836, and d. there April 16, 1837.

[2025.]   6. LINUS, b. in Lexington, now Jewett, N. Y., Jan. 13, 1838, and, in 1861, was living unm. in Windham, N. Y.

[2026.]   7. ADELAIDE B., b. in Lexington, now Jewett, N. Y., Oct. 15, 1840, and d. there March 16, 1854.

CHILDREN OF JOEL PECK (920) AND ANN E., HIS WIFE, BOTH
BORN IN WALLINGFORD, CONN.

[2027.]   1. SARAH .E., b. Oct. 7, 1842 ; m. Leonard Bishop, July 27, 1870, and, in 1875, was living in New Haven, Conn.

[2028.]   2. SAMUEL WILLIAM, b. Jan. 17, 1847, and, in 1875, was living in Wallingford, Conn.

CHILDREN OF SAMUEL PECK (922) AND ELIZA, HIS WIFE, BOTH
BORN IN WALLINGFORD, CONN. ·

[2029.]   1. ELLEN M., b. Nov. 3, 1850; m. Samuel Gilbert, June 15, 1875, and, in 1875, was living in New Haven, Conn.

[2030.]   2. ANNIE E., b. March 4, 1854, and, in 1875, was living in Wallingford, Conn.

CHILDREN OF ORIN PECK, (926) ALL BORN IN LEXINGTON, NOW
JEWETT, N. Y.

[2030.]   1. HARRIET D., b. May 15, 1825, and, in 1861, was living unm. in Harpersfield, N. Y.

[2031.]   2. PERMELIA, b. Oct. 28, 1827 ; m. William H. Sloat, and, in 1870, was living in Hobart, N. Y.

[2032.]   3. NEWTON G., b. Sept. 27, 1832 : m. Elizabeth Hubbard, and, in 1870, was living in Harpersfield, N. Y.

[2033.] 4. MEHITABLE A., b. June 15, 1834 ; m. Nicholas Mickle, and, in 1861, was living in Davenport, N. Y.

[2034.] 5. AMOS E., b. June 10, 1838, and, in 1861, was living unm. in Harpersfield, N. Y.

CHILDREN OF LEVI PECK (927) AND MARY, HIS WIFE, ALL BORN IN LEXINGTON, NOW JEWETT, N. Y.

[2035.] 1. ADELINE, b. March 13, 1829 ; m. Elias F. Peck. (1980) and, in 1870, was living in Great Barrington, Mass.

[2036.] 2. LUCINDA C., b. May 12, 1831, and, in 1876, was living unm. in Jewett, N. Y.

[2037.] 3. ELLEN J., b. May 11, 1833 ; m. Benjamin Barclay, and, in 1876, was living in Jewett, N. Y.

[2038.] 4. LYDIA A., b. Aug. 30, 1837 ; m. Alfred Edwards, May 1, 1866, and d. in Windham, N. Y.

[2039.] 5. CICERO C., b. Jan. 25, 1840 ; is a lawyer, and, in 1876, was living in Windham, N. Y.

[2040.] 6. EDGAR L., b. Feb. 15, 1848, and, in 1866, was living unm. in Jewett, N. Y.

CHILDREN OF CHARLES B. PECK (930) AND STATA, HIS WIFE, ALL BORN IN LEXINGTON, NOW JEWETT, N. Y.

[2041.] 1. OLIVER C., b. June 21, 1836 ; m. Luan Barkley, and, in 1876, was living in Jewett, N. Y.

[2042.] 2. LYMAN P., b. May 13, 1838 ; was in the U. S. Army in the war of the Rebellion, and d., in Falmouth, Va., Jan. 14, 1863.

[2043.] 3. GEORGE W., b. July 25, 1840 ; was in the U. S. Army in the war of the Rebellion, and d., at Key West, Oct. 16, 1862.

[2044.] 4. CATHARINE, b. Feb. 13, 1843 ; m. Newell Morse, and, in 1875, was living in Jewett, N. Y.

[2045.] 5. MARIA S., b. Nov. 1, 1845 ; m. George Rice, Dec. 25, 1865, and, in 1876, was living in Jewett, N. Y.

[2046.] 6. BRAINARD O., b. Nov. 4, 1848, and, in 1876, was living in Jewett, N. Y.

[2047.] 7. HORACE H., b. July 23, 1852, and, in 1875, was living in Jewett, N. Y.

CHILDREN OF MUNSON PECK (933) AND MARY, HIS WIFE, ALL BORN IN LEXINGTON, NOW JEWETT, N. Y.

[2048.] 1. EMILY F., b. Sept. 15, 1841; m. Putnam B. Dickerman, Sept. 12, 1865, and, in 1875, was living in Rockford, Ill.

[2049.] 2. ALFRED N., b. June 18, 1848, and d. in Great Barrington, Mass.

[2050.] 3. MARTHA J., b. Oct. 9, 1856, and, in 1875, was living in South Egremont, Mass.

CHILDREN OF JOEL PECK (939) AND ELIZA, HIS WIFE, ALL BORN IN FARMINGTON, OHIO.

[2051.] 1. DELIA M., b. Nov. 7, 1825; m. James C. Howard, Oct. 9, 1851, and, in 1861, was living in Covington, Ky.

[2052.] 2. ALLEN F., b. Feb. 15, 1828; m. ———— Fuller, and, in 1870, was living in Farmington, O.; had been a surgeon in the U. S. Army.

[2053.] 3. FLETCHER W., b. April 20, 1831; m. Coresta R. Smith, Aug. 28, 1855, and, in 1861, was living in Farmington, O.

ONLY CHILD OF CHARLES PECK, (942) BORN IN ORWELL, OHIO.

[2054.] AUSTIN DEAN, b. Jan. 20, 1865, and, in 1870, was living in Orwell, O.

CHILDREN OF BENJAMIN H. PECK (941) AND JULIA, HIS WIFE.

[2055.] 1. DANIEL M., b. in Farmington, O., Sept. 12 1826; m. Isabella A. McCorkle, June 2, 1854, and, in 1862, was living in Uniontown, Ind.

[2056.] 2. CHARLES W., b. in Farmington, O., July 27, 1829, and d. there May 23, 1846.

[2057.] 3. PHALLY A., b. in Farmington, O., June 10, 1832; m. David B. Ward, March 10, 1853, and, in 1862, was living in Uniontown, Ind.

[2058.] 4. ARZA B., b. in Farmington, O., June 5, 1834, and d. there March 16, 1841.

[2059.] 5. LYMAN M., b. in Farmington, O., Aug. 19, 1837, and, in 1862, was living unm. in Uniontown, Ind.

[2060.] 6. MATILDA M., b. in Delaware, O., Feb. 16, 1840, and, in 1862, was living unm. in Uniontown, Ind.

[2061.] 7. BENJAMIN H., b. in Farmington, O., Oct. 19, 1843, and, in 1862, was living unm. in Uniontown, Ind.

[2062.] 8. JOHN L., b. in Farmington, O., Sept. 23, 1846, and, in 1862, was living in Uniontown, Ind.

CHILDREN OF HENRY PECK (957) AND LAURA, HIS WIFE, ALL BORN IN BRISTOL, CONN.

[2063.] 1. CAROLINE, b. Feb. 7, 1836 ; m. Francis Johnson, May 15, 1858, and d., in Bristol, Conn., Nov. 22, 1861.

[2064.] 2. NOBLE, b. May 3, 1837 ; m. Anna Kendrick, Jan. 5, 1870, and, in 1872, was living in Bristol, Conn.

[2065.] 3. ALBERT C., b. Nov. 10, 1841 ; m. Grace A. Judson, Oct. 4, 1866, and, in 1874, was living in Woodbury, Conn.

[2066.] 4. GEORGE, b. May 4, 1847 ; m. Sarah Shary, March 25, 1869, and, in 1872, was living in Bristol, Conn.

CHILDREN OF GEORGE PECK (958) AND JANE, HIS WIFE.

[2067.] 1. ADELINE, b. in Hinsdale, N. Y., Oct. 5, 1831 ; m. John N. Brown, Jan. 24, 1855, and, in 1861, was living in Hinsdale, N. Y.

[2068.] 2. SARAH E., b. in Steuben Co., N. Y., July 23, 1837 ; m. John C. Knapp, Oct. 9, 1854, and, in 1861, was living in Hinsdale, N. Y.

[2069.] 3. ANN L., b. in Hinsdale, N. Y., Nov. 9, 1840 ; m. Julius Burlingame, Nov. 1, 1856, and, in 1861, was living in Hinsdale, N Y.

[2070.]   4. MAHLON C., b. in Hinsdale, N. Y., Dec. 4, 1842, and was in the U. S. Army in the war of the Rebellion.

CHILDREN OF JOHN PECK (962) AND MARIA, HIS WIFE, ALL BORN
IN BRISTOL, CONN.

[2071.]   1. EVELINE, b. Sept. 27, 1847 ; m. Josiah Cowles, Feb. 2, 1867, and, in 1872, was living in West Meriden, Conn.

[2072.]   2. JOHN F., b. April 19, 1853, and d., in Bristol, Conn., Dec. 3, 1853.

[2073.]   3. MARY, b. Jan. 5, 1856, and, in 1872, was living in West Meriden, Conn.

CHILDREN OF CHARLES PECK (963) AND LUCIA, HIS WIFE, ALL
BORN IN BRISTOL, CONN.

[2074.]   1. LUCINDA, b. May 15, 1852, and, in 1872, was living in Bristol, Conn.

[2075.]   2. ANDREW, b. Dec. 27, 1853, and, in 1872, was living in Bristol, Conn.

[2076.]   3. JANE, b. Feb. 12, 1856, and, in 1872, was living in Bristol, Conn.

[2077.]   4. WILLIAM, b. March 17, 1859, and, in 1872, was living in Bristol, Conn.

CHILDREN OF JESSE PECK (967) AND MARY ANN, HIS WIFE, ALL
BORN IN BUFFALO, N. Y., EXCEPT THE OLDEST, WHO
WAS BORN IN ALLENTOWN, PENN.

[2078.]   1. JAMES B., b. Sept. 16, 1820, and, in 1862, was living unm. at LaGrange, Cal.

[2079.]   2. SARAH E., b. March 11, 1824 ; m. B. F. Salisbury, and, in 1862, was living in Buffalo, N. Y.

[2080.]   3. JOHN S., b. Sept. 3, 1826, and, in 1862, was living unm. in Yreka, Cal.

[2081.]   4. WILLIAM C., b. Sept. 12, 1828 ; m. Mary J. Toomer, and, in 1862, was living in Durand, Wis.

[2082.]   5. FRANCIS, b. Feb. 9, 1831, and, in 1862, was living at Snellings, Cal.

[2083.] 6. CHARLES S., b. Sept. 11, 1834 ; m. Adeline Cook, and, in 1862, was living at Snellings, Cal.

[2084.] 7. GEORGE W., b. March 8, 1838, and, in 1862, was living unm, at Tidioute, Penn.

[2085.] 8. MARY, b. Sept. 22, 1846, and d., at Buffalo, N. Y., Sept. 30, 1849.

CHILDREN OF CHARLES PECK (968) AND MARY, HIS WIFE.

[2086.] 1. LOUISA, b. in Henderson, Ky., in 1821, and d., in Shawneetown, Ill., in 1821

[2087.] 2. SARAH ELIZABETH, b. Aug. 25, 1822 ; m. Henry Brown, and d., in Marshall, Mich., July 10, 1844.

[2088.] 3. OLIVE JANE, b. in Evansville, Ind., May 14, 1824 ; m. —— Preston, and, in 1862, was living at Evansville, Ind.

[2089.] 4. WILLIAM D., b. in Evansville, Ind., April 4, 1826, and d., in Louisville, Ky., Jan. 1, 1849.

[2090.] 5. OLIVER, b. in Buffalo, N. Y., in 1828, and d., in Dunkirk, N. Y., in 1832.

[2091.] 6. LUCINDA ANN, b. in Dunkirk, N. Y., Sept. 1, 1832 ; m. Nathaniel Bridges, and d. in Keokuk, Iowa.

[2092.] 7. JOHN, b. in Buffalo, N. Y., in 1834, and d. there the same year.

[2093.] 8. IRA BEACH, b. in Sheridan, N. Y., Oct. 23, 1834, and d. unm. in Louisville, Ky., April 10, 1850.

[2094.] 9. JULIA MARY, b. in Sheridan, N. Y., April 13, 1840, and, in 1872, was living in Madisonville, Hopkins Co., Kentucky.

[2095.] 10. MIRIAM, b. in Henderson, Ky., in 1842, and d. there in 1843.

CHILDREN OF MILES PECK (974) AND EMILY, HIS WIFE.

[2096.] 1. ALLYN S., b. in Wallingford, Conn., in April 1830. His present residence, if living, cannot be ascertained.

[2097.] 2. HENRY, b. in New Britain, Conn., and d., in infancy in New Britain, Conn.

CHILDREN OF JOEL PECK (976) AND CHARLOTTE M., HIS WIFE, ALL BORN IN FARMINGTON, CONN.

[2098.] 1. SUSAN F., b. July 4, 1835 ; m. Amos J. Beers, Oct. 6, 1856, and, in 1875, was living in New Haven, Conn.

[2099.] 2. JANE A., b. April 17, 1837 ; m. Edward M. Judd, March 23, 1859, and, in 1875, was living in Brooklyn, N. Y.

[2100.] 3. MARY B., b. June 17, 1839 ; m. William S. Toan, Oct. 25 1864, and, in 1875, was living in Hillsdale, Mich.

[2101.] 4. MARTHA A., b. April 25, 1843 ; m. R. D. Judd, June 19, 1862, and, in 1875, was living in New Britain, Conn.

[2102.] 5. JOEL WILBUR, b. Jan. 19, 1849, and, in 1875, was living in New Haven. Conn.

CHILDREN OF SAMUEL PECK (980) AND AMELIA, HIS WIFE, ALL BORN IN LEXINGTON, N. Y.

[2103.] 1. DELIA, b. Oct. 17, 1801 ; m. Thomas Strangham, and, in 1875, was living in Jewett, N. Y.

[2104.] 2. SAMUEL T., b. Jan. 22, 1803 ; m. Amelia Cornish, and, in 1875, was living in Windham, N. Y.

[2105.] 3. SAMANTHA, b. Oct. 2, 1805 ; m. John Goodsell, and d., in Jewett, N. Y., Jan. 15, 1859.

[2106.] 4. MIRANDA, b. June 12, 1807, and d. unm., in Lexington, N. Y., in Sept. 1825.

[2107.] 5. SOLOMON, b. Aug. 19, 1809 ; m. Abi Johnson, and, in 1875, was living in Jewett, N. Y.

[2108.] 6. AMELIA ANN, b. May 4, 1812 ; m. Lucas Van Valkenburgh, and, in 1875, was living in Lexington, N. Y.

[2109.] 7. ELIAKIM, b. Sept. 9, 1814 ; m. Louisa Whitcomb, and, in 1875, was living in Jewett, N. Y.

[2110.] 8. PHEBE C., b. Aug. 5, 1816 ; m. Hiram Bennett, and d., in Fulton, Ill., May 9, 1868.

[2111.] 9. ELIZABETH, b. April 9, 1818 ; m. James Kennedy, and, in 1875, was living in Lexington, N. Y.

[2112.] 10. MARY, b. June 6, 1820 ; m. Alexander Cornish, and d., in Lexington, N. Y., in January, 1854.

[2113.] 11. AMANDA L., b. Dec. 31, 1823, and, in 1875, was living unm. in Lexington, N. Y.

[2114.] 12. THEODORE, b. about 1825, and d. in infancy, in Lexington, N. Y.

CHILDREN OF RICHARD PECK (981) AND PERMELIA, HIS WIFE, ALL BORN IN WINDHAM, N. Y.

[2115.] 1. OLIVE, b. May 15, 1801 ; m. John P. More, and d., in Roxbury, N. Y., Aug. 15, 1849.

[2116.] 2. RICHARD, b. Sept. 25, 1803, and, in 1875, was living in New Comerstown, O.

[2117.] 3. PHILENA, b. Nov. 10, 1806 ; m. Henry Cole, and, in 1875, was living in Lexington, N. Y.

[2118.] 4. ERASTUS T., b. May 25, 1809 ; m. 1. Catharine Root, who d. Oct. 15, 1863 ; m. 2. Cynthia Goslee, and, in 1875, was living in Windham, N. Y.

[2119.] 5. PHILANDER, b. Nov. 24, 1811 ; m. Caroline Rowley, and d., in Durham, N. Y., Feb. 13, 1865.

[2120.] 6. PERMELIA, b. June 9, 1814 ; m. Owen Weeks, and d., in Roxbury, N. Y., Aug. 22, 1869.

CHILDREN OF TENNANT PECK (982) AND POLLY, HIS WIFE.

[2121.] 1. TENNANT, b. in Windham, N. Y., Jan. 21, 1806 ; m. Jane Card, in Sept. 1829, and d. in the U. S. Army, about 1863 or 1864.

[2122.] 2. POLLY, b. in Windham, N. Y., Feb. 23, 1808 ; m. William Webster, in Sept. 1830, and, in 1875, was living in Rensselaerville, N. Y.

[2123.] 3. RUSSELL, b. in Windham, N. Y., March 29, 1810 ; m. Margaret Applebee, in June 1831, and, in 1875, was living in Halcott, N. Y.

[2124.] 4. CATHARINE, b. in Windham, N. Y., Nov. 26, 1811 ; m. Sheldon Scoville, in June 1852, and, in 1875, was living in Freeport, Ill.

[2125.] 5. LYDIA, b. in Reading, N. Y., Sept. 21, 1814 ; m. Terry Ellis, Oct. 20, 1836, and, in 1875, was living in Freeport, Illinois.

[2126.] 6. SIDNEY, b. in Lexington, N. Y., May 25, 1817 ; m. Eliza Stanton, in April 1841, and, in 1875, was living at Point Pleasant, Iowa.

[2127.] 7. JAMES, b. in Lexington, N. Y., Jan. 6, 1820 ; m. Catharine Wilcox, in Jan. 1843, and, in 1875, was living at Yellow Creek, Ill.

[2128.] 8. LEWIS B., b. in Lexington, N. Y., Aug. 29, 1822; m. Elizabeth Wilcox, in Oct. 1844, and, in 1875, was living in Freeport, Ill.

[2129.] 9. NOAH D., b. in Lexington, N. Y., April 12, 1825 ; m. Sally Applebee, in May 1846, and, in 1875, was living in Freeport, Ill.

[2130.] 10. SARAH, b. in Lexington, N. Y., July 23, 1830 ; m. Benjamin Clow, in March 1848, and, in 1875, was living in Freeport, Ill.

CHILDREN OF JOHN C. PECK (990) AND NANCY, HIS WIFE.

[2131.] 1. SARAH ELIZABETH, b. in Lexington, N. Y. and d. unm. in Durham, N. Y., March 1, 1854.

[2132.] 2. HARRIET N., b. in Lexington, N. Y., June 24, 1830, and, in 1875, was living unm. in Durham, N. Y.

[2133.] 3. JOHN H., b. in Lexington, N. Y., Dec. 14, 1834 ; m. Henrietta F. Goslee, Nov. 14, 1860, and d., in Durham, N. Y., Nov. 25, 1865.

[2134.] 4. MARTHA A., b. in Durham, N. Y., Jan. 9, 1837 ; m. James A. Race, Dec. 7, 1865, and, in 1875, was living in Jewett, N. Y.,

[2135.]   5. NANCY ROSALINE, b. in Durham, N. Y., Sept. 2, 1845 ; m. Bissell Bascom, May 12, 1869, and, in 1875, was living in Durham, N. Y

CHILDREN OF PETER PECK (996) AND AMELIA, HIS WIFE, BOTH BORN IN ALBANY, N. Y.

[2136.]   1. EDWARD H., b. Aug. 17. 1830, and d. unm., in Albany, April 12, 1864.

[2137.]   2. MARY F., b. April 7, 1833 ; m. Henry S. Van Santford, April 14, 1857, and, in 1875, was living in Albany, N. Y.

CHILDREN OF ABNER PECK (998) AND REBECCA, HIS WIFE.

[2138.]   1. ALBERT, b. in Leverett, Mass , Aug. 11, 1818 ; m. Nancy C. Darling, Sept. 29, 1842, and, in 1868, was living in Shelburne, Mass.

[2139.]   2. ABNER, b. in Leverett, Mass., March 8, 1820 ; m. Lucretia Allen, Jan. 22, 1846, and, in 1868, was living in Shelburne, Mass.

[2140.]   3. ORILLA, b. in Leverett, Mass., Feb. 25, 1822 ; m. Pliny Fisk, Aug. 29, 1844, and, in 1868, was living in Shelburne, Mass.

[2141.]   4. AUSTIN, b. in Leverett, Mass., May 9, 1824 ; m. Lucia A. Severance, Sept. 17, 1841, and, in 1868, was living in Shelburne, Mass.

[2142.]   5. JOHN B., b. in Shelburne, Mass., June 13, 1826 ; m. Maria Jones, June 26, 1851, and d., in Shelburne, Mass., Nov. 22, 1866.

[2143.]   6. FANNY, b. in Shelburne, Mass., Oct. 19, 1828, and d. there June 5, 1844.

[2144.]   7. HARRIET, b. in Shelburne, Mass., June 21, 1832 ; m. Justin H. Tyler, Jan. 21, 1861, and, in 1868, was living in Napoleon, O.

CHILDREN OF PETER PECK (999) AND ARDELIA, HIS WIFE, ALL
BORN IN SHELBURNE, MASS.

[2145.] 1. FRANCIS P., b. May 18, 1825; m. Marietta
Knowlton, in Nov. 1850, and, in 1868, was living in Chicago,
Illinois.

[2146.] 2. HANNAH, b. Oct. 15, 1827 ; m. Oscar Bordwell
June 10, 1853, and, in 1868, was living in Shelburne, Mass.

[2147.] 3. WILLIAM T., b. May 23, 1831; m. Diana L.
Severance, Dec. 20, 1855, and, in 1868, was living in Shelburne, Mass.

[2148.] 4. MARSHALL, b. June 5, 1833, and d., in Shelburne, Mass., Sept. 22, 1836.

[2149.] 5. MARSHALL, again, b. Sept. 18, 1837, and d., in
Shelburne, Mass., Sept. 1, 1839.

[2150.] 6. ARDELIA T., b. June 23, 1841, and, in 1868,
was living unm. in Shelburne, Mass.

CHILDREN OF JASON W. PECK (1003) AND SUSAN, HIS WIFE.

[2151.] 1. ALANSON, b. in Reading, N. Y., Feb. 27, 1824 ;
m. Amanda Cross, June 6, 1848, and, in 1869, was living in
Lodi, N. Y.

[2152.] 2. BENONI, b. in Reading, N. Y., Dec. 15, 1825 ;
m. Sally Ann Travis, March 20, 1843, and, in 1869, was living
in Monterey, N. Y

[2153.] 3. LEANDER H., b. in Reading, N. Y., Aug. 24,
1829 ; m. Rachael Townsend, Feb. 6, 1853, and, in 1869, was
living at Cooper's Plains, N. Y

[2154.] 4. NORMAN, b in Reading, N. Y., Aug. 14, 1832 ;
m. Sally Ann Ayres, Feb. 6, 1857, and, in 1869, was living in
Watkins, N. Y.

[2155.] 5 WILLIAM R., b. in Tyrone, N. Y., Dec. 9, 1835;
m. Lydia Ann Washburne, March 4, 1855, and, in 1869, was
living in Madison, Mich.

[2156.] 6. GABRIEL, b. in Reading, N. Y., June 4, 1839,
and d. there June 10, 1839.

[2157.] 7. ORANDA, b. in Reading, N. Y., Nov. 18, 1840 ; m. Zeron Washburne, in 186₁, and, in 1869, was living in Madison, Mich.

[2158.] 8. MAHLON, b. in Reading, N. Y., March 8, 1843 ; m. 1. Sarah E. Jones, Feb. 7, 1865 ; m. 2. Eliza Short, June 7, 1868, and, in 1869, was living in Altay, N. Y.

[2159.] 9. CHILION, b. in Reading, N. Y., March 8, 1843, and, in 1869, was living unm. in Altay, N. Y.

CHILDREN OF ERASTUS PECK (1004) AND LYDIA, HIS WIFE, ALL BORN IN READING, N. Y.

[2160.] 1. FANNY O.. b. Feb. 4, 1827 ; m. Lewis LeFever, June 21, 1848, and, in 1869, was living in Hinsdale, N. Y.

[2161.] 2. JOEL S., b. March 28, 1829 ; m. 1. Eliza Culver, Sept. 23, 1856, and m. 2. Lowly Culver, Nov. 19, 1863, and, in 1869, was living in Altay, N. Y.

[2162.] 3. MARTIN H., b. Oct. 16, 1831 ; m. Maria Osborn, and, in 1869, was living in Altay, N. Y.

[2163.] 4. ARTHUR, b. April 5, 1835 ; m. Lucinda D. Nav, April 18, 1860, and, in 1869, was living in Clinton, Ill.

[2164.] 5. NANCY, b. Sept. 29, 1837 ; m. John Jackson, Sept. 13, 1857, and, in 1869, was living in Altay, N. Y.

[2165.] 6. ANN E., b. Oct. 4, 1839 ; m. Alonzo Winters, March 29, 1857, and, in 1869, was living in Barrington, N. Y.

CHILDREN OF TENNANT PECK (1005) AND DURINDA, HIS WIFE, ALL BORN IN READING, N. Y.

[2166.] 1. MIRANDA, b. Aug. 14, 1825 ; m. Jonathan Davison, and, in 1869, was living in Corydon, Penn.

[2167.] 2. ELIZA J., b. July 22, 1828 ; m. Jeremiah Turk, and, in 1869, was living at Jenkins' Bridge, Va.

[2168.] 3. JOHN S., b. Sept. 16, 1830, and, in 1869, was living unm. in Reading, N. Y.

[2169.] 4. FERNANDO, b. April 9, 1833 ; m. Mary J. Masters, and, in 1869, was living in Thurston, N. Y.

[2170.] 5. SIMON S., b. Dec. 9, 1835 ; m. Phebe J. Clark, and, in 1869, was living in Tyrone, N. Y.

[2171.] 6. LYDIA, b. April 20, 1838 ; m. Thomas Holley, and, in 1869, was living in Reading, N. Y.

[2172.] 7. SOPHRONA, b. Jan. 22, 1841, and d., in Reading, N. Y., March 17, 1844.

[2173.] 8. ERASTUS, b. Dec. 11, 1843, and d., in Reading, N. Y., April 6, 1844.

[2174.] 9. CANDACE, b. Aug. 24, 1845, and d., in Reading, N. Y., April 26, 1854.

CHILDREN OF BENONI PECK (1007) AND CLARISSA, HIS WIFE, ALL BORN IN WATKINS, N. Y.

[2175.] 1. SARAH JANE, b. Aug. 10, 1832 ; m. George H. Freeman Dec. 22, 1851, and, in 1869, was living in Irving, Mich.

[2176.] 2. EDWARD Q., b. Jan. 25, 1835 ; m. Nellie Upton, and, in 1869, was living in Hornellsville, N. Y.

[2177.] 3. GEORGE, b. Feb. 17. 1837, and d., in Watkins, N. Y., May 16, 1839.

[2178.] 4. JUDSON A., b. March 13, 1839 ; m. Anna Green, and, in 1869, was living in Niles, Mich.

[2179.] 5. WALLACE, b. Feb. 24, 1841 ; m. Maria Anthony, July 3, 1866, and, in 1869, was living in Niles, Mich.

[2180.] 6. ADRAIN, b. Nov. 17, 1845, and d. unm. Sept. 19, 1865, being drowned in the Alleghany river.

CHILDREN OF JOEL PECK, (1013) ALL BORN IN HECTOR, N. Y.

[2181.] 1. ANN ELIZA, b. March 3, 1815 ; m. 1. John C. Hotchkiss Oct. 17, 1833 ; m. 2. Avery S. Hutchins, May 8, 1853, and, in 1869, was living in Nevada, Iowa.

[2182.] 2. POLLY, b. Oct. 9, 1816 ; m, John Woodward, Oct. 15, 1834, and d., in Hector, N. Y., Nov. 26, 1864.

[2183.] 3. MARTIN B., b. July 7, 1819, and d., in Hector, N. Y., Nov. 9, 1823.

[2184.]　4. LEVI H., b. June 22, 1821, and d., in Hector. N. Y., June 1, 1822.

[2185.]　5. ALBERT, b. April 12, 1823, and d., in Hector, N. Y., Aug. 24, 1825.

[2186.]　6. HARRIET P., b. June 24, 1825 ; m. 1. David Brown, April 4, 1842 ; m. 2. A. D. Retun, Jan. 6, 1863, and, in 1869, was living in Hudson, Mich.

[2187.]　7. LYDIA ANN, b. June 24, 1827 ; m. Philip S. Sked, March 29, 1849, and, in 1869, was living in Pennington, N. J.

[2188.]　8. ELON G., b. Sept. 16, 1830 ; m. Emma E. Bradford, May 13, 1852, and, in 1872, was living in Hector, N. Y.

[2189.]　9. SYLVESTER B., b. May 23, 1832 ; m. 1. Adelia J. Everts, Sept. 23, 1857, who d. Oct. 28, 1871 ; m. 2. Fannie A. Reynolds, Nov. 27, 1872, and, in 1876, was living in Tioga, Penn.

[2190.]　10. HORACE S., b. April 23, 1835 ; m. Mary E. Coburn, Sept. 13, 1856, and, in 1869, was living in Crown Point, N. Y.

[2191.]　11. SOPHIA, b. May 1, 1837 ; m. Eli Bennett, June 27, 1858, and, in 1869, was living at Crown Point, N. Y.

CHILDREN OF ELISHA PECK, (1020) ALL BORN IN PHELPS, N. Y.

[2192.]　1. ALVIRA, b. March 24, 1814 ; m. Richard Hallett April 10, 1834, and, in 1869, was living in Hillsdale, Mich.

[2193.]　2. LEWIS, b. May 13, 1816 ; m. Sarah Long, Oct. 27, 1854, and, in 1869, was living in Phelps, N. Y.　He graduated at Madison University, in the class of 1844, and was a member of the New York Legislature, in 1860.

[2194.]　3. LYDIA, b. Feb. 6, 1818 ; m. Daniel Crouch, in Oct. 1844, and d., in Phelps, N. Y., Aug. 11, 1850.

[2195.]　4. JOHN, b. Nov. 29, 1819 ; m. Amanda Gates, in 1841, and, in 1869, was living in Hillsdale, Mich.

[2196.]　5. IRA, b. Nov. 18, 1821 ; m. Marcia B. Dixon, Dec. 18, 1845, and, in 1869, was living at Port Byron, N. Y.

[2197.] 6. JESSE, b. Feb. 29, 1824 ; m. Hattie Walthart, in July 1861, and, in 1869, was living in Brownsville, Penn.

[2198.] 7. SARAH, b. Dec. 13, 1825 ; m. Luther Worden, in Jan. 1846, and d. Sept. 14, 1853.

CHILDREN OF HORACE PECK (1021) AND SEBE, HIS WIFE, ALL
BORN IN PHELPS, N. Y.

[2199.] 1. DAMARIS, b. May 4, 1815 ; m. A. Frank Ranney, and d., in Hillsdale, Mich., Jan. 12, 1847.

[2200.] 2. HIRAM, b. June 30, 1817 ; m. Louisa Whittemore, and, in 1869, was living in Phelps, N. Y.

[2201.] 3. WILLIAM, b. Nov. 26, 1819 ; m. Ellen Case, and, in 1872, was living in Phelps, N. Y.

[2202.] 4. DOROTHY, b. Feb. 13, 1823 ; m. John Green, and d., in Genoa, N. Y., Aug. 19, 1848.

[2203.] 5. CLARISSA, b. Nov. 1, 1824 ; m. Rev. Jacob A. Wader, and, in 1869, was living in Orleans, N. Y.

[2204.] 6. HORACE, b. Oct. 28, 1832 ; m. Elizabeth Reals, and, in 1869, was living in Phelps, N. Y.

[2205.] 7. ELLEN, b. June 27, 1835, and d. unm. in Phelps, N. Y., March 6, 1851.

[2206.] 8. CHARLES D., b. Jan. 28, 1838 ; m. Mary Homan, and, in 1869, was living in Phelps, N. Y.

CHILDREN OF DARIUS PECK, (1023.)

[2207.] 1. MORTIMER, b. in Barre, N. Y., in 1820 ; m. Ursula Sage, and, in 1871, was living in Benton, Mo.

[2208.] 2. MARY ANN, b. in Barre, N. Y., June 12, 1823 ; m. Eli Dixon, and d., in Aroma, Ill., in 1865.

[2209.] 3. DARIUS, b. in Fairport, N. Y., Jan. 20, 1831 ; m. Susan Wilson, and, in 1871, was living in Benton, Mo.

[2210.] 4. MARTHA, b. in Mentz, N. Y., Dec. 8, 1833 ; m. J. V. White, and d., in Port Byron, N. Y., in 1870.

[2211.] 5. SARAH, b. in Mentz, N. Y., Dec. 30, 1836 ; m. W. A. White, and, in 1871, was living in Auburn, N. Y.

CHILDREN OF ENOCH PECK, (1026.)

[2212.]   1. EZRA J., b. in Castleton, N. Y., Dec. 19, 1830 ; m. Annie L. Bartlett, March 31, 1856, and, in 1869, was living in Phelps, N. Y.   He graduated at Williams College in 1851.

[2213.]   2. HENRY J., b. in Castleton, N. Y., July 20, 1834 ; m. Mary Gray, Oct. 18, 1859, and, in 1869, was living in Phelps, N. Y.

[2214.]   3. HATTIE C. A., b. in Baldwinsville, N. Y., Nov. 9, 1846, and, in 1869, was living unm. in Phelps, N. Y.

[2215.]   4. MARY J., b. in Canoga, N. Y., Dec. 21, 1849, and, in 1869, was living unm. in Phelps, N. Y.

CHILDREN OF IRA PECK (1027) AND POLLY, HIS WIFE, ALL BORN IN SENECA, N. Y.

[2216.]   1. CHARLES, b. Sept. 6, 1830 ; m. Harriet N. Pierson, Nov. 29, 1860, and, in 1869, was living in Seneca, N. Y.

[2217.]   2. BETSEY E., b. April 1, 1833 ; m. Alonzo Carson, Sept. 22, 1852, and, in 1869, was living in Hudson, Mich.

[2218.]   3. ESTHER A., b. Nov. 5, 1837 ; m. 1. Jerome Guilford, Aug. 22, 1853 ; m. 2. Enoch Hallett, in March 1863, and, in 1869, was living in Hudson, Mich.

[2219.]   4. HENRY H., b. Aug. 31, 1840 ; m. Ophelia Dibble, July 3, 1862, and, in 1869, was living in Seneca, N. Y.

CHILDREN OF SETH MARVIN PECK (1031) AND SARAH, HIS WIFE, ALL BORN IN BETHANY, N. Y.

[2220.]   1. SARAH E., b. Feb. 22, 1826 ; m. Alvin Rockwood, and, in 1869, was living in Bethany, N. Y.

[2221.]   2. PHEBE R., b. Sept. 18, 1827 ; m. Benjamin F. Peck (1337), and, in 1869, was living in Bethany, N. Y.

[2222.]   3. LAURA, b. Jan. 23, 1829 ; m. Horace Ensign, and, in 1869, was living in Bethany, N. Y.

[2223.]   4. SETH M., b. April 14, 1831 ; m. Lucy Jane Peck (1338), and, in 1869, was living in Bethany, N. Y.

[2224.] 5. ALMIRA, b. March 10, 1833 ; m. Chauncey Rogers, and, in 1869, was living in Bethany, N. Y.

[2225.] 6. HENRY, b. Sept. 7, 1836, and, in 1869, was living unm. in Bethany, N. Y.

CHILDREN OF JOHN MOORE PECK (1032) AND LUCINDA, HIS WIFE, ALL BORN IN BETHANY, N. Y.

[2226.] 1. DANIEL B., b. March 18, 1827 ; m. Ruana Freeman, and, in 1869, was living in Jackson, Mich.

[2227.] 2. WILLIAM O., b. June 15, 1828 ; m. Louisa Hallock, and. in 1869, was living in Bethany, N. Y.

[2228.] 3. RUSSELL S., b. July 29, 1830 ; m. Betsey Down, and, in 1869, was living in Jackson, Mich.

[2229.] 4. EMILY, b. Dec. 7, 1832, and, in 1869, was living unm. in Jackson, Mich.

[2230.] 5. JOHN N., b. Dec. 27, 1834 ; m. Emma E. Peck (1053), April 22, 1852, and, in 1869, was living in Jackson, Michigan.

[2231.] 6. GEORGE W., b. Oct. 22, 1836, and, in 1869, was living unm. in Jackson, Mich.

[2232.] 7. LUCINDA B., b. Jan. 4, 1839, and, in 1869, was living unm. in Jackson, Mich.

[2233.] 8. CALISTA A., b. March 3, 1841, and, in 1868, was living unm. in Jackson, Mich.

[2234.] 9. ELLEN A., b. Dec. 14, 1842 ; m. Alonzo Blossom, and, in 1869, was living in Jackson, Mich.

[2235.] 10. EDWARD M., b. April 10, 1845, and d., in Bethany, N. Y., Oct. 12, 1846.

[2236.] 11. JAMES M., b. July 7, 1847, and, in 1868, was living unm. in Jackson, Mich.

[2237.] 12. HARRISON D., b. Oct. 2, 1849, and, in 1868, was living unm. in Jackson, Mich.

[2238.] 13. ALBERT A., b. June 6, 1852, and, in 1868, was living in Jackson, Mich.

CHILDREN OF WILLIAM PECK (1034) AND PAMELIA, HIS WIFE,
ALL BORN IN MIDDLEBURY, N. Y.

[2239.] 1. FANNY, b. July 16,1828; m. Hiram Ewell, and,
in 1869, was living in Bethany, N. Y.

[2240.] 2. JANE, b. Oct. 11, 1830; m. William Bishop, and,
in 1869, was living in Bethany, N. Y.

[2241.] 3. HELEN, b. April 24, 1832; m. Alonzo Pierce,
and, in 1869, was living in Bethany, N. Y.

[2242.] 4. WILLIAM, b. May 29, 1833; m. Ardelia Miller,
and, in 1869, was living in Bethany, N. Y.

[2243.] 5. PAMELIA, b. Dec. 19, 1834; m. Alanson Miller,
and, in 1869, was living in Bethany, N. Y.

[2244.] 6. DELIA, b. Aug. 29, 1836; m. Jacob Smith, and,
in 1869, was living in Bethany, N. Y.

[2245.] 7. WARREN, b. March 30, 1839, and, in 1868, was
living unm. in Bethany, N. Y.

[2246.] 8. ADELE, b. Aug. 16, 1848, and, in 1868, was living in Bethany, N. Y.

CHILDREN OF DANIEL B. PECK, (1036).

[2247.] 1. CLARISSA A., b. in Bethany, N. Y., Dec. 5,
1830; m. David Soules, Dec. 26, 1855, and, in 1877, was living
in Whitehall, Mich.

[2248.] 2. DAVID A., b in Bethany, N. Y., Dec. 27, 1832;
m. Mary Chase, in 1856, and, in 1868, was living in Middlebury, N. Y.

[2249.] 3. CYRUS O., b. in Bethany, N. Y., July 8, 1836;
m. Wilmina Tranger, May 1, 1867, and, in 1877, was living in
Clinton, Iowa.

[2250.] 4. ELISHA S., b. in Bethany, N. Y., May 29, 1839;
m. Melvina Minard, Oct. 3, 1860, and d., near Richmond, Va.,
June 4, 1864.

[2251.] 5. LORETTA E., b. in Bethany, N. Y., May 26,
1841; m. Francis W. Brown, Nov. 15, 1860, and, in 1877, was
living in Rochester, N. Y.

[2252.]   6. ESTHER A., b. in Bethany, N. Y., Jan. 11, 1843; m. Algeroy Aikin, in Oct. 1863, and, in 1877, was living in Warsaw, N. Y.

[2253.]   7. DANIEL W., b. in Bethany, N. Y., Dec. 6, 1845; m. Mary A. Goodrich, Nov. 24, 1868, and, in 1877, was living at Clam Lake, Mich.

[2254.]   8. SARAH C., b. in Middlebury, N. Y., June 16, 1848, and, in 1877, was living unm. in Wyoming, N. Y.

[2255.]   9. CHARLES F., b. in Middlebury, N. Y.. Sept. 23, 1851, and, in 1877, was living unm. in Warsaw, N. Y.

[2256.]   10. JOHN F., b. in Middlebury, N. Y., Jan. 28, 1854, and, in 1877, was living in Rockford, Ill.

[2257.]   11. ANNA E., b. in Warsaw, N. Y., Jan. 22, 1865, and, in 1877, was living in Warsaw, N. Y.

CHILDREN OF JOSHUA PECK, (1035).

[2258.]   1. HARRIET, b. in Bethany, N. Y., Oct. 12, 1828 ; m. Alfred Harris, and, in 1869, was living in Rutland, Mich.

[2259.]   2. JOHN M., b. in Dumfries, C. W., Jan. 30, 1832 ; m. Catharine Munger, in April 1854, and d. in 1863.

[2260.]   3. ELIAS, b. in Dumfries, C. W., July 1, 1833 ; m. 1. Frances Fullerton, in 1862 ; m. 2. ——— ———, and, in 1869, was living in Rochester, Ind.

[2261.]   4. GEORGE, b. in Dumfries, C. W.. April 30, 1836 ; m. Harriet Andrus, in 1865, and, in 1869, was living in Rutland, Mich.

[2262.]   5. LUCINDA, b. in Dumfries, C. W., July 25, 1837 ; m. Garry Garrison, and, in 1869, was living in Rutland, Mich.

[2263.]   6. EMMA, b. in Dumfries, C. W., Sept. 15, 1846 ; m. Albert Bowen, in 1863, and, in 1869, was living in LaCrosse, Wisconsin.

[2264.]   7. IDA, b. in Rutland, Mich., Sept. 13, 1863, and, in 1869, was living in Rutland, Mich.

[2265.]   8. WILLIAM, b. in Rutland, Mich., July 27, 1867, and, in 1869, was living in Rutland, Mich.

[2266.] 9. BETSEY, b. in Rutland, Mich., Feb. 21, 1869, and, in 1869, was living in Rutland, Mich.

CHILDREN OF JOSEPH PECK (1039) AND JULIET, HIS WIFE.

[2267.] 1. FRANCES, b. in LeRoy, N. Y., in 1841 ; m. Seth Howard, and, in 1869, was living in Wyoming, N. Y.

[2268.] 2. ADELAIDE, b. in LeRoy, N. Y., in 1843. and d. unm. in Bethany, N. Y., in 1861.

[2269.] 3. CAROLINE, b. in LeRoy, N. Y., in 1850, and, in 1869, was living unm. in Lockport, N. Y.

[2270.] 4. SOPHIA, b. in Bethany, N. Y., and d. there in 1860.

CHILDREN OF BENJAMIN PECK (1040) AND EMILY, HIS WIFE.

[2271.] 1. SEYMOUR W., b. in Bethany, N. Y., July 1, 1842 ; m. Lizzie Kline, Oct. 12, 1864, and, in 1868, was living in Dickeysville, Wis.

[2272.] 2. CHAUNCEY J., b. in Jamestown, Wis., Sept. 13, 1843, and d. unm. in the army, at Jefferson Barracks, St. Louis, Mo., Aug. 12, 1862.

[2273.] 3. SAMUEL E., b. in Jamestown, Wis., March 24, 1846, and, in 1868, was living in Staceyville, Iowa.

[2274.] 4. THEODORE, b. in Jamestown, Wis., March 3, 1848, and, in 1868, was living in Staceyville, Iowa.

[2275.] 5. FLORA EVA, b. in Jamestown, Wis. Oct. 27, 1849, and, in 1868, was living in Staceyville, Iowa.

[2276.] 6. ELLEN E., b. in Jamestown, Wis., Sept. 24, 1852, and, in 1868, was living in Staceyville, Iowa.

[2277.] 7. WALTER R., b. in Dickeysville, Wis., May 25, 1855, and, in 1868, was living in Staceyville, Iowa.

[2278.] 8. EMILY O., b. in Staceyville, Iowa, Dec. 29, 1858, and, in 1868, was living in Staceyville, Iowa.

ONLY CHILD OF ELISHA S. PECK (1045) AND CAROLINE, HIS WIFE, BORN IN LYME, CONN.

[2279.] SMITH ELY, b. June 14, 1857, and, in 1869, was living in Lyme, Conn.

CHILDREN OF TIMOTHY HOLLIS PECK (1046) AND IRENE, HIS WIFE, BOTH BORN IN LYME, CONN.

[2280.] 1. ELIZABETH L., b. Dec. 21, 1846 ; m. Christopher C. Brockway, July 3, 1866, and, in 1869, was living in East Haddam, Conn.

[2281.] 2. CHARLES L., b. Jan. 28, 1850, and, in 1869, was living in Lyme, Conn.

CHILDREN OF ELISHA PECK, (1054) ALL BORN IN HARTFORD, CONN.

[2282.] 1. MARY R., b. Nov. 29, 1826 ; m. Charles W. Allen, July 14, 1846, and d., in New Haven, Conn., Feb. 5, 1856.

[1283.] 2. JULIA W., b. June 10, 1829 ; m. Rev. Dwight W. Marsh, (missionary) Oct. 19, 1852, and d., in Mosul, Turkey, Aug. 12, 1859.

[2284.] 3. CHARLES McLEAN, b. in Aug. 1841; m. Lucy Eaton, of Ogdensburgh, N. Y., and, in 1868, was living in New York city.

CHILDREN OF DANIEL A. PECK (1058) AND JOANNA, HIS WIFE.

[2286.] 1. ERASMUS D., b. in Stafford, Conn., May 21, 1837 ; m. Harriet A. Whitney, Nov. 26, 1863, and, in 1868, was living in Toledo, O.

[2287.] 2. ALONZO H., b. in Stafford, Conn., Nov. 29, 1839; m. Martha Tiffany, June 24, 1860, and, in 1868, was living in Ellington, Conn.

[2288.] 3. CAROLINE A., b. in Washington, Conn., Feb. 24, 1842, and, in 1868, was living unm. in Ellington, Conn.

[2289.] 4. EMMA ANN, b. in Ellington, Conr., July 28, 1844, and. in 1868, was living unm. in Ellington, Conn.

[2290.] 5. RIAL S., b. in Ellington, Conn., Dec. 22, 1847 and, in 1868, was living unm. in Troy, N. Y.

ONLY CHILD OF ERASMUS D. PECK (1059) AND LUCY E., HIS WIFE.

[2291.] HENRY E., b. May 1, 1838, and, in 1867, was living unm. in Perrysburgh, O.

CHILDREN OF ELEAZER A. PECK (1062) AND LUCY E., HIS WIFE.

[2292.] 1. ELIZABETH, b. in Hartford, Conn., July 11, 1840 ; m. Amasa R. Moore, Oct. 18, 1865, and, in 1875, was living in Troy, N. Y.

[2293.] 2. WILLIAM A., b. in Hartford, Conn., Nov. 20, 1844, and, in 1875, was living unm. in Troy, N. Y.

[2294.] 3. ALFRED G., b. in Troy, N. Y., Oct. 9, 1846 ; m. Charlotte E. Avery, Dec. 11, 1867, and, in 1877, was living in Troy, N. Y.   He has the following children, all b. and, in 1877, all living in Troy, N. Y., viz: *Lottie A.*, b. Dec. 16, 1869 ; *Frederick William*, b. Oct. 5, 1871, and *Eleazer Adorno*, b. May 14, 1874.

CHILDREN OF DANIEL PECK (1064) AND MARIA, HIS WIFE, ALL BORN IN EAST HADDAM, CONN.

[2295.] 1. DANIEL A., b. Nov. 14, 1833, and, in 1868, was living in East Haddam, Conn.

[2296.] 2. MARY J., b. Nov. 7, 1835 ; m. Edward G. Beinet, Nov. 20, 1866, and, in 1868, was living in Newark, N. J.

[2297.] 3. HENRY, b. May 4, 1837, and d., in East Haddam, Conn., July 19, 1838.

[2298.] 4. HENRY, again, b. Oct. 4, 1838, and, in 1868, was living unm. in East Haddam, Conn.

[2299.] 5. GEORGE, b. Dec. 25, 1843, and, in 1868, was living unm. in East Haddam, Conn.

[2300.] 6. THEODORE D., b. April 13, 1846, and, in 1868, was living in East Haddam, Conn.

CHILDREN OF EZEKIEL Y. PECK (1067) AND ESTHER J., HIS WIFE, ALL BORN IN AKRON, OHIO.

[2301.] 1. NORA F., b. Oct. 2, 1843, and d., in Akron, O., June 30, 1852.

[2302.] 2. CLARENCE M., b. Aug. 2, 1845 ; m. Avilda Haggerty, in 1866, and, in 1868, was living in Akron, O.

[2303.] 3. HERBERT C., b. Dec. 5, 1847 ; m. Lydia Clowner, in 1867, and, in 1868, was living in Akron, O.

[2304.] 4. THEODORE H., b. Dec. 5, 1851, and, in 1868, was living in Akron, O.

[2305.] 5. A SON (not named) b. April 13, 1853, and d., in Akron, O., April 15, 1853.

[2306.] 6. HELEN F., b. June 5, 1854, and d., in Akron, O., July 27, 1856.

CHILDREN OF ERASTUS F. PECK (1068) AND SOPHIA, HIS WIFE, ALL BORN IN EAST HADDAM, CONN.

[2307.] 1. CLARISSA M., b. Dec. 14, 1835 ; m. Edwin A. Emmons, Dec. 25, 1856, and, in 1868, was living in East Haddam, Conn.

[2308.] 2. ALBERT F., b. April 26, 1839 ; m. Margaret E. Day, and, in 1868, was living in East Haddam, Conn.

[2309.] 3. CHARLES D., b. Jan. 4, 1842, and, in 1868, was living unm. in East Haddam, Conn.

CHILDREN OF ROSWELL C. PECK (1070) AND ELIZABETH S., HIS WIFE.

[2310.] 1. WASHINGTON C., b. in New London, Conn., June 21, 1852, and d., in infancy, in New London, Conn.

[2311.] 2. WILLIE C., b. in Willington, Conn., Jan. 11, 1854, and d., in Willington, Conn., Aug. 24, 1855.

[2312.] 3. FREDERICK H., b. in Hartford, Conn., Dec. 25, 1855, and d., in Hartford, Conn., Jan. 26, 1858.

[2313.] 4. EDWARD P., b. in Hartford, Conn., April 1, 1857, and, in 1868, was living in East Haddam, Conn.

[2314.]   5. WILLIE E., b. in Springfield, Mass., Jan. 22, 1860, and, in 1868, was living in East Haddam, Conn.

[2315.]   6. MARY E., b. in Long Meadow, Mass., Oct. 21, 1864, and d., in East Haddam, Conn., Feb. 16, 1865.

[2316.]   7. LIZZIE, b. in East Haddam, Conn., July 16, 1867, and, in 1868, was living in East Haddam, Conn.

CHILDREN OF JOSEPH V. PECK (1074) AND ABECCA, HIS WIFE, ALL BORN IN PENN'S MANOR, IOWA.

[2317.]   1. LUCINA, b. April 5, 1856, and, in 1868, was living in Penn's Manor, Iowa.

[2318.]   2. WALLACE R., b. June 7, 1857, and d., in Penn's Manor, Iowa, July 26, 1858.

[2319.]   3. EDITH, b. Dec. 6, 1858, and d., in Penn's Manor, Iowa, July 29, 1859.

[2320.]   4. EMMA V., b. Oct. 1, 1859, and d., in Penn's Manor, Iowa, Oct. 1, 1859.

[2321.]   5. EMMA J., b. Sept. 29, 1861, and d., in Penn's Manor, Iowa, March 26, 1863.

[2322.]   6. CLARA M., b. April 26, 1863, and, in 1868, was living in Penn's Manor, Iowa.

CHILDREN OF RICHARD E. PECK (1075) ALL BORN IN MONROE, O.

[2323.]   1. AMELIA M., b. June 19, 1835, and d., in Monroe, O., June 18, 1851.

[2324.]   2. JEDEDIAH, b. Oct. 19, 1836, and, in 1867, was living in the State of Indiana.

[2325.]   3. CLARISSA F., b. Sept. 8, 1841, and, in 1867, was living in Sheffield, O.

[2326.]   4. FRANK E., b. March 11, 1853, and, in 1867, was living in Monroe, O.

[2327.]   5. WILBER E., b. Sept. 14, 1858, and, in 1867, was living in Monroe, O.

[2328.]   6. DENNIS E., b. June 3, 1861, and, in 1867, was living in Monroe, O.

[2329.] 7. MERTON, b. June 27, 1864, and, in 1867, was living in Monroe, O.

CHILDREN OF ERASTUS PECK (1076) AND CANDACE, HIS WIFE.

[2330.] 1. ESTHER A., b. in Kingsville, O., June 23, 1833; m. Bryan C. Smith, Feb. 29, 1860, and, in 1867, was living in Sheffield, O.

[2331.] 2. URSULA S., b. in Monroe, O., Nov. 4, 1835; m. Augustus B. Maltby, Oct. 2, 1853, and, in 1867, was living in Denmark, O.

[2332.] 3. SARAH A., b. in Kingsville, O., March 23, 1838, and d., in Kingsville, O., April 4, 1841.

[2333.] 4. MALVINA A., b. in Kingsville, O., June 12, 1842, and, in 1867, was living unm. in Kingsville, O.

CHILDREN OF ELISHA PECK (1078) AND AMANDA, HIS WIFE, ALL BORN IN SHEFFIELD, O.

[2334.] 1. HARRIET E., b. Nov. 8, 1844; m. Reason A. J. Debolt, Oct. 18, 1866, and, in 1867, was living in Elkhart, Ind.

[2335.] 2. CAROLINE A., b. Oct. 17, 1846; m. Henry D. Cleveland, Jan. 15, 1867, and, in 1867, was living in Denmark, Ohio.

[2336.] 3. MYRON W., b. Sept. 16, 1848, and, in 1867, was living in Elkhart, Ind.

[2337.] 4. THEODORE E., b. Oct. 19, 1850, and, in 1867, was living in Elkhart, Ind.

[2338.] 5. ELLEN A., b. July 14, 1855, and. in 1867, was living in Elkhart, Ind.

CHILDREN OF ELIJAH PECK (1079) AND ADALINE, HIS WIFE, ALL BORN IN SHEFFIELD, O.

[2339.] 1. SIDNEY S., b. Sept. 4, 1844, and, d., in Sheffield, O., May 23, 1852.

[2340.] 2. SARAH A., b. Oct. 18, 1853, and, in 1867, was living in Sheffield, O.

[2341.] 3. CLARISSA L., b. Oct. 23, 1855, and, in 1867, was living in Sheffield, O.

CHILDREN OF DAVID W. PECK (1081) AND JULIA A., HIS WIFE, ALL BORN IN SHEFFIELD, O.

[2342.] 1. MARY A., b. Feb. 1, 1857, and d. in Sheffield, O., Jan. 23, 1864.

[2343.] 2. LAURA A., b. Nov. 9, 1858, and d., in Sheffield, O., Jan. 27, 1864.

[2344.] 3. TERNIA J., b. June 23, 1861, and, in 1867, was living in Denmark, O.

CHILDREN OF PETER PECK, (1086).

[2345.] 1. PAULINA J., b. in Fredericktown, O., Sept. 30 1838 ; m. Benjamin F. Johnson, Dec. 25, 1855, and, in 1867, was living in Edgewood, Ill.

[2346.] 2. SARAH S., b. in Fredericktown, O., March 14, 1841; m. James Pugh, June 15, 1855, and d., in Huntersville, O., Aug. 9, 1856.

[2347.] 3. WILLARD S., b. in Fredericktown, O., Jan. 15, 1844 ; m. Ellen Buchanan, Feb. 8, 1866, and, in 1868, was living in Huntersville, O.

[2348.] 4. ESTHER M., b. in Amity, O., June 3, 1849 ; m. Joseph Burdick, March 26, 1866, and, in 1868, was living in Niles, Mich.

[2349.] 5. MARY E., b. in Liverpool, O., Sept. 13, 1853, and, in 1868, was living in Millburgh, Mich.

[2350.] 6. JOHN T., b. in Huntersville, O., April 24, 1858, and d., in Huntersville, O., June 8, 1858.

[2351.] 7. PETER J., b. in Huntersville, O., Jan. 27, 1862, and, in 1868, was living in Millburgh, Mich.

CHILDREN OF MYRON H. PECK (1101) AND DELIA M., HIS WIFE.

[2352.] 1. MYRON H., b. in Victor, N. Y., June 6, 1850, and, in 1869, was living in Batavia, N. Y.

[2353.] 2. WILLARD P., b. in Canandaigua, N. Y., Jan. 3, 1852, and d., in Batavia, N. Y., Jan. 4, 1860.

[2354.] 3. CHARLES B., b. in Canandaigua, N. Y., Nov. 8, 1856, and, in 1869, was living in Batavia, N. Y.

[2355.] 4. JULIA M., b. in Batavia, N. Y., June 1, 1858, and, in 1869, was living in Batavia, N. Y.

[2356.] 5. WILLIAM O., b. in Batavia, N. Y., Nov. 18, 1859, and, in 1869, was living in Batavia, N. Y.

[2357.] 6. ELLA D., b. in LeRoy, N. Y., May 6, 1862, and, in 1869, was living in Batavia, N. Y.

CHILDREN OF NELSON C. PECK, (1117).

[2358.] 1. MARY JANE, b. in Pittsfield, N. Y., Oct. 8, 1839, and, in 1870, was living unm. in Schenectady, N. Y.

[2359.] 2. CHARLES A., b. in Bern, N. Y., April 11, 1845; m. Abbie Lappens, July 8, 1865, and, in 1870, was living in Clifton Park, N. Y.

[2360.] 3. ALBINA, b. in Clifton Park, N. Y., Aug. 12, 1848; m. Henry Watson, Nov. 10, 1866, and, in 1870, was living in Albany, N. Y.

[2361.] 4. ANNA M., b. in Clifton Park, N. Y., Aug. 23, 1850, and, in 1870, was living unm. at Tribe's Hill, N. Y.

[2362.] 5. LYMAN Z., b. in Clifton Park, N. Y., June 13, 1853, and, in 1870, was living unm. in Clifton Park, N. Y.

[2363.] 6. ELLA, b. in Clifton Park, N. Y., Aug. 17, 1854, and, in 1870, was living at Tribe's Hill, N. Y.

CHILDREN OF LYMAN Z. PECK (1119) AND MARIA A., HIS WIFE.

[2364.] 1. DAVID D., b. in Glen, N. Y., Dec. 28, 1840, and d. there March 7, 1842.

[2365.] 2. AMBROSIA J., b. in Glen, N. Y., June 9, 1843; m. Albert H. Sarle, July 14, 1867, and, in 1870, was living in Pittsfield, N. Y.

[2366.] 3. ANNIE E., b. in Clifton Park, N. Y., June 18, 1846, and, in 1870, was living unm. in Pittsfield, N. Y.

[2367.] 4. LYMAN Z., b. in Clifton Park, N. Y., Jan. 13, 1849, and, d. there Sept. 18, 1852.

[2368.] 5. CALISTA, b. in Clifton Park, N. Y., Sept. 10, 1856, and d. there Aug. 17, 1857.

[2369.] 6. GEORGE H. C., b. in Clifton Park, N. Y., Oct. 1, 1859, and, in 1870, was living unm. in Pittsfield, N. Y.

CHILDREN OF HIRAM PECK (1127) AND HARRIET, HIS WIFE.

[2370.] 1. WILSON b. in New Lyme, O., March 10, 1852, and. in 1870, was living in Rome, O.

[2371.] 2. FLORENCE, b. in New Lyme, O., Nov. 7, 1853, and, in 1870, was living in Rome, O.

[2372.] 3. LOIS, b. in Rome, O., Oct. 14, 1864, and, in 1870, was living in Rome, O.

[2373.] 4. HIRAM L., b. in Rome, O., March 14, 1859, and, in 1870, was living in Rome, O.

ONLY CHILD OF EDWARD C. PECK, JR., (1128).

[2374.] WESLEY, b. in New Lyme, O., Dec. 22, 1851, and, in 1870, was living in Colebrook, O.

CHILDREN OF MATTHEW G. PECK (1129) AND WEALTHY, HIS WIFE, ALL BORN IN NEW LYME, O.

[2375.] 1. EUGENE, b. Sept. 25, 1855, and, in 1870, was living in New Lyme, O.

[2376.] 2. IDA, b. Sept. 25, 1858, and, in 1870, was living in New Lyme, O.

[2377.] 3. OTIS, b. Jan. 29, 1860, and, in 1870, was living in New Lyme, O.

[2378.] 4. ANNA, b. May 23, 1862, and, in 1870, was living in New Lyme, O.

[2379.] 5. URINA A., b. March 18, 1864, and, in 1870, was living in New Lyme, O.

ONLY CHILD OF FENNIMORE E. PECK (1133) AND MARION, HIS WIFE.

[2380.] STRONG L., b. in New Lyme, O., Aug. 6, 1869, and was living there in 1870.

CHILDREN OF WILLIAM S. PECK (1135) AND ELIZABETH, HIS WIFE, ALL BORN IN KANE CO., ILL., EXCEPT CHARLES D., WHO WAS BORN IN GRUNDY CO., IOWA.

[2381.] 1. WILLIAM HENRY, b. Nov. 20, 1839; m. Esther L. ———, and, in 1872, was living in Fairfield, Grundy Co., Iowa.

[2382.] 2. RACHEL A., b. June 5, 1844; m. Pravella A. Bronson, Jan. 19, 1864, and, in 1870, was living in Plymouth Co., Iowa.

[2383.] 3. GEORGE G., b. Jan. 19, 1847; m. Myra Prichard, Nov. 18, 1868, and, in 1870, was living in Beaver, Grundy Co., Iowa.

[2384.] 4. MARY E., b. Oct. 16, 1849; m. Charles Collins Sept. 13, 1866, and, in 1870, was living in Plymouth Co., Iowa.

[2385.] 5. ALVIRA E., b. Feb. 9, 1852; m. Charles Waite, July 17, 1870, and was then living in Spencer, Iowa.

[2386.] 6. CHARLES D., b. in Grundy County, Iowa, July 27, 1857, and was living there in 1870.

CHILDREN OF JOSIAH J. PECK (1139) AND CATHARINE, HIS WIFE.

[2387.] 1. MARY E., b. in Kane Co., Ill., July 13, 1851, and m. Luchar Walker.

[2388.] 2. ELLA R., b. in Kane Co., Ill., March 24, 1853, and m. Robert Post.

[2389.] 3. WALLIS U., b. in Kane Co., Ill., April 29, 1855.

[2890.] 4. RACHEL O., b. in Grundy Co., Iowa, April 25, 1857.

[2391.] 5. WILLIAM B., b. in Grundy Co., Iowa, Feb. 24, 1860.

CHILDREN OF SILAS PECK (1140) AND MARIA, HIS WIFE, BOTH
BORN IN GRUNDY CO., IOWA.

[2392.] 1. EVART, b. April 3, 1861, and was living in Beaver, Iowa, in 1870.

[2393.] 2. C. WILBUR, b. April 18, 1867, and d., in Fairfield, Iowa, April 3, 1868.

ONLY CHILD OF NELSON H. PECK (1141) AND JANE, HIS WIFE,
BORN IN GRUNDY CO., IOWA.

[2394.] FREDERICK A., b. July 27, 1865, and d., in Beaver, Iowa, in Feb. 1870.

CHILDREN OF LESTER S. PECK (1142) AND CLARA, HIS WIFE,
ALL BORN IN GRUNDY CO., IOWA.

[2395.] 1. FLORENCE, b. Jan. 14, 1860, and, in 1870, was living in Beaver, Iowa.

[2396.] 2. CORA F., b. Sept. 7, 1864, and d., in Fairfield, Grundy Co., Iowa, in Nov. 1870.

[2397.] 3. HATTY A., b. May 2, 1868, and d., in Fairfield, Grundy Co., Iowa, in Feb. 1870.

CHILDREN OF JOSIAH PECK (1145) AND MINERVA, HIS WIFE, ALL
BORN IN COLEBROOK, OHIO.

[2398.] 1. CLAYTON L., b. June 19, 1860, and, in 1870, was living in Colebrook, O.

[2399] 2. LOVANDO B., b. Sept. 30, 1862, and, in 1870, was living in Colebrook, O.

[2400.] 3. URBINE, b. June 16, 1865, and, in 1870, was living in Colebrook, O.

[2401.] 4. BETSEY D., b. Nov. 9, 1867, and, in 1870, was living in Colebrook, O.

[2402.] 5. MYRON C., b. Nov. 6, 1869, and, in 1870, was living in Colebrook, O.

CHILDREN OF JOHN B. PECK (1146) AND BETSEY, HIS WIFE.

[2403.] 1. LEONA, b. in Colebrook, O., July 24, 1857, and d. there in Feb. 1867.

[2404.] 2. CORNELIA, b. in Colebrook, O., in Jan. 1861, and, in 1870, was living at Grand Rapids, Mich.

[2405.] 3. CHARLES, b. in Venango, Penn., in Jan. 1866, and, in 1870, was living in Ashtabula, O.

CHILDREN OF SAMUEL PECK (1147) AND JANE, HIS WIFE, BOTH BORN IN COLEBROOK, OHIO.

[2406.] 1. ELON, b. Aug. 31, 1862, and d., in Colebrook, O., in Aug. 1863.

[2407.] 2. CLARENCE, b. Aug. 14, 1868, and, in 1870, was living in Colebrook, O.

CHILDREN OF JOHN S. PECK (1150) AND ANTOINETTE, HIS WIFE, ALL BORN IN NEW LYME, OHIO.

[2408.] 1. ELLEN V., b. Oct. 30, 1853, and, in 1870, was living in New Lyme, O.,

[2409.] 2. ASHLEY S., b. March 27, 1855, and d., in New Lyme, O., March 10, 1866.

[2410.] 3. MARY D. E., b. Feb. 9, 1857, and, in 1870, was living in New Lyme, O.

[2411.] 4. INEZ A., b. Feb. 21, 1867, and, in 1870, was living in New Lyme, O.

CHILDREN OF EDWIN A. PECK (1160) AND URANA, HIS WIFE.

[2412.] 1. ELMER A., b. in Orwell, O., April 1, 1858, and was living there in 1870.

[2413.] 2. EDNA A., b. in Orwell, O., Jan. 24, 1860, and was living there in 1870.

[2414.] 3. MELVILLE, b. in Union, Iowa, March 18, 1863, and, in 1870, was living in Orwell, O.

[2415.] 4. LEANDER R., b. in Orwell, O., Feb. 17, 1868, and, in 1870, was living in Orwell, Vt.

CHILDREN OF AMOS A. PECK (1161) AND ELIZABETH, HIS WIFE.

[2416.] 1. WILLARD S., b. in Warren, Penn., Aug. 5, 1858, and, in 1870, was living in Rome, O.

[2417.] 2. ALMIRA S., b. in Orwell, O., March 21, 1860, and, in 1870, was living in Rome, O.

[2418.] 3. CHARLES G., b. at Cedar Falls, Iowa, April 12, 1863, and, in 1870, was living in Rome, O.

[2419.] 4. LEWIS A. L., b. in Rome, O., June 29, 1865, and was living there in 1870.

[2420.] 5. ALLEN J., b. in Rome, O., March 1, 1868, and was living there in 1870.

CHILDREN OF STEPHEN L. PECK (1166) AND PRUDENCE, HIS WIFE.

[2421.] 1. MALISSA P., b. in Clarence, N. Y., Jan. 31, 1820 ; m. 1. John W. Bodge, Oct. 14, 1839, who d. in Feb. 1862, and m. 2. Rev. George Reid, May 17, 1864, and, in 1871, was living in Nevada, O.

[2422.] 2. PRUDENCE, b. in Clarence, N. Y., March 19, 1822 ; m. Rev. J. C. Kingsley, Aug. 14, 1844, and, in 1871, was living in Urbana, O.

[2423.] 3. ELIAS, b. in Clarence, N. Y., May 5, 1823, and d., in Clinton, O., in the Fall of 1828.

[2424.] 4. STEPHEN L., b. in Clinton, O., Sept. 18, 1828 ; m. Mary Morse, and d., in Worthington, O., Oct. 19, 1858.

[2425.] 5. WILLIAM CHARLES, b. in Clinton, O., Dec. 9, 1833 ; m. Rosa B. Foss, March 9, 1857, and, in 1876, was living in Springfield, Mo.

[2426.] 6. HENRY, b. in Clinton, O., Sept. 8, 1838, and d. unm., in Worthington. O., Dec. 22, 1858.

CHILDREN OF NATHANIEL PECK (1169) AND LYDIA, HIS WIFE.

[2427.] 1. ELVIRA, b. in Clarence, N. Y., in 1822 ; m. 1. Alfred Fox, who d. in 1852 ; m. 2. George Turner, and, in 1872, was living in Millington, Mich.

[2428.]   2. MARY A., b. in Clarence, N. Y., Oct. 18, 1825 ; m. L. H. Husted, July 4, 1847, and, in 1872, was living in Groveland, Mich.

[2429.]   3. LYDIA A., b. in Clarence, N. Y., Feb. 4, 1827 ; m. H. N. Jennings, Feb. 24, 1853, and, in 1872, was living in Fenton, Mich.

[2430.]   4. CHARLES W., b. in Clarence, N. Y., Aug. 15, 1829 ; m. Sophia Francis, Oct. 16, 1859, and, in 1872, was living in Holly, Mich.

[2431.]   5. JOHN T., b. in Clarence, N. Y., Jan. 8, 1831 ; m. Julia Johnson, July 13, 1858, and d., in Groveland, Mich., May 11, 1872.

[2432.]   6. MELISSA M., b. in Clarence, N. Y., April 4, 1833 ; m. Joseph Phipps, in Oct. 1848, and, in 1872, was living in Groveland, Mich.

[2433.]   7. CAROLINE C., b. in Clarence, N. Y., Nov. 4, 1835 ; m. Eber P. Taylor, Aug. 16, 1856, and, in 1872, was living in Groveland, Mich.

[2434.]   8. LOUISA H., b. in Groveland, Mich., Nov. 3, 1840, and, in 1872, was living unm. in Groveland, Mich.

[2435.]   9. ABNER A., b. in Groveland, Mich., Dec. 21, 1844 ; m. Augusta Valette, July 3, 1866, and, in 1872, was living in Groveland, Mich.

CHILDREN OF CHARLES L. PECK, (1170).

[2436.]   1. HARRIET, b. at Mulberry Gap, Tenn., Aug. 2, 1827 ; m. John W. Lowery, May 31, 1843, and, in 1871, was living in Green Co., Mo.

[2437.]   2. STEPHEN L., b. at Mulberry Gap, Tenn., Feb. 1830 ; m. Mary Killingworth, June 4, 1851, and, in 1871, was living in Green Co., Mo.

[2438.]   3. JAMES L., b. in Lee Co., Va., June 15, 1832 ; m. Mary C. Bingham, in Dec. 1855, and d., in California, Oct. 18, 1864.

[2439.]   4. WILLIAM L., b. in Lee Co., Va., June 30, 1834; m. Nancy McClure, Nov. 16, 1865, and, in 1871, was living in Forsyth, Mo.

[2440.]   5. MARTHA, b. in Greene Co., Mo., Sept. 19, 1837 ; m. Webb B. Grant, Feb. 23, 1858, and, in 1871, was living in Greene Co., Mo.

[2441.]   6. HANNIBAL, b. in Greene Co., Mo., May 10, 1840; m. Elizabeth Clark, Nov. 25, 1863, and, in 1871, was living in Granby, Mo.

[2442.]   7. MARY ANN, b. in Greene Co., Mo., March 13, 1842 ; m. Hugh L. Hale, Jan. 17, 1861, and d., in Siderly, Mo., Nov. 5, 1864.

[2443.]   8. ELIZABETH, b. in Greene Co., Mo., March 13, 1842 ; m. John W. Hale, Sept. 4, 1862, and, in 1871, was living in Arkansas.

[2444.]   9. ELVIRA, b. in Greene Co., Mo., June 12, 1844 ; m. John W. Hudgeon, Dec. 30, 1866, and, in 1871, was living in Greene Co., Mo.

[2445.]   10. JOHN, b. in Greene Co., Mo., Aug. 22, 1849 ; m. Nancy Jane Rooks, Feb. 11, 1869, and, in 1871, was living in Greene Co., Mo.

[2446.]   11. LOUISA, b. in Greene Co., Mo., Jan. 25, 1833, and was living there in 1871.

[2447.]   12. ORLINA, b. in Greene Co., Mo., Jan. 3, 1869, and was living there in 1871.

CHILDREN OF HARRIS PECK, JR., (1173) AND MARTHA, HIS WIFE.

[2448.]   1. ELIZA JANE, b. in Mendow, N. Y., Dec. 26, 1828 ; m. Chauncey Cooley, Feb. 5, 1848, and, in 1872, was living in St. Dervin, Nemaha Co., Neb.

[2449.]   2. WILLIAM C., b. in New London O., April 6, 1832 ; m. Sarah A. Green, Feb. 28, 1854, and, in 1872, was living in Chicago, Ill.

[2450.]   3. MARTHA A., b. in Cleveland, O., Nov. 6, 1836 ; m. Irvin Barnard, in Sept. 1856, and, in 1872, was living in San Buenaventura, Cal.

[2451.]   4. MARY L., b. in New London, O., April 2, 1841; m. Horatio D. Brown, Dec. 19, 1861, and, in 1872, was living in Albert Lea, Minn.

CHILDREN OF COLEMAN C. PECK (1178) AND BETSEY, HIS WIFE.

[2452.]   1. ⎧ HE is said to have three daughters, whose
[2453.]   2 ⎪ names, dates of birth, and present residence
[2454.]   3: ⎨ are unknown. They are supposed to have
         ⎩ lately resided in Marcellus, Cass Co. Mich.

CHILDREN OF RICHARD L. PECK (1180) AND ROXANA, HIS WIFE.

[2455.]   1. HORACE L., b. in LaGrange, O., May 18, 1841, and, in 1872, was living in Wellington, O.

[2456.]   2. MARION, b. in Wellington, O., Feb. 12, 1843, and was living there in 1872.

[2457.]   3. ⎧
[2458.]   4. ⎨ . THERE are said to be three other children,
[2459.]   5. ⎩ whose names, &c., are unknown.

CHILDREN OF SAMUEL I. PECK (1181) AND CAROLINE, HIS WIFE.

[2460.]   1. CHARLES M., b. in Wellington, O., Jan. 1, 1850, and, in 1872, was living unm. in Pittsfield, O.

[2461.]   2. TRACY L., b. in Wellington, O., Nov. 27, 1853, and was living unm., in Pittsfield, O., in 1872.

[2462.]   3. ELLEN IDA, b. in Pittsfield, O., May 12, 1854, and was living there in 1872.

[2463.]   4. ADA A., b. in Pittsfield, O., May 20, 1860, and was living there in 1872.

CHILDREN OF OSCAR J. PECK (1182) AND CHARLOTTE, HIS WIFE, ALL BORN IN WELLINGTON, OHIO.

[2464.]   1. HARRIS W., b. Sept. 22, 1856, and, in 1872, was living in Wellington, O.

[2465.]   2. HENRY JAY, b. March 11, 1858, and, in 1872, was living in Wellington, O.

[2466.] 3. GEORGIA, b. Feb. 29, 1860, and, in 1872, was living in Wellington, O.

[2467.] 4. { IT is said there are two additional children,
[2468.] 5. { whose names, &c., have not been ascertained.

CHILDREN OF JOHN CLARK PECK (1183) AND HULDAH, HIS WIFE.

[2469.] 1. LEON GIBBS, b. in Wellington, O., Oct. 16, 1866, and, in 1872, was living in Pittsfield, O.

[2470.] 2. THERE is said to be another child, whose name, &c., has not been ascertained.

CHILDREN OF JASPER C. PECK (1188) AND MARY C., HIS WIFE, ALL BORN IN WEST BLOOMFIELD, N. Y.

[2471.] 1. CASSIUS C., b. Dec. 10, 1844 ; m. Mary D. Kelly, Oct. 1, 1867, and, in 1874, was living in West Bloomfield, N. Y. His wife d., in Chicago, Ill., Feb. 15, 1871, where he then resided.

[2472.] 2. MARY E., b. April 17, 1846, and, in 1871, was living unm. in West Bloomfield, N. Y.

[2473.] 3. LYRA R., b. Nov. 1, 1854, and, in 1871, was living in West Bloomfield, N. Y.

[2474.] 4. FLORENCE H., b. Feb. 3, 1862, and d., May 25, 1874, in West Bloomfield, N. Y.

CHILDREN OF ABEL H. PECK (1189) AND SARAH, HIS WIFE.

[2475.] 1. CAROLINE A., b. in West Bloomfield, N. Y., Dec. 20, 1833 ; m. William Satterlee, in 1855, and, in 1869, was living in Bloomfield, Mich.

[2476.] 2. FRANK C., b. in Pontiac, Mich., Aug. 16, 1838 · m. Lizzie Valandingham, Nov. 30, 1861, and, in 1869, was living at Fort Harker, Kan.

[2477.] 3. MARCUS H., b. in Pontiac, Mich., Nov. 17, 1842, and, in 1869, was living in Leavenworth, Kan.

CHILDREN OF JOSEPH A. PECK (1190) AND SUSAN, HIS WIFE, ALL
BORN IN PONTIAC, MICH.

[2478.]   1. ANNING R., b. Jan. 31, 1846, and, in 1869, was
living unm. in Adrian, Mich.

[2479.]   2. HELEN M., b. Feb. 28, 1850, and, in 1869, was
living unm. in Kalamazoo, Mich.

[2480.]   3. ISRAEL P., b. May 10, 1854, and, in 1869, was
living in Kalamazoo, Mich.

[2481.]   4. CLARA M., b. Oct. 8, 1857, and, in 1869, was
living in Kalamazoo, Mich.

CHILDREN OF SAMUEL D. PECK (1197) AND NANCY W., HIS WIFE.

[2482.]   1. ANN E., b. in West Bloomfield, N. Y., Feb. 13,
1845, and, in 1867, was living unm. in Colony, Iowa.

[2483.]   2. RUTH E., b. at Turkey River, Iowa, Sept. 23,
1847, and, in 1867, was living unm. in Colony, Iowa.

[2484.]   3. MARTHA C., b. at Turkey River, Iowa, March
16, 1850, and, in 1867, was living unm. in Colony, Iowa.

[2485.]   4. SARAH F., b. at Peck's Ferry, Iowa, Aug. 14,
1852, and, in 1867, was living in Colony, Iowa.

[2486.]   5. FLORENCE, b. in Colony, Iowa, May 25, 1857,
and was living there in 1867.

[2487.]   6. PALMER D., b. in Colony, Iowa, Dec. 18, 1860,
and was living there in 1867.

[2488.]   7. ELMER E., b. in Colony, Iowa, Dec. 11, 1862,
and was living there in 1867.

[2489]   8. MARCUS S., b. in Colony, Iowa, Feb. 24, 1864,
and was living there in 1867.

CHILDREN OF DOUGLASS PECK, (1198).

[2490.]   1. ELLEN M., b. in East Mendon, N. Y., March
15, 1851, and d. there Oct. 5, 1851.

[2491.]   2. RICHARD W., b. in Colesburgh, Iowa, Aug. 11,
1859, and was living there in 1867.

[2492.] 3. ALBERT D., b. in Colesburgh, Iowa, Oct. 22 1861, and was living there in 1867.

[2493.] 4. MARY C., b. in Colesburgh, Iowa, July 25, 1864, and was living there in 1867.

[2494.] 5. not named, b. in Colesburgh, Iowa, Jan. 25, 1867, and was living there in 1867.

ONLY CHILD OF OLIVER PECK (1199) AND HULDAH MARIA, HIS WIFE, BORN IN SHEFFIELD, MASS.

[2495.] CATHARINE E., b. Nov. 20, 1826, and, in 1875, was living in Sheffield, Mass.

CHILDREN OF MATTHEW J. PECK (1205) AND MARIANNA, HIS WIFE, BOTH BORN IN WEST BLOOMFIELD, N. Y.

[2496.] 1. HOWARD H., b. Dec. 6, 1858, and, in 1869, was living in West Bloomfield, N. Y.

[2497.] 2. MARY A., b. March 9, 1864, and, in 1869, was living in West Bloomfield, N. Y.

CHILDREN OF RICHARD H. PECK (1206) AND MARY, HIS WIFE.

[2498.] 1. FANNY H., b. in Chatham, N. Y., April 26, 1843, and, in 1869, was living unm. in Austin, Texas.

[2499.] 2. FREDERICK T. E., b. in Chatham, N. Y., Oct. 27, 1844, and, in 1869, was living unm. in Austin, Texas.

[2500.] 3. MARY E., b. in Chatham, N. Y., Oct. 3, 1846, and, in 1869, was living unm. in Austin, Texas.

[2501.] 4. SARAH T. E., b. in Austin, Texas, Jan. 29, 1853, and was living there in 1869.

[2502.] 5. PHEBE C., b. in Austin, Texas, Oct. 17, 1854, and, was living there in 1869.

CHILDREN OF OLIVER J. PECK (1207) AND ANGELINE R., HIS WIFE, BOTH BORN IN CHATHAM, N. Y.

[2503.] 1. ROBERT H., b. Aug. 13, 1850, and d., in Chatham, N. Y., Nov. 10, 1862.

[2504.]   2. BESSIE, b. Feb. 28, 1863, and, in 1869, was living in Chatham, N. Y.

CHILDREN OF EDWARD R. PECK (1208) AND MARY, HIS WIFE, BOTH BORN IN KINDERHOOK, N. Y.

[2506.]   1. CHARLES J., b. July 20, 1859, and, in 1869, was living in Kinderhook, N. Y.

[2507.]   2. HERBERT E., b. Feb. 28, 1863, and, in 1869, was living in Kinderhook, N. Y.

ONLY CHILD OF PALMER PECK (1210) AND SELA, HIS WIFE, BORN IN WEST BLOOMFIELD, N. Y.

[2508.]   ELISHA T., b. March 2, 1827 ; m. Marion Rowley, and, in 1869, was living in San Francisco, Cal.

CHILDREN OF JEREMIAH PECK (1212) AND JULIA A., HIS WIFE, ALL BORN IN WEST BLOOMFIELD, N. Y.

[2509.]   1. JOHN S., b. Dec. 17, 1833 ; m. Mary Hines, and, in 1869, was living in Adrian, Mich.

[2510.]   2. HILAND A., b. Dec. 3, 1834 ; m. Myra Woodruff, Aug. 10, 1833, who d. May 9, 1864, and, in 1869, was living in Rochester, N. Y.

[2511.]   3. FRANKLIN W., b. May 1, 1836 ; m. Mary Sullivan, and, in 1869, was living in Brockport, N. Y.

[2512.]   4. SARAH A., b. Feb. 7, 1838 ; m. John Y. Raines, Aug. 13, 1859, who d., Dec. 18, 1864, and, in 1869, was living in West Bloomfield, N. Y.

CHILDREN OF NATHAN PECK (1213) AND MARY, HIS WIFE, ALL BORN IN LIMA, N. Y.

[2513.]   1. ELIZABETH, b. Nov. 19, 1837, and d., in Lima, N. Y., Oct. 15, 1858.

[2514.]   2. CAROLINE, b. March 28, 1839, and d., in Lima, N. Y., Aug. 30, 1840,

[2515.]   3. ANN V., b. Dec. 18, 1840, and, in 1869, was living unm. in Lockport, N. Y.

[2516.]   4. MARITTA A., b. April 23, 1842, and, in 1869, was living unm. in Buffalo, N. Y.

[2517.]   5. EMILY C., b. Dec. 9, 1843, and d., in Lima, N. Y., Sept. 11, 1845.

[2518.]   6. MARVIOR, b. Nov. 7, 1846, and, in 1869, was living unm. in Lima, N. Y.

[2519.]   7. SARAH L., b. March 20, 1848 ; m. John E. Wager, Dec. 29, 1869, and was then living in West Bloomfield, N. Y.

[2520.]   8. JOHN S., b. May 30, 1850, and, in 1869, was living in Lima, N. Y.

[2521.]   9. CHARLES W., b. March 8, 1853, and, in 1869, was living in Lima, N. Y.

[2522.]   10. GEORGE E., b. June 17, 1854, and, in 1869, was living in Lima, N. Y.

[2523.]   11. JENNIE C., b. Nov. 3 1857, and, in 1869, was living in Lima, N. Y.

CHILDREN OF HENRY PECK, (1214).

[2524.]   1. HENRY G., b. in Lima, N. Y., Feb. 11, 1828 ; m. Theresa M. Jacobs, Jan. 3, 1855, and, in 1869, was living in Victor, N. Y.

[2525.]   2. JENETTE, b. in Lima, N. Y., Sept. 14, 1830; m. Martin Hall, April 11, 1855, and, in 1869, was living in Hamburgh, Mich.

[2526.]   3. JAMES, b. in Lima, N. Y., in 1835, and d. there Feb. 3, 1845.

[2527.]   4. DELIA, b. in Lima, N. Y., May 23, 1840 ; m. Martin Boughton, Dec. 28, 1856, and, in 1869, was living in East Bloomfield, N. Y.

CHILDREN OF RICHARD PECK (1219), ALL BORN IN LIMA, N. Y.

[2528.]   1. JAMES B., b. May 4, 1835 ; m. Juliet Sprague, Oct. 20, 1858, and, in 1869, was living in Lima, N. Y.

[2529.] 2. ASAHEL B., b. Jan. 21, 1837 ; m. Helen M. Steele, Sept. 12, 1860, and, in 1769, was living in Lima, N. Y.

[2530.] 3. MARY ELIZABETH, b. Nov. 8, 1846, and, in 1869, was living unm. in Lima, N. Y.

CHILDREN OF SYLVANUS PECK (1222) AND JEMIMA, HIS WIFE, ALL BORN IN LIMA, N. Y.

[2531.] 1. GEORGE, b. June 2, 1845 ; m. Frances Rice, June 20, 1865, and, in 1869, was living in Salamanca, N. Y.

[2532.] 2. THOMAS, d. while in service in the army, in the war of the Rebellion.

[2533.] 3. SARAH, b. Jan. 31, 1851.

CHILDREN OF EDWARD W. PECK (1224) AND LUCY B., HIS WIFE.

[2534.] 1. LUCY A., b. in Troy, Mich., April 27, 1834 ; m. David H. Jerome, June 15, 1859, and, in 1869, was living in Saginaw, Mich.

[2535.] 2. BETSEY M., b. in Troy, Mich., Feb. 2, 1836 · m. Byron B. Buckhout, Nov. 18, 1857, and, in 1869, was living in East Saginaw, Mich.

[2536.] 3. EDWARD I., b. in Pontiac, Mich., May 11, 1855, and, in 1869, was living in Pontiac, Mich.

CHILDREN OF JOSEPH FRANKLIN PECK (1225) AND CLARISSA, HIS WIFE.

[2537.] 1. CHARLES H., b. in West Bloomfield, N. Y., Sept. 28, 1835, and d., in Lima, N. Y., Feb. 6, 1836.

[2538.] 2. JULIA E., b. in Lima, N. Y., July 24, 1837, and, in 1870, was living unm. in Springfield, Mass.

[2539.] 3. SARAH L., b. in Lima, N. Y., Sept. 28, 1839 ; m. Harvey B. Hazeltine, Dec. 8, 1858, and, in 1870, was living in Henrietta, N. Y.

[2540.] 4. FRANCES S., b. in Lima, N. Y., Aug. 2, 1843, and, in 1870, was living unm. in Springfield, Mass.

CHILDREN OF JOHN SEARS PECK (1228) AND MARY, HIS WIFE, ALL BORN IN WEST BLOOMFIELD, N. Y.

[2541.] 1. EMILY E., b. Jan. 19, 1849, and, in 1869, was living unm. in Oberlin, O.

[2542.] 2. MARY A., b. Dec. 13, 1850, and, in 1869, was living unm. in Oberlin, O.

[2543.] 3. JOHN F., b. Nov. 29, 1853, and, in 1869, was living in Oberlin, O.

[2544.] 4. EDWARD W., b. July 10, 1856, and, in 1869, was living in Oberlin, O.

[2545.] 5. CHARLES F., b. May 23, 1859, and d., in West Bloomfield, N. Y., June 10, 1859.

CHILDREN OF DESMOND G. PECK (1231) AND HARRIET, HIS WIFE, ALL BORN IN WEST BLOOMFIELD, N. Y.

[2547.] 1. AMELIA E., b. July 15, 1837 ; m. Nathan Hicks Lee, and, in 1869, was living in Romeo, Mich.

[2548.] 2. WATROUS, b. Dec. 28, 1840, and, in 1869, was living at Cedar Rapids, Iowa.

[2549.] 3. GILBERT W., b. Feb. 2, 1842 ; m. Libbie Gilbert, Jan. 1, 1869, and was then living in Richmond, N. Y.

[2550.] 4. FRANCES E., b. Feb. 15, 1844, and, in 1869, was living unm. in Richmond, N. Y.

CHILDREN OF VINTON PECK (1240), ALL BORN IN WEST BLOOMFIELD, N. Y.

[2551.] 1. CURTIS V., b June 2, 1847, and, in 1869, was living unm. in West Bloomfield, N. Y.

[2552.] 2. LLEWELLYN C., b. Nov. 9, 1850, and, in 1869, was living in West Bloomfield, N. Y.

[2553.] 3. NELLIE A., b. Nov. 13, 1859, and, in 1869, was living in West Bloomfield, N. Y.

[2554.] 4. WILLIAM H., b. in Jan. 1869, and was living in West Bloomfield, N. Y., in 1869.

CHILDREN OF THOMAS R. PECK (1244) AND JULIA F., HIS WIFE,
THE OLDEST BORN IN WEST BLOOMFIELD, AND
THE OTHERS IN WATERLOO, N. Y.

[2554.] 1. HERBERT H., b. Sept. 19, 1858, and, in 1869, was living in Waterloo, N. Y.

[2555.] 2. THOMAS REYNOLD, b. Jan. 4, 1864, and, in 1870, was living in Waterloo, N. Y.

[2556.] 3. BERTHA AMELIA, b. Dec. 8, 1865, and, in 1870, was living in Waterloo, N. Y.

[2557.] 4. HARRISON HOPKINS, b. July 21, 1869, and, in 1870, was living in Waterloo, N. Y.

CHILDREN OF THOMAS R. GOLD PECK (1254) AND SUSAN, HIS WIFE.

[2559.] 1. WILMOT D., b. in Brooklyn, N. Y., Aug. 22, 1860, and, in 1875, was living at Hastings upon Hudson, N. Y.

[2560.] 2. HENRY GOLD, b. at Hastings upon Hudson, N. Y., Dec. 16, 1861, and was living there in 1875.

CHILDREN OF HENRY DWIGHT PECK (1257) AND JENNIE M. HIS WIFE.

[2561.] 1. JENNIE M., b. in Lyme, Conn., June 7, 1869, and, in 1875, was living in Staunton, Va.

[——.] 2. JOHN S., b. in New Haven, Conn., Nov. 20, 1871, and, in 1875, was living in Staunton, Va.

[——.] 3. HORACE S., b. in Staunton, Va., Aug. 3, 1875 and was living there in 1876.

CHILDREN OF JOHN HENRY PECK (1267) AND JULIA E., HIS WIFE
ALL BORN IN CHICAGO, ILL.

[2562.] 1. JULIA AUGUSTA, b. Nov. 9, 1860, and d., in Chicago, the next day.

[2563.] 2. CARRIE WHITE, b. Dec. 10, 1863, and d., in Chicago, Ill., Aug. 11, 1864.

[2564.] 3. MAY AUGUSTA, b. in July 1869, and d., in Chicago, Ill., in 1871.

[2565.] 4. CAROLINE MITCHELL, d. at two years of age.

CHILD OF WILLIAM K. PECK (1276) AND ELIZA, HIS WIFE.

[2566.]   WILLIAM HENRY, b. in June 1839.

CHILDREN OF CHARLES C. PECK (1277) AND ANGELINE, HIS WIFE,
ALL BORN IN NEW YORK CITY.

[2567.]   1. EMILY SOMERS, b. in May 1856, and d. Nov.
25, 1859.
[2568.]   2. MARY LOUISA, b. Sept. 24, 1858.

CHILD OF HORACE E. PECK (1278) AND EMMA, HIS WIFE.

[2569.]   HERMAN K., b. in Sept. 1850.

CHILDREN OF ELEAZER C. PECK (1279) AND EUNICE H., HIS WIFE
ALL BORN IN LYME, CONN.

[2570.]   1. CHARLES E., b. Oct. 29, 1842.
[2571.]   2. ORRIN M., b. May 22, 1844.
[2572.]   3. WARREN J., b. Feb. 8, 1846.
[2573.]   4. HARRIET E., b. April 27, 1849.
[2574.]   5. SARAH E., b. April 4, 1851 ; m. Ebenezer Brockway, in Old Lyme, Conn., Jan. 22, 1874.
[2575.]   6. ALBERT W., b. in May 1853.
[2576.]   7. ELIZA C., b. in Sept. 1855 ; m. Charles H.
Morley, Jan. 22, 1874.
[2577.]   8. ANGELINE S., b. in April 1859, and d., in Lyme,
the same year.

CHILDREN OF GEORGE R. PECK (1285) AND ELIZABETH S., HIS
WIFE, ALL BORN IN LYME, CONN.

[2578.]   1. SETH L., b. Dec 6, 1825 ; m. Eunice Gallup,
June 6, 1849, and, in 1870, was living in Norwich, Conn.
[2579.]   2. JOSEPH, b. Aug. 1, 1828, and, in 1870, was living unm. in Lyme, Conn.
[2580.]   3. ESTHER, b. July 27, 1830, and, in 1870, was
living unm. in Lyme, Conn.

[2581.] 4. RICHARD W., b. Sept. 22, 1832 ; m. 1. Sarah A. Mather, Nov. 12, 1858 ; m. 2. Ellen E. Crosby, June 28, 1860, and, in 1870, was living at Deep River, Conn.

[2582.] 5. GEORGE, b. Nov. 5, 1834 ; m. Sarah F. Butler, and, iu 1868, was living in Detroit, Mich.

[2583.] 6. JAMES H., b. June 23, 1837 ; m. Mary E. Champlin, April 29, 1861, and, in 1870, was living in Pennsylvania.

[2584.] 7. FRANCIS E., b. July 11, 1839, and, in 1870, was living unm. in New Haven, Conn.

[2585.] 8. MARY E., b. Aug. 7, 1841, and, in 1870, was living unm. in New Haven, Conn.

[2586.] 9. JOHN H., b. Feb. 19, 1843, and d., in Lyme, Conn., Dec. 7, 1845.

[2587.] 10. WALTER S., b. July 14, 1846, and, in 1870, was living unm. in Lyme, Conn.

CHILDREN OF GILBERT M. PECK (1286) AND SARAH B., HIS WIFE, ALL BORN IN EAST BETHANY, N. Y.

[2588.] 1. HENRY C., b. April 12, 1838, and d. unm , in East Bethany, N. Y., June 12, 1861.

[2589.] 2. WILLIAM G., b. May 9, 1840 ; m. Ida D. Comstock, Oct. 28, 1868, and, in 1869, was living in New London, Conn.

[2590.] 3. S. FRANCES, b. Sept. 16, 1843, and d., in East Bethany, N. Y., June 10, 1845.

[2591.] 4. ANNER C., b. Jan. 18, 1847, and, in 1869, was living in East Bethany, N. Y.

CHILDREN OF NEWTON L. F. PECK (1294) AND SAMANTHA, HIS WIFE, ALL BORN IN SPRINGVILLE, LINN CO., IOWA, EXCEPT GEORGE H., WHO WAS BORN IN MIDDLETOWN, OHIO.

[2592.] 1. MARY I., b. Oct. 9, 1849 ; m. Isaac R. Worrall, Jan. 1, 1868, and, in 1870, was living in Springville, Iowa.

[2593.] 2. CHARLES N., b. Jan. 5, 1852, and, in 1870, was living in Springville, Iowa.

[2594.] 3. GEORGE H., b. in Middletown, O., April 8, 1854, and, in 1870, was living in Springville, Iowa.

[2595.] 4. DELIA A., b. May 2, 1857, and, in 1870, was living in Springville, Iowa.

[2596.] 5. JOHN F., b. Aug. 5, 1858, and, in 1870, was living in Springville, Iowa.

[2597.] 6. DOUGLASS C., b. Oct. 27, 1860, and, in 1870, was living in Springville, Iowa.

[2598.] 7. VENIE CUSH, b. June 29, 1862, and, in 1870, was living in Springville, Iowa.

CHILD OF OVANDO S. X. PECK, (1295).

[2599] CHARLES M., b. at Frederick, Md., Sept. 16, 1852, and was living there in 1871.

CHILDREN OF HOMER P. K. PECK, (1296).

[2600] 1. MARY H., b. in Middletown, O., March 13, 1850; m. Edward N. Freshman, May 24, 1870, and, in 1871, was living in Cincinnati, O.

[2601.] 2. ARTHUR, b. in Middletown, O., May 6, 1852, and, in 1871, was living in Rochester, N. Y.

[2602.] 3. SALLIE, b. in Washington City, Aug. 14, 1854, and, in 1871, was living in Rochester, N. Y.

[2603.] 4. EMMA, b. in Washington City, July 30, 1858, and, in 1871, was living in Rochester, N. Y.

[2604.] 5. WILLARD, b. in Washington City, Oct. 23, 1860, and, in 1871, was living in Rochester, N. Y.

[2605.] 6. HELEN BELLE, b. in Middletown, O., March 8, 1862, and, in 1871, was living in Rochester, N. Y.

[2606.] 7. FLORA REBECCA, b. in Middletown, O., Aug. 1, 1867, and, in 1871, was living in Middletown, O.

CHILDREN OF JOHN P. P. PECK, (1297).

[2607.] 1. DELIA E., b. in Sharonville, O., Sept. 10, 1844, and, in 1870, was living in Hamilton, O.

[2608.] 2. ALICE I., b. in Sharonville, O., Aug. 11, 1847, and, in 1870, was living in Hamilton, O.

[2609.] 3. MARY, b. in Sharonville, O., April 26, 1851, and, in 1870, was living in Hamilton, O.

[2610.] 4. ROBERT M., b. in Hamilton, O., Sept. 15, 1859, and was living there in 1870.

[2611.] 5. JOHN P. P., b. in Hamilton, O., April 3, 1867, and was living there in 1870.

[2612.] 6. JAMES F., b. in Hamilton, O., July 29, 1872, and was living there in 1872.

CHILDREN OF MATTHEW G. PECK, (1315).

[2613.] 1. MARY A., b. in Pontiac, Mich., June 26, 1855, and, in 1869, was living in Pontiac, Mich.

[2614.] 2. EMILY B., b. in Rochester, N. Y., Sept. 26, 1858, and, in 1869, was living Pontiac, Mich.

CHILDREN OF PASCAL P. PECK (1317) AND ALEXINE, HIS WIFE, BOTH BORN IN NASHVILLE, TENN.

[2615.] 1. WILLIAM H., b. March 14, 1852, and, in 1869, was living in Nashville, Tenn.

[2616.] 2. MYRON K., b. March 22, 1857, and, in 1869, was living in Nashville, Tenn.

ONLY CHILD OF NATHANIEL PECK (1332) AND ALTHEA M., HIS WIFE, BORN IN STAFFORD, N. Y.

[2617.] CATHARINE M., b. April 25, 1847, and d. in Newstead, N. Y., in Feb. 1858.

CHILDREN OF RICHARD PECK (1333) AND SYLVIA, HIS WIFE.

[2618.] 1. CHARLES G., b. in Stafford, N. Y., March 25, 1854, and, in 1869, was living in Palmyra, Ill.

[2619.] 2. MARY H., b. in Round Grove, Ill., Oct. 1, 1861, and, in 1869, was living in Palmyra, Ill.

[2620.] 3. KATIE LOUISE, b. in Round Grove, Ill., March 10, 1864, and, in 1869, was living in Palmyra, Ill.

CHILDREN OF ISRAEL M. PECK (1334) AND FRANCES C., HIS WIFE,
ALL BORN IN STAFFORD, N. Y.

[2621.] 1. ELIZABETH F., b. July 5, 1857, and, in 1871,
was living in Stafford, N. Y.

[2622.] 2. ALVAN VAN EPPS, b. Jan. 19, 1862, and d.,
in Stafford, N. Y., Oct. 13, 1862.

[2623.] 3. JUNIUS MATSON, b. June 8, 1865, and, in
1871, was living in Stafford, N. Y.

[2624.] 4. WINFIELD S., b. Oct. 15, 1868, and, in 1871,
was living in Stafford, N. Y.

CHILDREN OF BENJAMIN F. PECK (1337) AND PHEBE R., HIS WIFE,
ALL BORN IN EAST BETHANY, N. Y.

[2624.] 1. FLORENCE, b. July 17, 1855, and, in 18/1, was
living in East Bethany, N. Y.

[2625.] 2. RICHARD, b. Oct. 12, 1857, and, in 1871, was
living in East Bethany, N. Y.

[2626.] 3. MARY ANN, b. July 15, 1869, and, in 1871, was
living in East Bethany, N. Y.

NINTH GENERATION.[1]

CHILDREN OF DARIUS PECK (1363) AND HARRIET M., HIS WIFE,
ALL BORN IN THE CITY OF HUDSON, N. Y.

[2628.] 1. JOHN HUDSON, b. Feb. 7, 1838; graduated at
Hamilton College, N. Y., in 1859 ; was admitted to the bar of
the Supreme Court of the State of New York in 1862, and
settled as a lawyer in the city of Troy, N. Y., where, in 1877,
he was living and in practice as such, being one of the law firm
of Tracy & Peck, of that city.

---

1. It was not originally designed to continue the Genealogy further than the Eighth
Generation.   A few, in the Ninth and Tenth Generations, have been added in deference to the wishes of some members of the family.

[2629.]   2. HORACE ROBINSON, b. Dec. 9, 1839 ; graduated at Hamilton College, N. Y., in 1859 ; was admitted to the bar of the Supreme Court of the State of New York in 1863 ; settled as a lawyer in the city of Hudson, N. Y., and, in 1877, was living there in the practice of his profession. He was married to Anna Van Deusen, of Greenport, N. Y., Nov. 14, 1867. He has one son, an only child, *Bayard Livingston*, b. Aug. 16, 1869.

[2630.]   3. SARAH LUCRETIA, b. March 19, 1842 ; was educated at the Female Seminary, Troy, N. Y. ; m. Martin Hoffman Philip, of the town of Claverack, N. Y., Oct. 19, 1859, and d. there Oct. 25, 1876. She had children : 1. *Katharine Maud*, b. in the city of Hudson, N. Y., Sept. 13, 1860 ; 2. *Harry Van Ness*, b. Aug. 9, 1862, and 3. *Laura Johnson*, b. Dec. 10, 1863 ; both b. in the town of Claverack, N. Y.

[2631.]   4. WILLARD, b. March 2, 1844 ; graduated at Hamilton College, N. Y., in 1864, and was admitted to the bar of the Supreme Court of the State of New York in 1867. He settled as a lawyer, has continued his professional career, and, in 1877, was living and practicing his profession in the city of Hudson, N. Y.   He was married to Mary Langford Curran, of Utica, N. Y., June 16, 1869, and has had children : 1. *Harriet Hudson*, b. in Utica, N. Y., April 2, 1870, and d. there April 5, 1870 ; 2. *Philip Curran*, b. Feb. 7, 1874, and 3. *Darius*, b. May 5, 1877 ; both b. in the city of Hudson, N. Y.

[2632.]   5. NORA, b. Sept. 16, 1846 ; was educated at the Female Seminary, Troy, N. Y. ; m. Frederick Folger Thomas, of San Francisco, Cal., June 18, 1873.   Her children, b. in Oakland, Cal., where she was living in 1877, are : 1. *William Shepard*, b. March 23, 1874, and 2. *Maud Angeline*, b. Feb. 10, 1876.

[2633.]   6. THEODOSIA, b. Oct. 24, 1848, and d., in the city of Hudson, N. Y., Aug. 23, 1849.

[2634.]   7. EMMA WILLARD, b. May 9, 1852 ; was educated at the Female Seminary, Troy, N. Y., and, in 1877, was living in the city of Hudson, N. Y.

CHILDREN OF PHILETUS B. PECK (1366) AND NANCY M., HIS WIFE.

[2635.] 1. DARIUS M., b. in Cazenovia, N. Y., Oct. 15, 1832 ; m. Josephine McCormick, at Lock Haven, Penn., Aug. 30, 1865, and, in 1877, was living in Williamsport, Penn.   His children were : 1. *Catharine Hood*, b. at Lock Haven, Penn., Feb. 24, 1867, and 2. *Josephine McCormick*, b. at Owego, N. Y., Oct. 26, 1868 ; both of whom d. March 16, 1876, of diphtheria, then prevailing as an epidemic.

[2636.] 2. SPENCER T., b. in Hamilton, N. Y., Dec. 19, 1837 ; m. Isabella Crawford, Dec. 28, 1865, and, in 1877, was living in Williamsport, Penn.   He has no children.

[2637.] 3. JULIA A. M., b. at Owego, N. Y., May 9, 1840 ; was educated at the Female Seminary, Troy, N. Y. ; m. George A. Madill, a lawyer, of Owego, N. Y., Dec. 24, 1862 ; removed three or four years afterwards from Owego to St. Louis, Mo., where her husband soon became a prominent lawyer, and has occupied a high judicial position, and where they were living in 1877.   Her children, b. in St. Louis, Mo., are : 1. *George Alexander*, b. Oct. 10, 1867, and *Charles Peck*, b. Sept. 10, 1872.

[2638.] 4. SARAH N., b. at Owego, N. Y., June 22, 1844 ; was educated at the Female College, Elmira, N. Y., and, in 1877, was living at Owego, N. Y.

ERRATA.

———————

ADDITIONS AND CORRECTIONS, MOSTLY FROM INFORMATION RECEIVED TOO
LATE FOR THEIR APPROPRIATE INSERTION.

———————

Page 11 in line 12 from bottom for "(32)" read "(22)."

" 83 in line 12 from bottom after the word "Conn." add the words "and d. there in May, 1877."

" 135 in line 9 from bottom for "(2629)" read "(2635.)"

" 138 and 139 strike out "(2630)," "(2631)," "(2632)," "(2633)," "(2634)" and "(2635)."

" 165 in line 13 from top for "Abner" read "Albert."

" 167 in lines 2 and 8 from bottom for "1873" read "1877," and in line 10 from bottom after the word "and" insert "in 1877," strike out all after the word "was" and add "living at Grand Rapids, Mich."

" 173 in line 6 from top strike out the 3d letter "N" from "Annnie."

" 175 in line 6 from bottom between the words "Peck" and "and" insert (848).

" 239 of Index in line 15 from bottom of 3d column for "138" read "158."

INDEX

OF CHRISTIAN OR GIVEN NAMES OF ALL IN THE WORK OF THE
SURNAME OF PECK, BETWEEN PAGES 6 AND 237.

The figures refer to the pages. When more than one of the same name is upon the same page, only the first one is designated in the index ; the others on that page being omitted.

INDEX

OF SURNAMES IN THE WORK OTHER THAN PECK.

The figures refer to the pages. When the same name occurs more than once on the same page only the first is mentioned by name ; the others on that page being designated by figures.

CPSIA information can be obtained at www.ICGtesting.com
Printed in the USA
LVOW07s2326031215

465275LV00025B/229/P